The events described in *Possess the Air* begin in Italy one hundred years ago, when war, corruption, and economic uncertainty had shaken a people's confidence in the fundamental institutions of democracy.

At a crucial time, Benito Mussolini rose to power by promising to make Italy great again. Before declaring himself dictator, though, Mussolini was democratically elected to the Italian parliament. His success was enabled by elites—both Conservatives and Liberals—who chose to remain silent, or to maintain their power by cutting deals with a man they knew advocated division, winked at brutality, and exalted war. Mussolini became Il Duce because too many Italians undervalued the free institutions underlying the modern democratic state—institutions that previous generations had battled to establish and defend, often at the cost of their lives. The willingness to trade liberty for a spurious promise of security, prosperity, and glory allowed an opportunistic autocrat to implement the tenets of Fascism, an ideology that would visit unspeakable terror and bloodshed on Europe and the world.

Not everybody accepted Mussolini's vision of the future. Many Italians were willing to sacrifice their careers, their freedom, and even their lives to oppose the hate, violence, and warmongering they saw taking over the public life of the country they loved.

This is the story of how, in a period of rising authoritarianism, some patriots found a way to fight for the liberty that many of their fellow citizens had come to take for granted, or even spurn.

Which is what makes this—as the memory of the consequences of succumbing to the empty promises of a strongman appears to be fading—a story for our time.

POSSESS THE AIR

LOVE, HEROISM, AND THE BATTLE FOR THE SOUL OF MUSSOLINI'S ROME

TARAS GRESCOE

BIBLIOASIS
WINDSOR, ONTARIO

FIRST EDITION

Library and Archives Canada Cataloguing in Publication

Title: Possess the air : love, heroism, and the battle for the soul of Mussolini's Rome / Taras Grescoe.
Names: Grescoe, Taras, author.

Description: Series statement: Untold lives

Identifiers: Canadiana (print) 20190119039 | Canadiana (ebook) 20190119276 | ISBN 9781771963237 (softcover) | ISBN 9781771963244 (ebook)

Subjects: LCSH: Bagnani, Gilbert, 1900-1985. | LCSH: Bagnani, Stewart, 1903-1996. | LCSH: De Bosis, Lauro, 1901-1931. | LCSH: Political activists—Italy—Biography. | LCSH: Anti-fascist movements—Italy—History—20th century. | LCSH: Italy—History—1914-1945.

Classification: LCC DG556.A1 G74 2019 | DDC 945.091—dc23

Edited by Janice Zawerbny
Copy-edited and indexed by Allana Amlin
Cover designed by Michel Vrana
Interior designed by Ingrid Paulson

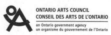

Published with the generous assistance of the Canada Council for the Arts, which last year invested $153 million to bring the arts to Canadians throughout the country, and the financial support of the Government of Canada. Biblioasis also acknowledges the support of the Ontario Arts Council (OAC), an agency of the Government of Ontario, which last year funded 1,709 individual artists and 1,078 organizations in 204 communities across Ontario, for a total of $52.1 million, and the contribution of the Government of Ontario through the Ontario Book Publishing Tax Credit and Ontario Creates. This is one of the 200 exceptional projects funded through the Canada Council for the Arts' New Chapter program. With this $35M investment, the Council supports the creation and sharing of the arts in communities across Canada.

PRINTED AND BOUND IN CANADA

For Victor,
who, from the get-go,
has known that
life is so great.

CONTENTS

"Minos may possess everything, but he does not possess the air."

–Ovid, *Daedalus and Icarus*

PROLOGUE **THE VIEW FROM THE JANICULUM**

A lucky walker in Rome, weary of dodging gelato-eaters and rushing *motorini*, may be lured out of the teeming streets of Trastevere by the prospect of the upward-sloping paving stones of the sycamore-shaded Via Garibaldi. To the right, a side street dead-ends in flights of well-worn stone steps, bordered on one side by fortifications built by a third-century emperor to repel barbarous Germanic tribes.

The staircase ascends, alongside crumbling bricks overgrown with wildflowers and canary-grass, to a piazza dominated by a striking monument in luminous travertine limestone. The Fontana dell'Acqua Paola is a confection of the high Baroque, built around five niches—divided by columns of red granite and topped by high-perched griffins, lines of stone-cut Latin, and a gossamer iron cross—out of which water gushes into a cerulean basin, as shallow as it is enticing. The pet project of a seventeenth-century Pope, it is fed by the same ancient aqueduct that once filled Trastevere's *naumachia*, the artificial lake where the Emperor Trajan staged mock naval battles using galleys rowed by real slaves. Taxi drivers know it simply as the *fontanone*, the big fountain.

The Fontana dell'Acqua Paola, however, is merely the backdrop to a far more impressive spectacle. Crossing the paving stones of the semi-circular piazza, the fortunate stroller approaches a curved stone balustrade, which projects like a proscenium over the most sumptuous of playhouses. Just beyond the high canopies of thin-trunked umbrella pines, the first metropolis of the world unscrolls to the limits of peripheral vision.

Ecco: Roma.

In the foreground, quadrilaterals of weathered stucco in hues of ochre and pink form a Cubist jumble, jostling around the bend in the Tiber that snags Trastevere, the most ancient and authentic of Rome's *rioni*, or central neighbourhoods, like a bishop's crozier. Across the river, the hemispheric roof of the two-millennia-old Pantheon, the largest dome in the world until well into in the twentieth century, protrudes from Rococo cupolas, a concrete barnacle cemented fast to the medieval and Renaissance city. And, white as sun-bleached baleen, the Brescian marble of the Vittoriano, that pretentious monument to the earthiest of Italy's kings, rises against the Impressionist smear of blue on the eastern horizon, the foreboding Sabine and Alban Hills.

The Latin satirist Martial, who owned a villa near the crest of this hill, the Janiculum, wrote of the vista: "From here you can see the seven lordly hills, and measure the whole of Rome."

The only reminders that this is the second decade of the twentieth-first century are the cellphone masts that bristle from certain strategic eminences, and the occasional contrail of an airplane that scumbles a sky notably unscraped by towers of glass and steel.

It is a view that has consoled generations of visitors, suggesting that humans and their problems come and go, but Roma—the

Urbs Aeterna, the *Caput Mundi*, the *Città Eterna*—will always abide. The city's persistence across the centuries seems to offer a salutary rebuke to an unhealthy obsession with the present.

But Rome has never been exempt from history. From the balcony of the Janiculum, observers have watched the flames that leapt up from the Temple of Jupiter as Sulla sacked the Forum, the cannonballs that burst in the Piazza Barberini after French gunners dislodged General Garibaldi from the Villa Aurelia, and the columns of smoke that rose from the rubble of the San Lorenzo district after it had been carpet bombed by Flying Fortresses in the darkest days of the Second World War.

On a warm autumn evening in the Ninth Year of the Fascist Era, families that had wandered up to the Janiculum were witness to another dramatic episode in the city's history. As the sun set on October 3, 1931, a dot appeared in the western sky. In the gathering twilight, it quickly resolved itself into a fuselage that sprouted crimson-tipped wings. People stopped to watch its progress, for aircraft were no longer a common sight in Rome. The Fascists liked to boast that not even a swallow dared to penetrate the sky over the capital without their permission.

Whoever the pilot was, he was flying silently, in a controlled downwards glide. Heads swivelled as the plane passed above the treetops, and crossed the Tiber on what seemed like a certain collision course with the palazzo where—as the day's newspapers had announced—Il Duce and the leading members of the Fascist Grand Council had gathered to work late into the night.

In the cockpit, a young man looked out over the rooftops of his hometown and wagged the wings of his little plane in triumph. Through a daring act of bravado, he was about to reveal what, for almost a decade, the dictatorship had been striving to conceal from the world.

Mussolini didn't know what was about to hit him.

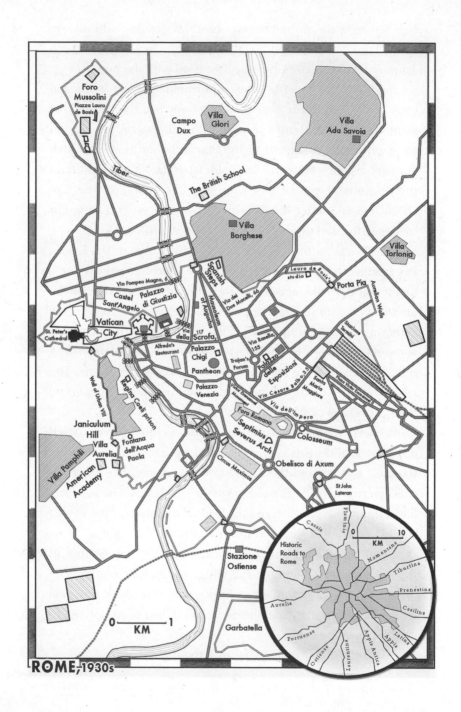

Foro Mussolini
Piazza Laura de Bosis
Campo Dux
Villa Glori
Villa Ada Savoia
Tiber
The British School
Villa Borghese
Villa Torlonia
Via Pompeo Magno, 6
Spanish Steps
Lauro de Bosis' studio
Porta Pia
Castel Sant'Angelo
Palazzo di Giustizia
Mausoleum of Augustus
Via del Due Macelli, 66
Aurelian Walls
Vatican City
St. Peter's Cathedral
Via della Scrofa, 117
Via Rasella, 155
Stazione Termini
Alfredo's Restaurant
Palazzo Chigi
Pantheon
Trajan's Forum
Palazzo delle Esposizioni
Via Cesare Balbo, 35
Santa Maria Maggiore
Piazza Vittorio Emanuele
Regina Coeli prison
Palazzo Venezia
Victor Emmanuel Monument
Foro Romano
Via dell'Impero
Wall of Urban VIII
Janiculum Hill
Villa Aurelia
Fontana dell'Acqua Paola
Septimius Severus Arch
Colosseum
Villa Pamphili
American Academy
Circus Maximus
Obelisco di Axum
St John Lateran

Stazione Ostiense

0 ——— 1
KM

Garbatella

Historic Roads to Rome
Cassia
Flaminia
0 ——— 10
KM
Nomentana
Tiburtina
Prenestina
Aurelia
Casilina
Portuense
Latina
Appia
Appia Antica
Ostiense
Laurentina

ROME, 1930s

PART I

"Dictators are always afraid of poets."
–Ursula K. Le Guin

PART I

1 THE BLACK DEVILS

Lilian Mowrer first saw them outside her apartment on the Via della Scrofa, in the opening weeks of 1921. Young men, dressed in tight black shirts, hollow-eyed white skulls embroidered over the left breast. She was inclined to chuckle at their long hair, often painstakingly marcelled into a permanent wave with hot curling tongs, and the way they strode through the streets chanting *"Eia, Eia, Eia, Alalà!"* with the accent on the last ringing note, as though they were beer-drunk university athletes on a spree.

But there was nothing funny about the effect they had on her neighbours.

"They carried carbines or revolvers," wrote Mowrer, "and walked with a tremendous swagger, not just the Don Juan swagger of the average Italian male out for a stroll, but a provocative business-like swagger that made people stand aside to let them pass. They called themselves *Fascisti*—Fascists."

Many were former *Arditi*, the shock-troops of the Italian army in the First World War, modelled on the German *Sturmtruppen*.

Better paid and fed than the regular troops, they'd been trained to travel light, without packs, storm foxholes with only daggers and grenades, and use hand-to-hand combat to fight the enemy to the death. On the front lines, operating under the slogan *me ne frego* ("I don't give a damn"), they'd cultivated a devil-may-care cult of death, and an aesthetic to match. With their long forelocks, and handsome black uniforms embroidered with flames, they resembled modern-day pirates. After the war, idle and adrift, they were a terrifying presence in Italian cities, drinking themselves into a stupor at cafés. Marching down Rome's Corso, they would force passersby to stand aside, and beat any man who failed to doff his hat with their weapon of choice, the lead-weighted *Santo Manganello*—the "Saint Bludgeon."

Until then, the life Lilian and her husband, Chicago *Daily News* correspondent Edgar Mowrer, lived in Rome had been an idyll. Their top-floor apartment in the Palazzo Galitzin had one-metre-thick walls, and its low-arched windows, designed by the High Renaissance architect Donato Bramante, looked across the river to St. Peter's. Edgar's office, on *the piano nobile* of a building near the Spanish Steps, was a ten-minute walk away. In the summer, the Mowrers would ride the streetcars beyond the walls, punctuating their hikes in the *campagna*, Rome's near-vacant countryside, with pauses at a country *osteria* for prosciutto, melon, and the white wine of Frascati. When it was too hot to walk, they'd go swimming at the bend in the Tiber near the Milvio Bridge.

But, after six years, the idyll was coming to an end. Every week seemed to bring reports of new violence. One day, a young friend, a journalist from Naples, came to their apartment in tears. In the nearby Piazza Colonna, she had made the mistake of commenting aloud how "disgusting" it was to see the offices of a newspaper ransacked by the Fascists.

The tassels atop two black fezzes, she told Lilian, twitched in her direction. A pair of burly Fascists who had overheard her comment seized her by the shoulders and frog-marched her to the nearest pharmacy, where the owner was ordered to produce a bottle of castor oil from under the counter. On the spot, a half pint of the "golden nectar of nausea" was forced down her throat. She was thrown into the back of a taxi, where they held her in place as the powerful purgative did its work. Vomiting and wracked by explosive diarrhea, she was driven around the Column of Marcus Aurelius in the open car. When the thugs were done with her, they pitched her into the street, shouting: "We think *you* are disgusting!"

No one, she sobbed to Lilian, had dared interfere. "They simply pushed me away as if I were dirt and drove off."

The Fascists were making Italy—which was still a heaven for those lucky enough to be insulated from its politics—a hell for many of its ordinary citizens.

The Romans had a name for the swaggering thugs. They called them *"i diavoli neri"*—the black devils.

2 TRAIN 112 FROM NAPLES

On the night of October 14, 1920, train 112, the *direttissimo* from Naples, pulled into Termini Station, two-and-a-half hours late.

As Thornton Niven Wilder, the youngest son of the former Consul General to Hong Kong and Shanghai, carried his suitcase through the deserted station, he cursed the Italian railways. The train had been overcrowded, even by Italian standards. Rumours of a cholera outbreak among the backstreet beggars of Naples had provoked an exodus of panicked tourists, and even first-class ticket holders were forced to stand. The twenty-three-year-old Yale graduate had been lucky to find a seat in an ill-heated second-class compartment. As he shivered in a heavy overcoat while watching the sun set between the broken arches of the aqueducts along the Via Appia Antica, he'd planned his first-night spree in Rome. He imagined himself dispatching a fiasco of red wine, and then running down the middle of Via Cavour, to gaze upon the moonlit ruins of the Forum, before collapsing at dawn within sight of the dome of St. Peter's.

By the time the train arrived, though, it was past midnight, and he was cold and tired. There was nowhere in the station, which was plastered with ads for mineral water and stank of ammonia, to purchase the longed-for glass of Chianti. Outside, the sky was moonless, and there was nothing, apart from a small Egyptian obelisk, on the rain-swept piazza outside that suggested ancient grandeur. Lugging his suitcase between the many hotels that surrounded the station, he finally found a vacancy at a large, modern hotel.

Alone in his small room, Wilder consoled himself by writing a letter to his family, a habit he'd picked up as a lonely boarder at the Inland Mission School at Chefoo, on the Chinese coast.

"I have this minute arrived in Rome, and am waiting up in my room for some supper. The train was late, and I know no more of Rome than can be gained on rainy evenings crossing the street that separates the station from the Hotel Continentale (The last room left for 22 lire)."

The fact that the room had cost a mere ninety cents, he knew, would cheer his father. Nine hundred dollars had been allotted him for his year of study abroad, a sum that, given the post-war weakness of the Italian lira, promised to go far. The plan to study in Rome had not come from his father, a strict Baptist and life-long teetotaller who had refused any temptation to enrich himself during his postings to China's Treaty Ports. It was his open-minded, idealistic mother who had suggested the idea of coming to Italy, after she'd read Stark Young's lyrical Roman dispatches in *The New Republic*, which also mentioned an exchange rate favourable to foreign visitors. The case for going to Italy was further strengthened when an old family friend, a director of the American School of Classical Studies before the war, mentioned study opportunities for bright young men in Rome.

Until then, the course of Wilder's life had been directed by missives from his father, who cheerfully admitted to moving his five offspring around the globe like chess pieces. At the age of 15, Wilder had been ordered to leave his Chinese boarding school, sail across the Pacific, and join his older brother Amos at a ranch-style school among the high mountains and avocado orchards of California's Ojai Valley. He'd then been instructed to transfer to Berkeley High School, where he first began to write playlets and perform on stage. (A paternal decree had forbidden him from donning drag as Lady Bracknell in a performance of Oscar Wilde's *The Importance of Being Earnest*.) He was then moved to Oberlin College in Ohio, a solidly Christian institution co-founded by his maternal great-grandmother, and the site of the establishment of the Anti-Saloon League. Any hope Wilder had of liberating himself in his last years of study ended when he was sent to New Haven, where his father, a Skull-and-Bones man, had taken a post directing the Yale-in-China Association.

Even when Amos Parker Wilder wasn't telling his son exactly what to do, his Puritanical commandments seemed to dominate Wilder's thoughts. "There are times," he would later confide to his older brother, "when I feel his perpetual and repetitive monologue is trying to swamp my personality, and I get an awful rage."

The letter that promised freedom from the yoke arrived the previous summer while he was wearing overalls in Litchfield, Connecticut, doing the outdoor labour that his father hoped would cure him of "his peculiar gait and certain effeminate ways." Despite misgivings about wine-drinking Catholics, Amos approved the plan to go to Italy. Thornton's time abroad would be used to gain a grounding in the Classics, one solid enough to secure him a reliable position teaching Latin when he returned to the United States.

Wilder had other plans. On board the French ocean liner *Providence*, which sailed from New York on the first day of September, he was delighted to find himself "largely in the company of *young men who had left their fathers at home.*" He slept in the upper-berth of a four-bunk cabin. At the boisterous bachelors' table in the second-class dining saloon, set with carafes of tongue-loosening wine, he met a Harvard graduate from Sorrento, who introduced him to his friends when they landed, after two weeks at sea, in Naples.

He wandered the city's Museo Archeologico in his baggy grey suit, blushing at the bulbous phalluses and leering satyrs rescued from the ruins of Pompeii in the museum's *Gabinetto Segreto*. He booked a room at the Cocumella, the grand hotel over the plunging cliffs of Sorrento that had welcomed Goethe and Mary Shelley, and scaled Vesuvius, scuffing his shoes as they sank into the volcano's blue-black dust. He started work on a new play, about an American widow in Capri duped by an Italian adventurer. Such was his pleasure that he wrote to the school in Rome, where he was expected, to say his constitution had been upset by the change of continents and that his arrival would be delayed for several days.

"I love Italy now indissolubly; and the Italians; and the language," he wrote to his family, after a week. After two, he'd boarded the express at Napoli Centrale, bound for Rome.

Though the proverbially inefficient Italian railways had ruined his plans that night, he couldn't contain his joy at being in Rome.

"I keep going to the window," he wrote. "Outside in wonderful Rome it is drizzling. Carriages and trams pass. Not far away the Pope and forty cardinals are sleeping, the Coliseum and the Forum are lying dampish, and silent and locked up, but with one burning light at least, the Sistine Chapel is glimmering, and somewhere further off, in the struggling starlight, your graves, John Keats and Percy Shelley, lie succeeding to establish, if anyone can, that it is better to lie in a moist hill with glory, than live in an elegant hotel with stupidity."

That night, as Wilder lay down, sober and alone in his single bed, he was grateful to note an absence. Italy seemed to be stilling the paternal voice that scolded him for perceived weaknesses and inadmissible affinities, telling him that he could never be what he was already becoming: a writer.

The following morning Wilder got his first glimpse of Rome by daylight. He stopped at the Spanish Steps, where Keats had succumbed to consumption, and shed a tear as he recalled some lines from his poem, "When I have fears that I may cease to be." As he walked up the flanks of the Janiculum, the sound of fleetly played notes hung in the air like a scent and signalled he was approaching his destination.

Inside the school, the sound of the pianist at work on his scales filled a leafy courtyard. In the broad corridors, women's voices and distant footsteps echoed. He was told at the administrative office that, though his room wouldn't be ready for another week, he was welcome to use the school's facilities. He was asked if he'd like to come upstairs, where the director's wife and twenty students and staff were having tea. After solicitous enquiries about the "illness" that had delayed his arrival from Sorrento, they set about making him feel at home.

"There are teachers here from Smith and Wellesley and St. Marks and Cornell," he wrote in that night's letter home, "taking a sabbatical among tomb inscriptions and fallen capitals; there are 'bright' homely girls writing theses on stucco bas-relief and the development of lettering. Everybody was having rum in their tea and feeling like the devil. But I had seen the Tiber only twenty minutes before and wanted nothing better than to edge toward the window."

Thornton Wilder, visiting scholar at the American Academy in Rome, had arrived for the academic year of 1920–21.

3 A VILLA IN ROME

The American Academy appears to be an institution as venerable as any in this, the most venerable of cities.

The campus consists of ten buildings near the crest of the Janiculum Hill. The highest-perched of them, just above the triumphal arch at Porta San Pancrazio, is the orange stucco Villa Aurelia. Originally built as a casino for a seventeenth-century Farnese cardinal, before being passed on to a family of commoners who manufactured candles for the Vatican, it rises from one-and-a-half hectares of classical gardens, on a sloping property that offers stunning sunset views over the rooftops of Rome all the way to the Tyrrhenian Sea.

The Academy's Main Building, whose facade is decorated with the medallion of a two-faced Janus ringed by terra cotta stars, could pass for the palazzo of some Renaissance count. In an oasis-like inner courtyard, water gushes into a shallow pool of travertine from the gaping jaws of a serpent being throttled by the naked baby Hercules. The reading room, modelled on the

Piccolomini Library in Siena's cathedral, offers views of the tile-roofed Casa Rustica, built on the foundations of the tower where Galileo Galilei gave a demonstration of his new invention, the telescope, on a moonless night in 1611. In the building's northeast corner, a broad staircase descends to the arch-roofed cryptoporticus, under whose stones flow the subterranean Aqua Traiana, the two-thousand-year-old aqueduct that supplies the Fontana dell'Acqua Paola with water from a lake some fifty kilometres distant.

Yet the Academy is a newcomer on the Roman landscape. A plaque in the vestibule honouring the founders is inscribed not with the names of Medicis and Borgias, but those of Vanderbilt, Morgan, Frick, Rockefeller, Carnegie, and other robber barons of America's Gilded Age. In a sitting room dominated by a grand piano, tables are spread with the latest issues of *The New York Times* and *The Wall Street Journal*. Part Roman villa, part medieval monastery, part Palladian palazzo, the Academy's Main Building is a mishmash, a New World confection that exuberantly, if indiscriminately, mingles the idioms of the Old.

In 1920, the Academy had just emerged from a long period of uncertainty. Italy's declaration of war on Austria, followed by the United States's entry into the First World War in 1917, had brought studies to a complete halt. The Villa Aurelia was rented to the head of the American Red Cross, and the Main Building was requisitioned, though never used, as a 380-bed hospital.

In its earliest years, the institution's purchase on Rome had been even more precarious. The idea for the Academy had been conceived in a makeshift log cabin, known as "The Shack," erected on the shores of Lake Michigan in 1893. There, the urban planner Daniel Burnham convened an elite group of architects, artists, and craftsmen to plan the White City, the temporary metropolis of white-painted plaster buildings on an artificial lagoon that would form the nucleus of the World Columbian Exposition. Among them was Charles Follen McKim, one of the few architects of his generation who had crossed the Atlantic to study at the École des Beaux-Arts. McKim, the stammering son of Pennsylvania Quakers, disapproved of Parisian manners, but, on a side-trip to the Mediterranean, fell in love with Rome. Back in the United States, he became a founding partner in McKim, Mead & White, the firm that would set the Neoclassical tone in American cities and campuses before the First World War. Clients eager for Continental panache hired McKim and his partners to design the Boston Public Library, modelled on Paris's Bibliothèque Nationale, and Manhattan's original Pennsylvania Station, whose waiting room was a replica of the Roman Baths of Caracalla, enlarged by a quarter.

Since 1666, France had its Académie Française, housed in the monumental Villa Medici near the top of the Spanish Steps. The Germans had their Archaeological Institute, with its world-renowned library, near the Vatican. There was no reason, McKim believed, the United States shouldn't have its own foreign school to train and "send men home who shall become a true leaven in America." It could only be located, he argued, in Rome, the true capital of western civilization. The applicants would have to be unmarried in order to ensure a monastic devotion to study, and willing to receive instruction in only the solidest Classical canons.

After the closing of the Columbian Exposition, the well-connected architect launched a fundraising campaign. A committee, made up of the heads of the fine arts and architecture departments of Harvard, MIT, Cornell, and three other universities, raised $15,000 to fund the new institution.

Even for the time, the sum was far from princely. Fortunately, turn-of-the-century Rome was amply stocked with duchesses and counts, many living in well-concealed poverty. The Americans had the money, and needed real estate. The Italians needed money, and had the real estate. Eight rooms were secured on the top floor of a palazzo on the Via dei Condotti, two blocks from Bernini's boat-shaped fountain in the Piazza di Spagna. The first incarnation of the

Academy, the American School of Architecture, opened in November 1894. The entire student body amounted to four young men, each expected to make do on a stipend of five hundred dollars a year. Its library consisted of a single volume, an already-superannuated copy of the guidebook *Ancient Rome in 1885*.

The Academy then moved to the Villa Mirafiori, a kilometre and a half outside the Aurelian Walls. Though spacious enough to welcome the archaeologists of the recently founded American School of Classical Studies, its location was positively suburban. Streetcars into the city stopped running at 9:30 at night, and the cab drivers that lurked outside the villa's gates charged the foreigners extortionate rates.

The Academy's secretary Frank Millet, who had dreamt up the scheme with McKim in The Shack, believed what was really needed was a brand-new structure, purpose-built for the Academy. "If we could build our own buildings and show these Johnnies what architecture is! I never felt so modern in my life as I did in Rome. Nor did I ever enjoy so much the glories of the past."

Not everyone shared the Americans' sanguine vision of the unshakable grandeur of Rome. To many Italians, the city was a shameful symbol of national decline. In 1910, as the energetic fellows of the American Academy started to explore the Forum and Hadrian's Villa, a former schoolteacher sat at a café in the town of Forli, a minor provincial capital in the Romagna, three hundred and fifty kilometres northeast of Rome.

He made a point of writing in public, commandeering a corner table to compose the fiery editorials that appeared in *La Lotta di classe* (The Class Struggle), the obscure Socialist newspaper whose editorship he'd recently assumed. That week he was working on a screed about the influence of the Eternal City. His fiercely furrowed brow and dark gaze warned away any passerby who contemplated interrupting his work.

"Rome, a parasitic city of landladies, shoeshine boys, prostitutes, priests and bureaucrats, Rome—a city without a genuine proletariat—is not the centre of the nation's political life, but rather the centre and source of its infection. Enough of this stupid obsession for unity, the insistence that absolutely everything must be concentrated in Rome—in that enormous vampire-city that drains the best blood of the nation."

The author was young, ambitious, and immensely frustrated. After crossing the border into Switzerland to avoid conscription, he'd been accused of theft in Trento, and ignominiously conducted back to the border by the Austrian authorities. As a would-be intellectual, who had already authored an anti-clerical bodice-ripper about a salacious cardinal, he longed for acclaim in Milan, Vienna, or Paris. But at the age of 27, he found himself back in Italy, only a few kilometres from the village of his birth, surrounded by pig farmers. For this provincial radical, steeped in the writing of Karl Marx, George Sorel, and Prince Kropotkin, the "vampire-city" of Rome represented all that was abhorrent: the enervating domination of the priesthood, the corruption of the Liberal elite, a despicable tradition of deference to wealthy tourists and condescending foreign scholars.

Yet Rome, he knew, also stood for power, empire, Italy's lost glory, and the hope of its revival. Everything that, in his heart, Benito Mussolini longed for.

The Academy, after its shaky early years in rented *palazzi*, had acquired some wealthy and influential allies. Among them was the financier considered the most powerful man in America.

John Pierpont Morgan Sr., after repeatedly rebuffing McKim's entreaties for funds, finally agreed to pledge $100,000 for the

Academy's endowment, a sum soon matched by John D. Rocke-feller, William Vanderbilt, Henry Frick, and six other founders. Late in life, Morgan had taken to travelling in Europe, and his Italian sojourns introduced him to attractive real estate opportunities in Rome. He settled on the Janiculum Hill as the most fitting home for the Academy. He was particularly interested in a property put on the market by an eccentric Philadelphian widow. Clara Jessup Heyland had acquired the Villa Aurelia at a discount, buying it at auction after its role as Garibaldi's headquarters had made it the target of the cannons of the French. She fixed up the partially ruined villa in dubious Victorian style, installing Colonial-style bay windows and decorating its salons with looped velvet *portières* and tufted chairs.

Heyland, after "languishing on a blue satin sofa with a basket of kittens, each wearing a blue bow," died in 1909. In her will, she bequeathed the Villa Aurelia to her compatriots at the American Academy.

If the acquisition of Mrs. Heyland's villa was a consummation for McKim, it was a brief one. He died just weeks after the bequest was announced. (His comrade from The Shack, Frank Millet, was last seen on April 14, 1912, waving to the passengers he'd helped onto a lifeboat on the deck of the *Titanic*.) It fell on his partners at McKim, Mead & White to complete the construction of the nearby Main Building. Unlike the Academy's former rented quarters, the building's 128 rooms would be more than sufficient to house, feed, and instruct cohorts of young artists, architects, and classicists. Its location would put it within walking distance of the *trattorie* of Trastevere and the principal attractions of Rome.

On the eve of the First World War, the campus, cobbled together from some of Rome's most coveted noble estates, was almost complete. One holdout remained. Prince Giovanni Torlonia had built a home for his mistress on the lot immediately to the left of the Main Building's entrance. As work progressed, he threatened legal action against the Academy. Aware that the Prince would likely triumph in any lawsuit, Morgan agreed to pay $40,000, an exorbitant sum for the small Arts and Crafts villa. Though Torlonia's mistress stripped the villa of its light fixtures and precious chandeliers as she vacated the premises, Morgan was able to present the Villino Bellacci to the Academy on March 29, 1913.

Morgan died two days later, at the age of 75, in a $500-a-night suite at Rome's Grand Hotel.

A week after arriving in Rome, Wilder left his room at the Hotel Continentale, and moved into his new quarters at the American Academy. The fellows lived in dormitory rooms, with shared bathrooms, on the upper floor of the Main Building. As a late-arriving visiting scholar, Wilder was accommodated in the little villa next to the sculptors' pavilion, the Villino Bellacci.

"My new school is too serene and beautiful to be described. A villa overlooking Rome, all mine!" Wilder exulted in a letter to his family. "I have a bedroom, dressing-room and the bath all in a row." He enclosed a playful sketch intended for his youngest sister, Janet. "A tiny darling house, with a garden and a great grille gate, and a little side door for the middle-sized bear and a tiny back gate by a box hedge for a tiny bear."

It was an excellent time to be an American in Rome. An Italian lira, worth twenty cents before the First World War, could now be had for just four. The United States, a late entrant into the conflict, had come out with its wealth and prestige unscathed, indeed strengthened. North American travellers were rich and, as the stock market boomed, they would become ubiquitous in Europe, forming Bohemian enclaves in Paris, Berlin, Florence, and Athens.

Stark Young, whose *New Republic* dispatches had been a decisive factor in Wilder's parents approving his plan to go to Italy, marvelled: "In the shops there were Parker's Fountain Pens at two dollars, straw hats for twenty lire. For a leather address book one sees on Fifth Avenue for fourteen dollars, Mr. Cole in the Borgo San Iocopo was asking twelve lire."

The Academy, set to release a new cohort of architects, archaeologists, and artists into the streets of Rome, was especially well positioned. Indeed, it had surpassed its original model, an outcome that would have cheered founder McKim: the Villa Aurelia now faced down its French counterpart, visible across the Tiber River on the lesser eminence of the Pincian Hill.

Just a few hundred steps from Wilder's door was the Fontana dell'Acqua Paola, with its vista of rooftops and ruins. Rome, and all it had to offer a young man eager for independence and experience, lay at his feet.

4 A BEAUTIFUL BACKWATER

A century before Wilder's arrival, the Romantics discovered Rome, fixing it in the poetic imagination as a setting immune to the passage of time. The city has never since been the same.

Goethe set the tone by describing a Coliseum awash in moonlight, its dilapidated archways occupied by beggars. "One is, so to speak, reborn, and one's former ideas seem like child's swaddling clothes," the German traveller exulted. "Here the most ordinary person becomes somebody." Lord Byron, who spent just twenty-two days in the city in 1817, concurred, composing an ode to the statue known as the *Dying Gladiator*, which turned the Capitoline Museum into a site of pilgrimage for generations of literary travellers.

"The impression," wrote a twenty-six-year old Percy Bysshe Shelley in 1818, "exceeds anything I have ever experienced in my travels. It is a city, as it were, of the dead, or rather of those who cannot die, and who survive the puny generations which inhabit and pass over the spot which they have made sacred to eternity."

Just four years later, Shelley would become a permanent inhabitant of Rome when a storm scuppered his custom-made sailing ship, the *Don Juan*, in the Gulf of La Spezia. After he was cremated on a pyre on a Tuscan beach, his ashes—and unburnt heart—were interred near Keats's grave in the Protestant Cemetery, in the shadow of the Pyramid of Cestius.

The Rome known to Goethe, Madame de Staël and other *forestieri* (as Italians label outsiders from less civilized lands) was, in the true sense of the word, *romantic*. Under the Emperor Trajan, the city known as *Caput Mundi*—the capital of the world—had 1.4 million inhabitants. Only 25,000 remained by the sixteenth century, and, by time the Romantics began to sing its praises, the population had barely surpassed a hundred thousand. The Forum, once the sacred and administrative centre of an Empire that stretched from modern-day Syria to Portugal, was then known to the locals as the *Campo Vaccino*, the "cow field," for the gaunt cattle that grazed amidst its half-buried columns. On the southern slopes of the Capitoline Hill, laundry was hung out to dry on the Tarpeian Rock, where in antiquity traitors and murderers were flung to their deaths. In the Piazza Navona, Abruzzese shepherds still came down from the mountains at Christmas to play their bagpipes. The Coliseum, quarried by Pope Nicholas V to provide the stonework for St. Peter's, had become a moss-covered garbage dump and a vast public latrine. In the ruins of the mighty amphitheatre, one English botanist counted 420 distinct species of plants growing amidst the broken masonry and cracked marble. Along with knapweed, myrtle, wild olives, and fig trees were rare flowers thought to have germinated from seeds in the dung of African carnivores that had feasted on gladiators and Christians.

To be sure, the Rome of the Popes, with its seven pilgrimage churches, thirteen obelisks, and countless Baroque fountains, retained its majesty. But for Grand Tourists, Romantics, and Victorians, the essence of Rome, that beautiful backwater, was in its ruins. To set an easel in front of the Portico of Octavia, where beggars and fish vendors convened beneath the crumbling brickwork of an arch in the Jewish ghetto, was to muse on the greatness that was Rome, the puniness of its current inhabitants, and the vanity of all human ambition. *Sic transit gloria mundi*—"so passes the glory of the world"—was the City of the Dead's comforting message to the sentimental traveller.

Things changed—for a while—after the unification of Italy, and the relocation of the national capital to Rome from Florence in 1871. As politicians, courtiers, and civil servants from the more industrialized north flooded in, and labourers from the south came to build the new quarters to house them, *Romanos* became a minority in their own city. A population that had long consisted of nobles, priests, and the poor was swollen by a new middle class. Atmospheric medieval and Baroque neighbourhoods were levelled to make way for the thoroughfares of Via Nazionale, the Via Cavour, and the Corso Vittorio Emanuele, which were lined with identical modern buildings with pretentious facades. Thousand-year-old olive groves were cut down to build new housing projects. High embankments, similar to those in London and Paris, were built on the Tiber, making the city safe from floods, but also erasing the moody riverfront, whose houses used to crowd right up to the river's edge.

Augustus Hare, author of the Victorian guidebook *Walks in Rome*, lamented that the new regime had done "more for the destruction of Rome than all the invasions of the Goths and the Vandals." All moonlight romance, other expatriates complained, had been dispelled by street lights, and weed killer had forever effaced the evocative power, immortalized by Shelley in *Prometheus Unbound*, of the "odoriferous thickets" that once grew on the bricks of the Baths of Caracalla. Post-unification urban renewal was particularly hard on the poor. Large parts of the Ghetto, Europe's oldest continuously occupied Jewish neighbourhood, were razed to create sixty-foot-wide riverside boulevards, lined with "London" plane trees, along the banks of the Tiber.

By the beginning of the twentieth century, the real estate boom had gone bust. Fortunes were destroyed, as were the reputations of Liberal politicians, their public dreams of national unity tarnished by private acts of peculation and corruption in the redevelopment of Rome. Italy remained rent by internal divisions, the majority of Italians illiterate, poor, and uneducated. Symbolic of the dashed hopes of the Risorgimento—the "resurgence" of national pride that followed the unification of the nation under King Victor Emmanuel II of Sardinia—was the monument erected to his glory overlooking the Piazza Venezia. Dozens of medieval buildings, and even some ancient churches, were razed to make way for the blinding white construction of plaster, painted wood, and Botticino marble. (The equestrian statue of the king that topped it was so vast that twenty-one workers were photographed drinking vermouth in its belly.) When it first began to rise, in 1884, the monument was respectfully known as the Vittoriano. By the time it was inaugurated in 1911, it had been labelled "Sacconi's Heap," a mocking allusion to its overreaching architect. When it was finally completed, a half-century after work began, Romans had taken to calling it "The Wedding Cake," "The White Typewriter," or "The National Urinal."

The abortive Risorgimento attempt to build a new capital to rival the metropolis of antiquity and the popes was definitively ended by Italy's entry into the First World War. Unlike the French and the British, Italians, only recently united as a nation, were unenthusiastic about the conflict. Of the five and a half million men who went into battle, only eight thousand were volunteers. Peasant conscripts, the vast majority who spoke dialects incomprehensible to their commanders, were poorly paid, ill fed, and under-armed. A defeat at Caporetto on the Austro-Italian front was followed by the spectacle of Italian soldiers in retreat, many of them barefoot and without rifles. Enemy bombs rained down on Venice. The Italian navy, in spite of promises made to the Allies to patrol the Mediterranean, preferred to keep its ships in port. But by then the Austro-Hungarian empire was crumbling, and their troops couldn't be reinforced by the Germans, who were pinned down in the trenches of the western front. Rallying under the leadership of General Armando Diaz, and with the support of British and French troops, Italian forces entered the northeastern town of Vittorio Veneto, splitting the enemy line in two. The Austrians signed an armistice, and for Italy, the war ended on November 4, 1918.

But it was, in a phrase that became a rallying cry for patriots, a "mutilated victory." Hopes for renewed pride and glory, first raised in the glory days of Garibaldi and the Risorgimento, were dashed with the 1919 Treaty of Versailles. France, Britain, and America, busy creating new nations in the Balkans from the remains of Austro-Hungary, and their amused contempt for Italy, the "least of the great powers," was all too obvious. President Woodrow Wilson, initially a hero to Italians, scoffed at Italy's claims to Dalmatia and the Croatian port of Fiume. The term *"figlio di Wilson"*—"son of Wilson"—became an insult hurled at Americans in the streets of Rome.

The effort to throw off the yoke of the Austro-Hungarian empire had exhausted the nation. The only ones who seemed to have come out ahead were the *pescicani*—or "dogfish"—the newly rich war profiteers. To ordinary Italians, who saw them dressed in their furs and motoring goggles outside Rome's most expensive hotels, the *pescicani* gobbled up everything they could find.

Yet, a century after Keats and Shelley first saw it, large parts of the Rome that Wilder encountered were what the Romantics had seen: an atmospheric labyrinth of churches and ruins, populated by priests and beggars. The walls on the grounds of the American Academy still marked the western limits of the city and the beginning of the countryside. Shepherds drove their flocks with pipes and whistles through the Porta San Pancrazio, and Academy fellows were often awakened by the crowing of roosters. Within the city walls, cars, apart from the occasional Fiat of a *pescicane*, were still a rare sight. The streets of Trastevere were dominated by the sounds of human voices, church bells, and plashing fountains.

"How incredibly stirring the place is," Wilder wrote to this family. "How wise and philosophical, without didacticism, it makes you feel to see the little vegetable shops built into the arches of the Theatre of Marcellus, and the great big quivering rats that dart among the mossy capitals on the lawn that is called Temple of Hermes."

It was also a place where even an impecunious student could enjoy the best life had to offer.

"I have just come up from lunch, a beautifully served little thing for 14 lire [56 cents]," he wrote to his family that autumn. "The only continentals who can do it look bloatedly rich and deliberately immoral. There was such a tableful of *pescicani* sitting in the middle of the room about a whooping centerpiece of carnations."

For Rome and Italy, everything was about to change. Out of the dashed hopes of expansion that followed the First World War, voices were already demanding the resurrection of the dream of a Third Rome. This one would not be some quaint relic doted on by foreigners, but the capital of a new Mediterranean empire, with a Caesar fit for a new age.

5 MORTAL ITALY

Unlike most British and American expatriates, Edgar and Lilian Mowrer were keenly attuned to current events in Italy.

They'd met on a Liverpool-bound train from London, where Lilian was born, and quickly bonded in their Bohemianism. Lilian was a budding theatre director and critic. Edgar, born in Bloomington, Indiana and educated in Chicago, had just spent a year at the Sorbonne, studying under the philosopher Henri Bergson. When war broke out, he traded the life of the detached Latin Quarter poet for a position as a politically savvy foreign correspondent. Offered a choice between Vienna and Rome, Lilian had enthusiastically voted in favour of Italian sunshine. Even when Edgar was asked by the Chicago *Daily News* to leave to cover the war at short notice—he had marched on the muddy roads with barefoot soldiers retreating from defeat at Caporetto, and witnessed Italy's redeeming victory at Vittorio Veneto a year later—she hadn't regretted her choice.

Lilian engaged with the local avant-garde, dodging projectiles as she danced in a raucous performance at the Argentina, Rome's municipal theatre, by a controversial Futurist with pointed moustaches named Filippo Marinetti, who encouraged audiences to lob vegetables at the performers. An accomplished pianist, Lilian kept a small salon, which was frequented by Sardinian guitarists, Italian librettists, and musicians from the American Academy. On his first visit to Italy, Ezra Pound, sporting a pointed satyr's beard, a single turquoise earring, and a mane of reddish-blond hair tucked under a broad-brimmed hat, stopped by to read from his work-in-progress, *The Cantos*. After the United States entered the war, Lilian had volunteered for the Red Cross, which cut through Italian red tape with Yankee efficiency, distributing food and stores from its temporary offices in the American Academy.

Edgar's work made him aware of a deep undercurrent of discontent and violence in Italy's public life. Tipped off by a hotel porter about a meeting of Socialists in Milan in 1915, he'd entered an ill-lit hall where a stocky, bald man with a jutting chin was haranguing a crowd. While other Socialists favoured neutrality, the speaker counselled waging war on Austria.

"This," the man had told the crowd in ringing tones, "is a crusade of liberty!" Impressed by his energy and decisive gestures, Edgar introduced himself, and they had a long conversation in French. Benito Mussolini, until recently the editor of the Socialist daily *Avanti!*, invited his fellow newspaperman to look him up any time he was in Milan.

Since then, the Mowrers had followed the rise of this young, pop-eyed speechifier with growing alarm. During the war, Mussolini served in the light-infantry in the mountains near Caporetto, where he was wounded by shrapnel from one of his own company's grenades in a behind-the-lines exercise. (Though expelled from the Socialist party for urging his fellow citizens to go to war,

Mussolini did not volunteer, but was drafted into service. Nor did he fight with the cutthroat *Arditi*, but as a simple corporal in a light-infantry unit, one soldier among many.) A half million Italians were killed during the war; an equal number were counted among the *mutilati*, or wounded. Mussolini, exaggerating his own wounds and service record, emerged as the voice of the veterans, exploiting their conviction that Italy had been cheated of territory that it deserved by their stronger Allies. On March 23, 1919, he called together representatives of *Fasci di combattimento* (veterans' leagues) from twenty cities in Italy in a rented hall on Milan's Piazza San Sepolcro.

The first meeting of what would become the Fascist Party—named for the bundle (*fascio*) of rods tied around an axe carried by the bodyguards of ancient Roman magistrates—heralded a wave of violence across the country. After Mussolini spoke, the Futurist poet Marinetti denounced the Socialists for encouraging a wave of strikes that would soon see 400,000 workers occupying factories and shipyards. The strikers were asking for a wage increase to match inflation. The Liberal government, under the leadership of the elderly prime minister Giovanni Giolitti, feared Italy could become the next Soviet Union. For almost two years, the public life of an already troubled nation became even more chaotic. Telephones stopped working, trains failed to reach their destinations, gas and electricity were regularly cut. Flag-bearing veterans marched on uncultivated land and, to the consternation of property owners, started digging. When the garbage men struck during a summer heat wave, Lilian realized why the ruins of Rome were so much lower than the cobblestones of the modern city: people took to hurling rubbish from windows, as they had in ancient times, creating evil-smelling hills that rapidly raised the level of the streets.

All over the country, Communists and Anarchists were raising red and black flags raised over factories. Even the industrial giant

Fiat offered to sell its factory in Turin to its employees. In August 1920, Edgar talked his way into a worker-occupied electrical factory in Milan. He found machine guns mounted on the roof, electrified wires strung over vulnerable entry points, and workers and their families bivouacked next to the forges and dynamos, ready for a long siege. When it became clear Britain and France would not allow a revolution to occur in their backyard, the leadership of the Socialist party withdrew their support of the strikers. Fifty thousand troops were sent to Turin to suppress the strikes. By the end of the summer, the last of the occupations had come to an end.

But the Fascists, Futurists, and *Arditi* had seen an opportunity to target an enemy within: the "Bolshevist" workers who had opposed the war, scorned the returning veterans, and now seemed intent on impeding Italy's progress. After local elections in November brought many Socialist candidates to power, a wave of thuggery, intimidation, and murder began to unfurl across the country. Three hundred armed Fascists marched on Bologna's town hall as a new administration was being sworn in; in the ensuing melee, ten Socialists were killed. Ex-servicemen organized themselves into squads with names borrowed from companies of *Arditi*: "Dauntless," "Desperate," "Lightning," "Satan." Priming themselves with cherry brandy and cocaine, they would fan out through the countryside in the Fiat 18BL trucks mass-produced during the war, and besiege trade union offices and the *case del popolo*, the clubs where workers socialized. Sympathetic policemen often rode along, minus their uniforms. Local army barracks could be counted on to contribute grenades and rifles.

"The *carabinieri* travel around with them in their trucks," reported one disgusted priest from the Veneto, "sport their party badge in their button holes, sing their hymns and eat and drink with them." Near Ferrara, where a red flag had been raised over the Renaissance town hall, Edgar bore witness to the Fascists' tactics.

"They appear before a little house, and the order is heard, 'Surround the building.' There are twenty to a hundred persons armed with rifles and revolvers. They call to the *capolega* (head of a Red League), and order him to come down. If he refuses they cry, 'We'll burn your house, your wife, your children if you don't'... If he opens the door, they seize and tie him, carry him away on a camion, subject him to indescribable torture, pretending to kill or drown him, and then abandon him in open country, naked and tied to a tree.

"If he is a brave man and does not open the door and defends himself with arms, then it is immediate assassination, in the heart of the night, a hundred against one."

Edgar was horrified at the violence, which he likened to the tactics of the Ku Klux Klan and the more intolerant elements of the American Legion, and outraged at the complicity of local magistrates, who rarely prosecuted Fascist crimes. Within months, the thugs had cowed the countryside. Just fifty of them, Edgar observed, could control a large town; it took only four to dominate a village of two thousand. In the cities, stories of sadistic Fascist tortures circulated. Labour leaders were made to chew up live toads, swallow a corrosive mix of laxatives and gasoline, or defecate on red flags. One squad in Mantua became infamous for beating opponents around the head with dried codfish.

Squadrismo, the orgy of beatings, intimidation, and humiliation whose beginnings Lilian was witnessing on the streets of Rome in 1921, seemed to have no end. In the name of fighting Bolshevism, three thousand Socialists would be killed, tens of thousands of people wounded, an equal number run out of their communities. Mussolini himself had little control over the violence that had overtaken northern Italy, where the *ras* (local Fascist leaders, a title taken from the word for an Ethiopian chieftain) turned Ferrara, Cremona, Bologna and other cities into personal fiefdoms.

Mussolini may have given a name to Europe's new brand of right-wing populism, but in Fascism's early days he was, at best, a kind of sorcerer's apprentice. The movement's energy came from rage at the outcome of the First World War, and the frustrated desire to make Italy great again—as great as it had been in the Renaissance, or at the height of the Roman Empire.

If any one man was responsible for Fascism's militaristic spirit—and much of its outward trappings—it was not Mussolini, but a short, bald, bow-legged poet, who had long been known to his adoring followers as Il Duce.

Edgar Mowrer had first seen Gabriele d'Annunzio speaking in Genoa in 1915. Arriving by train from France, a country already at war with Germany, d'Annunzio was met at every station by throngs of admirers. On the quayside in Genoa, where a new statue of General Garibaldi was being dedicated, the poet harangued a crowd of thousands, blasphemously turning the Sermon on the Mount into a call to wage war on Austria:

Blessed are the young who hunger and thirst for glory, for they shall be satisfied...

Blessed are they who return with victories, for they shall see the new face of Rome.

The newspaperman was witnessing the exact moment when a decadent literary dandy was transformed into Italy's national redeemer. Mowrer found d'Annunzio's rhetoric repulsive, but his delivery—an incantatory style borrowed from Catholic liturgy, readily absorbed by his listeners—hypnotic. The speeches that followed d'Annunzio's triumph in Genoa would incite riots against Liberal politicians who favoured neutrality. More than any single person, he bore responsibility for drawing Italians into the First World War, and for the subsequent chaos that would give birth to Fascism.

The son of a wine merchant from the Abruzzi, d'Annunzio first made his name in Rome in the 1890s by promoting a story about his own premature death after a fall from horseback. While his writing style, in such novels as *Pleasure, The Triumph of Death,* and *The Virgins of the Rocks,* was studded with obscure archaisms and as convoluted as wrought-iron grillwork, he was obsessed by all that was modern: airplanes, automobiles, mechanized war. Though contemptuous of democracy, he ran for, and won, a seat as a Liberal member from his home riding in the Abruzzi, before crossing the floor to join the Socialists, only to denounce them in one of the few speeches he could be bothered to deliver in Parliament.

In his private life, d'Annunzio epitomized every cliché of *fin de siècle* decadence. He ran up, and ran out on, huge bills collecting Orientalist bric-a-brac. He was said to go through a pint of cologne—which he personally concocted from the most obscure essences—every day. At various times, he was addicted to opiates, cocaine, and sugar cubes soaked in ether. Though he seduced and abandoned the most celebrated beauties of the day, including Eleonora Duse, Italy's most famous actress, most people found him lacking in physical charm. He'd lost his curly black locks early in life, going bald, he claimed, after being wounded in a duel. The French poet Romain Rolland called him "a low-life Adonis." A celebrated Parisian courtesan, hoping to meet Italy's new Casanova, was disappointed to encounter "a frightful gnome with red-rimmed eyes and no eyelashes, no hair, greenish teeth, bad breath, and the manners of a mountebank." Utterly without empathy—he preferred his lovers sick or dying, and lost interest in them when they recovered—he was probably bipolar, and certainly a sociopath.

D'Annunzio was also, even skeptics like Edgar Mowrer had to admit, very brave. After urging Italians to enter the First World War, he joined them at the front lines, carrying a vial of poison should he be taken prisoner, while composing morbid odes to Italy's regrowth out of the bloodied mud of the trenches. Obsessed with aviation since seeing the Wright brothers instructing Italian aviators at a 1909 air-show, he became an early advocate of aerial warfare. Though he never learned to fly himself, he devised and participated in a series of spectacular raids on enemy positions.

In 1918, d'Annunzio climbed into the lead plane of a squadron of thirty-six aircraft, and flew over the Alps to drop fifty thousand red-white-and-green pamphlets on Vienna. The text urged Austria to surrender, and read in part: "Viennese! We could now be dropping bombs on you! Instead we drop only a salute."

D'Annunzio's greatest *beffa*, or stunt, was the occupation of Fiume, on the opposite side of the Adriatic Sea from Venice. The city now known as Rijeka was then a thriving port that served as Budapest's main outlet to the Mediterranean. Ruled by Hungary, Fiume was mostly populated by Croats, though the Venetian-built alleys in its old town were peopled by a well-to-do Italian minority, who enjoyed *caffè nero* and zabaglione in its many coffee shops. After the war, irredentists in Italy, feeling they'd been stabbed in the back at the Treaty of Versailles, claimed Fiume as "unredeemed" territory in an illusory Greater Italy. When the Croatian flag was hoisted over the neo-Renaissance Governor's Palace, local Italians sent an urgent telegram to d'Annunzio: "We look to the only firm and intrepid *Duce* of the Italian people. Command us." In modern times, only General Garibaldi had been deemed worthy of the ancient Roman title that described a guide or commander.

The Italian government, which had dispatched a warship to maintain order, was ambivalent about Fiume, but most Italian troops—and many of their commanders—were sympathetic to the irredentists. Leaving from Venice in a red sports car, d'Annunzio led a band of hijackers towards a military depot, where they commandeered twenty-six trucks. By the time they reached Fiume, two thousand men had joined them. On September 12, 1919, the column entered the city unopposed by the Allied command. Flowers rained down from balconies, turning d'Annunzio's open car into a moving pyramid of petals.

For the next sixteen months, d'Annunzio ruled, from his command post in the Governor's Palace, a pirate city-state he dubbed the "City of the Holocaust." Battalions-worth of disillusioned Italian soldiers arrived by motorboat and train, and were soon joined by shady adventurers from all over Europe. Eventually twenty thousand legionaries pledged to defend the city. D'Annunzio's followers shaved their heads and grew pointy beards in homage to their "Commandant." There were parades by day, and torch-lit processions and cocaine-fuelled parties by night, but the carnival atmosphere masked day-to-day brutality. Croats were expelled from their residences, and in one shocking incident, Italian police opened fire on a party of children returning from a picnic who refused to shout *"Viva Italia!",* killing nine of them.

When d'Annunzio refused to recognize the government's treaty with Yugoslavia, making Fiume an independent city-state linked to Italy by a strip of land, Italian troops besieged the city. After three days of fighting over Christmas, 1920, the six thousand remaining legionaries surrendered. (When the palace was shelled, the Commandant reportedly panicked, shouting "Help! Save me!") Fiume would be the last great drama in d'Annunzio's life. In the early weeks of the occupation, many acknowledged that he could have easily led three hundred thousand troops to Rome to become Il Duce of all Italy. But by the end, he was discredited in the eyes of his fellow citizens by his own eccentricities. He returned to Italy, where he spent the rest of his days turning the Vittoriale, his sprawling palazzo on the shores of Lake Garda, into a repository for biplanes, battleships, gilded Buddhas, and other souvenirs of his bizarre career.

Yet in Fiume, d'Annunzio and his followers had established both the style and substance of Fascism. Their ululating chant of *"Eia, Eia, Eia, Alalà!"*—d'Annunzio had swapped the barbaric "Hip! Hip! Hurrah!" with what he claimed was the battle yell of Achilles— would be adopted by the Fascist thugs who terrorized the cities.

Their marching hymn, *Giovinezza* ("Youth-time," an implicit rebuke to aged Liberal politicians), would become the movement's anthem. The black tunics of the *Arditi* would become Fascism's uniform, and the straight arm raised skywards, followed by the cry *A Noi!* ("To us!") would become its official salute. Even the tactic of feeding castor-oil to political enemies was first used by d'Annunzio's legionaries. The constitution of Fiume—in which "corporations" of workers and owners replaced trade unions— became the direct inspiration for the corporative-state of Fascist totalitarianism. And d'Annunzio's celebration of Fiume as the "City of the Holocaust"—until then an obscure term describing a sacrifice in which the victim is consumed by fire—would come to be applied to the twentieth-century's most fearsome human conflagrations.

Mussolini had watched events in Fiume closely, flying in for a visit in October, 1919. In national elections a month later, the new Fascist party received fewer than five thousand votes, and the Socialists gleefully paraded a coffin labelled with Mussolini's name through the streets of Milan. But as d'Annunzio's star fell, Mussolini's rose. The refinements of violence and mob rule per-fected in Fiume were employed to striking effect by the Fascists as they struck back against the "Bolshevists," while popular fatigue with labour unrest boosted the party's standing. In the elections of 1921, thirty-five Fascists were voted into office, includ-ing one "Professor Benito Mussolini."

D'Annunzio's one-time rival took up temporary residence in the elegant Hotel des Princes, next to the Spanish Steps, and Mus-solini began to assemble the team that would make him the first Duce of all Italy.

After six years in Italy, the Mowrers' feelings about the country and its people were mixed.

The young couple had become familiar figures in the serpentine streets in their neighbourhood in the historic heart of Rome. Lilian had learned to shop as early as possible for bargains at the Wednesday morning flea market in the Campo de' Fiori; the superstitious dealers considered it bad luck to refuse the first offer of the day, as long as it wasn't too unreasonable. The Mowrers ate at a modest *trattoria* a few doors down the Via della Scrofa, where the moustachioed owner, who bore a strong resemblance to Kaiser Wilhelm, oversaw the final preparation of every plate of *fettuccine alfredo*, mixing buttered noodles into a mound of shaved Parmesan with loose-wristed panache. When Edgar brought his friend, fellow Midwesterner Sinclair Lewis, he was so impressed with the dish that he included it in the novel he was then working on.*

Lilian loved life in Italy, though she found the circumscribed roles of the sexes limiting, and the men devastatingly vain, interested in a woman only if they thought they could bed her. And she was disgusted by the swaggering Fascist thugs she saw in the streets, and alarmed when friends reported their own experiences with castor-oil and beatings.

Edgar believed the violence a passing phenomenon. His first book, *Immortal Italy*, offered a synopsis of the good and the bad in the country.

"To associate long with Italians is to raise one's standards of personal beauty," he wrote, acknowledging: "many Americans learn through sojourn in Italy that all their lives they have been starving for art and never knew it." Even common apartment buildings, he noted, had staircases of white Carrara marble. "In

---

* The mention in *Babbitt*, proudly quoted on the restaurant's menus, would make the restaurant a fashionable destination for generations of tourists. Years later, when the owner Alfredo saw a long-legged, gaunt-faced American alone at a table, he condescendingly allowed Lewis to enter his name amidst those of stars of stage and screen whose photos covered the walls. The Nobel-Prize winning novelist signed the guest book "John Smith."

Rome the tenements are built of finer, more enduring material than American houses of the rich." He admired Italians' hedonism, their stamina, their good sense. "The Italian does not worry so much about his soul and he frankly enjoys good food, sunshine, public esteem and the opposite sex; but he puts up with discomfort without a murmur."

He deplored, though, the natives' superstition, vanity, and love of empty rhetoric. The fact that deadly formality burdened public institutions, while common life remained uncompromisingly individualistic, made him fear that for the Italians, "democracy will always be a hair shirt." But Edgar also believed Fascism could never become deeply rooted in the country. The old order, he believed, was already returning, as "Italy settled down to a condition of normal anarchy."

Edgar owed much of his optimism to his friendship with a remarkable Italian family, who lived a charmed existence in a villa off the ancient Via Toscolano. The father, Adolfo de Bosis, was a successful businessman, but also a respected lyric poet, who translated Shelley as he rode the streetcar to and from his office in the city. The mother, Lillian Vernon, was an American-born beauty, who had raised her six talented children to cherish and excel in the arts. Over long Sunday lunches in the Villa Diana's overgrown gardens, the Mowrers had shared the de Bosis family's dismay after the defeat at Caporetto, their ultimate faith in Italian victory, and their concern over the rise of Fascist violence. For Edgar, the de Bosis family represented the country's best qualities: its love of beauty, culture, liberty, and life itself. The violence they were witnessing, the Mowrers believed, was a response to the trauma of war. The good sense of the Italian people would eventually lead them to reject Fascism, as they had rejected d'Annunzio's occupation of Fiume.

As long as she was home to people like the de Bosises, Edgar believed that immortal Italy had no need to fear tyrants.

6 THE BRICK-LICKING BARBARIANS

Thornton Wilder was becoming accustomed to his life at the American Academy, with all its pleasant routines. At the Villino Bellacci, which he now shared with a fellow Yale graduate, a classicist named John C. Rolfe, he'd rise around eight, dress, walk the few steps to the metal grille of the Academy, nod at the porter, trot up the stairs of the Main Building, and signal his presence in the lofty dining room by yelling: *"Francesco! Sono qui!"* Over breakfast—*caffè latte* and hard brown bread with jam—he'd consider what the day had in store for him. Most mornings, lectures and coursework kept him at the Academy. He had enrolled in classes on Epigraphy, Roman Private Life, and Numismatics, and was working on a paper titled the "Mechanical Devices of the Pompeiian Stage," inspired by his experiences exploring the ruins at the foot of Vesuvius.

If the weather was fine, he might ask at the Academy office for a *permesso*, the letter of permission that would open the gates to a Renaissance garden villa just outside the Porta San Pancrazio.

There, catching glimpses of the dome of St. Peter's along the way, he would walk through sunken gardens where the heraldic devices of the princely Doria Pamphili family were recreated with plantings of primrose. From a semi-circular bench next to the main fountain, he could look up from his writing to watch flocks of sheep browsing in the adjacent pine woods, or the young seminarians who'd assembled on the lawn below, hoisting up their cassocks to play a noiseless game of soccer.

More often, though, Wilder would plunge into Rome. There was a little streetcar that wended its way from the Porta San Pancrazio to the Ponte Garibaldi—the carfare was just fifty *centesimi*, or two cents—but he generally opted to walk down the slopes of the Janiculum, crossing the narrow pedestrian Ponte Sisto to the Left Bank of the Tiber and into the historic heart of the city. At first, he'd been as disoriented as any tourist.

"Picture me backing up against a wall in a side street," he'd written to his family, "and unfolding my three-ft sq. map to find out where I am!"

A few weeks of this "wild wandering" had allowed him to master the geography of Rome. He'd visited the major churches, wondered at the rich red-and-purple vestments of the officiants at the high mass at St. John Lateran, and gazed upon the glittering ceiling of Santa Maria Maggiore, gilded with some of the first gold plundered from the Americas. He'd made literary pilgrimages to the graves of the Romantics, and tracked down the site of the English hospice where John Milton once stayed. At the Teatro Morgana, he'd attended a Verdi opera, where he was amused by the vehemence with which his seatmates glared and hissed at latecomers who dared interrupt an aria by their favourite baritone.

What really stirred Wilder's imagination, though, were the ruins. As a boy, he'd thrilled to the adventures of Heinrich Schliemann, the pioneering German archaeologist whose excavations of Troy had been the first to demonstrate that the feats of Achilles described in the *Iliad* might be based on real historical events. Now the ancient stones were brought to life for him by the Academy's archaeologists. He would join other students at the Temple of Castor and Pollux, where Ralph Magoffin, the head of classical studies, sat on a knoll, explaining that the site of the Forum was once a lake that had been drained by the Etruscans. When it began to rain, they would huddle beneath the dripping marble of the Arch of Septimius Severus, to hear a lecture on the typography of Republican Rome.

"I went with an archaeological party the other day to a newly discovered tomb of about the first century," he wrote to his family. "It was under a street near the center of the city, and while by candlelight we peered at faded paintings of a family called Aurelius, symbolic representations of their dear children and parents borne graciously away by winged spirits, playing in gardens, and adjusting their Roman robes, the street-cars of today rushed by over us."

His experience at excavations in Rome would forever change his perspective on history. "Once you have swung a pickax that will reveal the curve of a street four thousand years covered over which was once an active, much-traveled highway," he would tell an interviewer many years later, "you are never quite the same again. You look at Times Square as a place about which you can imagine some day scholars saying, 'There appears to have been some kind of public center here.'"

Wilder was well aware that he was a callow youth from a New World, eager to absorb all that a very old land had to offer. Within weeks, he would reflect to his father: "The dim churches, the pines, the yellow sunlight you will see in my eyes for years—it doesn't matter when I leave them... the very complexity of things flays one's peace of mind to the point of torment. You are haunted by the great vistas of learning to which you are unequal; continuous gazing at masterpieces leaves you torn by ineffectual conflicting aspirations."

Rome was changing Wilder, ineluctably, permanently, as it had changed so many before him.

Let the foreigners worship Rome. Most of the city's inhabitants would have found the exalted tributes of Goethe, Byron, and Shelley embarrassing, had they bothered to read them. Contact with priests and politicians, whose peccadilloes they were able to observe at close quarters, had made Romans notoriously irreverent; centuries of enduring foreign invasion had made them resistant and rueful; and living amidst ruins, ossuaries, and other symbols of death had made them habitually macabre. The literary tastes of the locals ran to Giuseppe Belli, who wrote in *Romanesco*, the city's rough-edged dialect. (A typical malediction in the local slang goes: *"L'anima de li mortacci tua!"* meaning "the soul of your rotting ancestors.") Frequently blasphemous, interlarded with obscene black humour, his verses reflected the long-suffering cynicism of the people of Trastevere, who still consider themselves the most ancient and authentic residents of the Eternal City.

"What does the Pope do?" Belli asked in a famous sonnet of 1835. "Drinks, and takes a nap / looks out the window, has a bite to eat / fiddles with the housemaid's garter strap / and makes the town a cushion for his feet."

Romans had a similarly flippant attitude to the ruins amidst which they spent their days. They built their apartments on foundations of *opus reticulatum* and cut marble from baths and temples to ornament church floors. Pagan ruins were the backdrop to real lives, roughly lived.

Real archaeological scholarship only began in earnest after 1809, the year Rome was annexed to the French Empire. Napoleon's enthusiasm for the artifacts of antiquity filled the squares of Paris with Egyptian obelisks and spread scientific-minded archaeologists through the newly conquered territories. Some of Rome's greatest treasures, including the Belvedere Apollo, the Laocoön, and masterpieces by Bernini, Caravaggio, and Raphael, were loaded onto wagons and carted off to Paris. The city's immovable monuments were treated with more respect, benefiting from systematic care and investigation for the first time since the fifth century. The French saved the outer wall of the Coliseum from collapse with a brick buttress, and their excavations revealed the full extent of Trajan's Market. The cattle market was evicted from the Forum, where diggers, many of them chained convicts, began to expose long-buried temples and earth-bound arches.

After the French occupation, which ended a year before Napoleon's death in 1815, Rome once again became a sleepy backwater, open to all comers. (One English visitor observed: "One can walk from one end of the city to the other without seeing a single thing to suggest that you are not still in the eighteenth century or to remind you that the French were once masters here for several years.")

For decades, foreign schools and academies in Rome, led by the German Archaeological Institute, became the chief drivers of research. In the abortive building boom that followed Rome's new status as capital of a unified Italy, streets were dug up, new artworks and ruins discovered, new museums built to house them. For the first time, scientific-minded Italian archaeologists, devoted not to Catholic relics but pagan antiquity, began to undertake excavations. Their dean was Giacomo Boni, a Venetian who oversaw the reconstruction of the Campanile after it toppled into St. Mark's Square. After studying in England and Germany, he pioneered the use of balloon photography and stratigraphic excavations in Italy, and began to oversee systematic digs in the Roman Forum in 1898.

Given his interest in archaeology, Wilder's sojourn was well-timed. Under Boni's guidance, scholars, both Italian and foreign, were exploring Rome with renewed purpose. The classicists of the American Academy were known for the energy they brought to their endeavours. They could be seen in the Forum, hammering together a 15-metre-high scaffold to photograph the reliefs atop the Arch of Septimius Severus, or hanging from the dome of St. Peter's, where they discovered a broad fissure—a defect at first denied, then hastily repaired, by Vatican officials. Some of the brightest stars were women, among them Marion Blake, who studied Roman mosaics and pavements, and Lily Ross Taylor, an authority on Roman mystery cults. Esther Van Deman, a fixture at the Academy since 1901, employed expert draftsmanship, cartography and photography to catalogue ancient Roman construction techniques. Her male colleagues, who nicknamed her the "*tufa* lady," after Rome's characteristic limestone, had at first mocked her for her dirt-smudged dresses and scuffed shoes. By the time she published her pioneering monograph "Methods of Determining the Date of Roman Concrete Monuments," scorn had turned to respect.

"She's the only archaeologist in Rome," a fellow scholar conceded, "who can date a brick by the taste of its mortar."

But the appreciation of Rome was no longer the exclusive purview of barbarians from beyond the Alps, or their brick-licking colleagues from across the Atlantic. Italians who had, until lately, taken Rome's antiquity for granted, were now studying it, cataloguing it, celebrating it, and refashioning it into a new ideology.

This was *Romanità*: the essence of "Roman-ness," and the belief that Rome's long-vanished glory would—sooner rather than later—reappear and raise the city to its rightful place as the Caput Mundi, "the capital of the world."

Two weeks after Wilder had taken up residence at the Academy, he was called into the office of the director, Gorham Stevens, who had a favour to ask him. Some men were wanted to carry the

American flag in a parade to honour the anniversary of Italy's defeat of Austria.

Wilder accepted with reluctance. "What could be more terrible," he fretted to his family, "than marching down these great streets packed with Romans, bearing the flag that every true Italian feels is partly responsible for his country's wrongs." Revolutionary demonstrations, and even pitched street battles, were anticipated along the parade route.

On the morning of the parade, Wilder went to the Palazzo San Marco, where he and several other students were provided with a flag. Inside, General Diaz, the man responsible for Italy's victory over Austria at Vittorio Veneto, presented him with a small maroon-and-yellow striped ribbon and a bronze medal of Romulus and Remus, a "token from Italy to America." The flag-bearers gathered on the steps of "Sacconi's Heap," the still-unfinished Vittoriano monument rising over the Piazza Venezia. Wilder gazed over the throngs that filled the piazza, which gradually filled with ranks of *bersaglieri*, the light infantrymen in their distinctive plumed helmets.

Wilder marched up the Corso, the elegant promenade that leads to the Piazza del Popolo, behind a group of veterans from Naples who sang lustily. The sidewalks were lined with onlookers, held back by lines of police. Some greeted the Stars-and-Stripes with pleased cries of "America!" and "Viva Harding!" But as they approached the Pincio hill, others responded with controlled but unmistakable hissing.

"This criticism had only the effect of making us more proud," he wrote. "In the light of it we saw America, quite differently, as a country that did not have to argue or defend against the misprision of remote peoples."

There were other signs that all was not well. "Everywhere one finds chalk-written 'Viva Lenin!'" he reported. "I'm told I'm standing on the despairing neck of an exhausted people."

But Wilder's ebullience at exploring Rome overcame such misgivings. In truth, as wonderful as the Academy was, it was also something of a bubble, cut off from the real life of the city. Table conversation among the male fellows seemed limited to alcohol, the figures of artists' models, and the price of overcoats.

"To whom can I communicate my pleasures of discovery and recognition?" he lamented. "These little East Side painters and sculptors with their limited talents; these Harvard architects with their conceit and phlegm?" (Wilder's stand-offishness was repaid with mockery. In a classroom wastepaper basket, he found an unflattering cartoon of himself, red-cheeked and bespectacled, captioned "Pop Wilder.")

Fortunately, his status as a visiting scholar, and his skills as a raconteur, had brought him invitations into the parlours of high society. He accepted with alacrity, especially when he learned he could make a meal of the pastries served at high tea, thus economizing the three-and-a-half lire the Academy charged for dinner.

It was as a result of an invitation to tea that his most important and lasting friendship came about. A Mrs. Jackson, head of the Academy's Boston committee, invited him to her parlour to read her his unfinished play. She was impressed, and begged him to share it with her friend, the American wife of the well-known Italian poet and translator of Shelley, Adolfo de Bosis. The de Bosises, she explained, knew everyone; Adolfo was rumoured to have been a lover of the great actress Eleonora Duse. They had been friends of the late Moses Ezekiel, a Jewish-American sculptor who had treated them like daughter and son. In the nineteenth century Ezekiel had kept his studio in the upper levels of the Baths of Diocletian, a complex once able to accommodate 3,200 bathers, and whose *frigidarium* (cold room) alone was large enough to contain an entire Michelangelo-designed church. Evicted when the government claimed the baths for the 1911 archaeological exposition commemorating fifty years of Italian unity, Ezekiel relocated to a tower at the top of the Via Veneto in the city walls. With royal approval, he had engineers turn the tower, built by the Byzantine general Belisarius in the sixth century, into his new residence. Before he died, Ezekiel willed the studio to Signor and Signora de Bosis.

Opening a nondescript iron door set into the wall on a stretch of the Via Campania, Wilder used a red silken rope to ascend a steep stairway walled with damp, pockmarked bricks. He found himself in a studio furnished with dusty divans, Renaissance chests, tiger skins, an enormous alabaster urn, and a piano. In this remarkable setting—a *fin de siècle* salon sequestered within ancient fortifications—a slightly intimidated Wilder read the third act of his play, *Villa Rhabini,* to the de Bosises. Two of their children were there, and listened attentively. Virginia, a brilliant student of Arabic and Aramaic, reminded him of a slightly plainer version of his sister Charlotte. The other was a lean, high-browed youth, whose earnest conversation was leavened by his skipping step and playful black-eyed gaze.

Lauro de Bosis, observed Wilder, was "*elegante,* delicately moustachioed, only nineteen, but conversant, even *passioné,* over higher philosophies, anxious to know if I accepted so-and-so's pluralism, or clung to the Neo-Hegelian realism; urging me to read Plato with a small group of his in the Greek."

Wilder accepted, and the following Sunday rode a streetcar that left Rome via the Porta San Giovanni, along tracks that led along the Via Toscolana deep into the *campagna.* Descending before the town of Frascati, he walked through an iron gateway flanked by two crouching stone lions, down a long avenue of pine and cedar trees, through overgrown garden plots where Ezekiel's cream-coloured marbles of nymphs and gladiators could be glimpsed through green leaves. Outside a reddish-yellow villa hung with flowering wisteria, the de Bosis family and their guests were gathered at an old marble table under a pergola of yellow roses.

"Things went merrily in and out of both languages. Lauro—my friend—and the Arabic-Aramaic sister I admire." From beneath shaggy eyebrows, their father beamed with pleasure at his brilliant children. "They began throwing at each other in Latin and from memory the ridiculous list of books which Rabelais says Pantagruel found at the library of Saint-Victor." Adolfo invited Wilder upstairs to the third-floor library, whose shelves ran the whole length of the villa, to ask his opinion about some thorny lines he was translating from Shelley's *Epipsychidion.*

Wilder became a regular guest at the de Bosis's Sunday open house. The company was invariably brilliant—sculptors, Italian nobles, philosophers, and American bohemians, including one red-headed poet with piercing eyes. (Years later Ezra Pound would tell Wilder that of course, they'd already met, in Rome, at the home of the de Bosises.) Tea with marchesas and the dull conversation at the Academy were quickly forgotten. Those sun-dappled afternoons of good food and heady talk at the Villa Diana were all that Wilder had hoped to find in Rome.

But it was the young de Bosis, with his pencil moustache and lighthearted intellectualism, who made the greatest impression. Lauro seemed to be a perfect product of America and Italy, combining the earnest good sense of his Puritan mother and the gentle Old-World cynicism of his father. Wilder was sure it was the beginning of a beautiful and lasting friendship.

7 THE NEXT SHELLEY

Nancy Cox McCormack was, by inclination and training, a head-hunter. Motherless at the age of three, fatherless by the age of fourteen, a bride by the age of eighteen, she had set out from Nashville, her birthplace, to study sculpture at the St. Louis School of Fine Arts and the Chicago Art Institute. By 1921, after extricating herself from a marriage of convenience, she'd made her way to Europe to study at the fonts of western civilization.

Surviving a difficult childhood had left Cox McCormack self-assured and full of drive; her training had made her into a connoisseur of limbs and skulls that cried out for sculpting. Observing the high cheekbones and expansive temples of a young American poet who sat down at her table at a restaurant in Paris to ask for news from America, she'd insisted on casting his "death mask." (Ezra Pound mailed a photo of the plaster to a hostile *Chicago Tribune* critic.) Arriving in Rome, where female sculptors were a vanishingly rare breed, she'd scoffed at the Italian myth that held that one had to possess the virility of a Bernini to cut marble or cast bronze.

Cox McCormack rented an apartment on Via Margutta, the little dog-legged street that for generations has formed an intimate artists' enclave backing onto the Villa Borghese gardens. Steps from her door was the heart of Rome's foreign enclave, the Piazza di Spagna, filled with cabmen waiting next to their horses, each with an erect pheasant's feather wagging between its ears. In the living profiles of modern-day Romans she saw delineated the same noble features she'd observed on the busts of the emperors in the Capitoline and Vatican museums. On the Spanish Steps lolled moustachioed layabouts dressed up in the traditional garb of herdsmen and peasants, artists' models hoping for a day's work. All around her were worthy heads, begging to be immortalized in stone.

One spring day, she found an apt and willing subject at a reception held in a neighbouring salon on a fifth-floor Via Margutta palazzo. As the first candles were being lit to illuminate the outline of St. Peter's for the last days of the Holy Eucharist, guests gazed down on leisurely couples and nurses pushing perambulators in the Pincio Gardens. Welcoming Cox McCormack with a cup of tea, her host, the head of the British Academy, told her he had someone to introduce her to.

"He presented a startling ivory-faced young man who had glided across the Turkish rugs to be introduced," she would recall. "I say 'glided' for that was the smooth toe-first manner in which Lauro de Bosis walked, as if unconscious of space itself." Cox McCormack noted the youth's features: he had "dark forward eyes, fine black hair and a tiny black mustache," a rounded chin and a full mouth that "curled up at the corners as if he were infinitely satisfied with the flavor of adventure."

Oblivious to the fact that he was in the midst of a formal gathering, the young man puckishly placed himself on the floor at her feet, and proceeded to grill her with questions about her life, her art, and her most deeply held beliefs. At once charmed and mortified by the attentions of this "sapling Hamlet in an burning mood," she extricated herself to talk to another guest, the director of the French Academy, who pointed out the walls of the nearby Villa Medici, around which hundreds of fork-tailed swallows were darting in the dying glow of the Roman twilight.

As she chatted, Cox McCormack continued to glance at the ardent youth with her keen hunter's eye, measuring his shapely skull, mentally adding another head to her list.

Lauro de Bosis, a young man destined to amaze the world, rarely failed to make a strong first impression. On the brink of adulthood, he was boyishly handsome, lithely athletic, almost princely in demeanour. Children gathered around when he entered a room, and he would delight them by swiftly confecting an origami frog or producing a flaming match from a handkerchief. His peers were astonished by his worldliness, eclectic interests, and precocious erudition. From his boyhood, his father had taught him to chant verse in ancient Greek, medieval Italian, and modern-day English. While other boys drew dragons and automobiles, his childhood sketchbooks were filled with images of flight: Icarus soaring on homemade wings, the winged horse Pegasus rising against the Mediterranean sun, Apollo driving fiery steeds through the heavens. His early schooling in literature, history, and ancient languages had made him at once discerningly romantic and proudly Roman in spirit. His conversation was studded with words like "glory," "imperishable," and "immortal," and he would walk away from anyone who suggested Wordsworth was a better poet than Keats or Shelley.

Lauro's penchant for high-minded conversation was leavened by physical prowess, playful energy, and an indomitable *joie de vivre.* Reciting lines from Virgil on a moonlit walk in the Campagna, he might impulsively shuck his clothes to go for a dip in a volcanic lake. A friend of his father's once witnessed a teenaged Lauro dive from a railway bridge over the shallow Tiber, swim with strong strokes to the riverbank, and rise from the water "like an ooze-covered Latium lake-god." Long days swimming in the Adriatic, where his parents had their summer residence, had earned him the nickname "Fofino"—"Fofo" for short—after the word in the local dialect for "little octopus."

He was, in short, a golden boy: half-Italian, half-American, wholly original. For Thornton Wilder, Edgar and Lilian Mowrer, Nancy Cox McCormack and others who encountered him in the early twenties, he seemed to blaze as vividly as a comet over a chaotic, war-darkened nation.

Lauro's origins were improbably poetic. His father's family came from Ancona, an Adriatic port founded by settlers from Syracuse where the local dialect was still peppered with words of ancient Greek origin. When Adolfo de Bosis was ten, his father, who had married his brother's widowed wife, shot himself with a revolver; after his death, fifty thousand lire were found missing from his stepchildren's accounts. Adolfo, who had suffered from bouts of depression since his infancy, was sent away to boarding school. Only the discovery of the work of a transcendent English poet lifted him out of his gloom. Taught the language by a blind, half-British tutor, Adolfo set about translating Percy Bysshe Shelley's "Time" into Italian at the age of sixteen.

The de Bosises had once been wealthy landowners, but Adolfo's father's death had left him only a small inheritance. Obliged to make his own way, he left Ancona to enroll at the University of Rome, where he graduated as a doctor-in-law. He was appointed executor to the House of Borghese, helping Prince Marcantonio, a nobleman bankrupt in Rome's post-Risorgimento building boom, to dispose of some forty thousand properties.

Allowed the run of the "Harpsichord"—as the Borghese Palace, now the home of the Spanish Embassy in the Piazza Borghese, is known to Romans for its trapezoidal ground plan—he turned a private chamber where Pope Paul V had once soaked in a marble bathtub under a frescoed vault into the editorial offices of *Il Convito* (The Banquet). Devoted to *fin de siècle* decadence, the literary review published the first instalments of a novel by a brilliant young writer named Gabriele d'Annunzio.

Adolfo de Bosis and d'Annunzio had much in common. They were both the same age, both enamoured of French decadence and British romanticism, both intent on making their way as ambitious provincials in Rome. But while de Bosis was high-minded, scrupulous, and hard-working, d'Annunzio was already embarking on his career as a mythomaniac, a serial womanizer, and a self-entitled sponger. He was also a spectacularly bad influence on de Bosis. In the summer of 1887, when d'Annunzio's young wife was in the last month of a pregnancy, he convinced de Bosis to sail out of the port of Pescara. The devil-may-care d'Annunzio anticipated an adventure like Shelley's ill fated voyage on the *Don Juan*. In a lightly fictionalized sketch describing the voyage, his surrogate's travel companion declares: "We will die like Percy!"

The boat they sailed on, a little cutter called the *Lady Clara*, belonged to de Bosis, but d'Annunzio took charge of the preparations, hiring two incompetent sailors to serve as crew on a whim because he liked the sound of their names. D'Annunzio spent his days sunbathing naked on the deck. When they spotted a deserted beach, they would row to shore, lay out Persian rugs, cushions, and a silver tea set and picnic in their white linens. One day, dangerously far from shore north of Rimini, an Adriatic squall picked up. The foundering *Lady Clara* was driven close to the coastal rocks, and it looked as though the poets would indeed share Shelley's fate. Some Italian navy ships happened to be doing maneuvers nearby, and the little boat was spotted, winched aboard the ironclad cruiser, and ignominiously deposited at Venice's Arsenal.

The escapade was a turning point for d'Annunzio. Being snatched from a wind-powered idyll by a mighty coal-driven warship seemed to transform him from a "mere poet" to a technology-inebriated advocate of the cleansing power of modern warfare. The following year, he published an ode *To a Torpedo Boat in the Adriatic*, describing it—in terms that anticipated the bellicose tropes of Futurism—as being as "beautiful as a naked blade." Revelling in his notoriety, d'Annunzio booked an expensive room in a hotel on the Venice's Riva degli Schiavoni. He begged his friend for money to cover the bill, initiating a habit of welching from de Bosis that would endure for years.

One good thing did come out of de Bosis's friendship with d'Annunzio. On a train bound for Naples, the two young writers began to squabble about which one of them had forgotten to bring the cigars. A foreigner who was sharing the compartment smiled and offered them the pick of his humidor. Talk turned to a recent exhibition in Rome, and de Bosis opined that the only good thing he'd seen was a modern work by an American sculptor.

"Oh, you liked it?" exclaimed the white-haired foreigner. "I did it!" Moses Ezekiel invited the erudite young lawyer to visit him at his studio in the Baths of Diocletian upon his return to Rome. De Bosis would end up moving in, paying the equivalent of seven cents a month for a room facing the clock atop the Termini train station, a rent that included breakfast, maid service, and cigars. Living in Ezekiel's lively and democratic artistic salon provided de Bosis an entree to bohemian Rome and a fast track to literary prominence.

One evening Ezekiel took de Bosis to a gathering organized by the American ambassador to the royal court in the Palazzo del

Drago, where he was introduced to a tall young woman, dressed simply in a brown robe decorated with a bouquet of pansies. Lillian Vernon was American, but spoke perfect Italian, and impressed him by repeating her favourite line from the *Ode to the West Wind*: "If Winter comes, can Spring be far behind?" He responded by chanting, in a vibrating voice, his own translation of Shelley's "Time."

Lillian cut an unusual figure in Rome. She was pure American Gothic, a long-boned, large-framed Puritan with strong hands and an upright bearing, who favoured long grey, mauve, or black dresses. Though descended from pioneer stock that had crossed the Midwest in covered wagons to settle in Iowa, her life had taken an exotic turn when her clergyman father was selected to establish St. Paul's Methodist, the first Protestant church within the walls of Rome. Left by industrious parents in the care of teachers and governesses, she was speaking full sentences in Italian by the age of six.

"The resulting predilection of mine for everything Italian produced a detachment from my own people," Lillian would recall in an unpublished memoir. "I thirsted for caresses, but [my mother] told me that I was too effusive, too demonstrative, and she never came near me."

In an attempt to cleanse their daughter of her growing Italianness, her parents sent her to school in Syracuse, New York. But before leaving Rome, Lillian had visited the Trevi Fountain, and tossed in the handful of coins that, according to the venerable superstition, would ensure her return. For two years, Adolfo sent her daily letters, courting her by mail as only a poet could. Reunited in Rome, they were married in 1890. Their first child, born three years later, was named Percy in honour of the poet who had brought them together.

For the most part, the union of the Italianized Midwesterner and the brooding Latin Anglophile was a happy one. De Bosis, while remaining a loyal lawyer to the Roman nobility, became Italy's foremost translator of Shelley, and a respected composer of somewhat old-fashioned verse, a poet who could be counted on to deliver an oration at Keats's grave or recite for the German queen dowager. *Il Convito*, from its headquarters in the Borghese pope's former bathroom, became a platform for fashionable turn-of-the-century literary decadence; a dozen issues, printed on the most luxurious paper, would feature works by Oscar Wilde and d'Annunzio's novel *The Virgins of the Rocks*. In surroundings of Pre-Raphaelite luxury, Lillian's Puritanism was mellowed, and she became a loving and generous mother to six children. Only one tragedy afflicted their *belle époque* idyll: the death of their seventh-born child, sixteen-month-old Manlio, after a high fever.

Lauro was born two days later, on December 9, 1901. His parents, mourning the loss of Manlio, hoped that this—the last fruit of a union born of a shared love for poetry—might prove to be the reincarnation of Shelley.

Nancy Cox McCormack had found a strategy for coping with Lauro, who was all-too-obviously smitten with her. Following the reception on Via Margutta, he'd taken her on a stroll to the swan-filled pond in the adjoining Villa Borghese, serenading her with verse until the mounted police bugled the closing of the park. A series of letters, written in his still shaky English, followed, pleading to be allowed to see her again. ("Do you know what you are for me? Do you only know what you have done of me? Have I in any way offended you?... I kiss your hands with deep emotion.") It wouldn't do, of course; she was sixteen years his senior. "His head at the time was too boyish for the age of twenty-one years," she observed. It was, however, admirably shaped, and fit for sculpting.

So, when Lauro insisted on knocking at the door of her studio at odd hours, she asked him to take a seat on a high stool, and began to put up clay. "Sitting for a portrait, speaking continually in imperfect English which I constantly corrected, completely appealed to him." It also calmed his ardour, allowing her to establish a more fitting relationship with this importunate youth. "Repeatedly he would exclaim, 'What shall I do to be worthy of having my likeness in enduring bronze?'"

Between sittings, Lauro introduced her to his world. He was an expert *cicerone* to Rome, whose streets had been his playground when he was a child, and whose monuments and ruins were the font of his rich imaginative life. It was clear that for Lauro, the great figures of the past, from Adonis to Garibaldi, were contemporaries, as alive to him as any artist's model lolling on the Spanish Steps. He obtained a *permesso* to the Villa Doria-Pamphili, next to the American Academy, whose gardens Thornton Wilder used to write letters home, and took her to the church built over the third-century BC Mamertine prison where the condemned St. Peter was said to have made a spring appear to baptize his pagan guards. "His preference for Etruscan art, the Roman ruins, the Augusteo, and in fact all antiquities was somewhat fantastic—but Roman."

One day, Lauro invited her to meet him atop the Palatine, the hill that rises from the Forum, where the wealthiest citizens of Republican and Imperial Rome once had their residences.

"I was escorted by a positively glowing youth," Cox McCormack wrote in a lyrical essay, "who lilts as he leaps—Lauro de Bosis." Picking their way over ancient chariot-wheel ruts in hard-lava pavements, they arrived at a modern pavilion built over the arches of one of the hill's most impressive structures, the Palace of the Caesars. Now the Palatine Museum, where statuary and artifacts explicate the pre-history of the Imperial Forum, it was then the shambolic headquarters of Italy's most illustrious archaeologist. Without bothering to pull the visitors' bell rope, Lauro pushed open a wired "gate towards the veranda overgrown with clematis, jasmine, and rose vines not yet in flower. At the first door, he tapped rather restrainedly, calling in a musical voice: 'Vittoria! Vittoria!'"

Cox McCormack heard the thumping of bare feet on stone. A peasant girl appeared, smiled at Lauro, and invited them to wait in a private garden until "Il Commendatore" was ready to receive them.

They were invited into a high-ceiling study. Cox McCormack looked around in wonder. The walls were brocaded with reliefs taken from the houses of ancient senators and consuls. Perched on the severed trunk of an oak tree was a marble torso, recently discovered in the courtyard of the House of the Vestal Virgins. A table that ran the length of the studio was studded with inscribed stone fragments that peasants had discovered in the Roman *campagna*, awaiting identification and translation by the "Commander" of the Palatine.

In the midst of it all was a white-bearded man dressed in tweeds, seated behind a table on a hard wooden chair. This was Giacomo Boni, the Venetian who over two decades had revolutionized the excavations in the Forum with the most up-to-date archaeological techniques.

"To look into his face brought one within the magic circle of the potentialities of an evolved soul. On his features, so strongly modelled, not a trace of hardness lurked to mar the philosophical serenity of approaching age." In fluent and mellifluous English, acquired during his studies at Oxford, Boni chatted with the persuasive American, and nodded his assent when she proposed sculpting his bust.

Cox McCormack had found an ideal subject for her next work, and she had Lauro to thank for it. Over many mornings, Boni sat patiently in a hard wooden chair, sharing stories of his childhood in Venice, where he earned money guiding English tourists to the lagoon's islands, all the while planting the pine cones to fulfill a private dream of restoring the forests of Italy as Dante had known them.

Lauro also introduced Cox McCormack to his family, who welcomed her at their main residence, an eighteenth-century palazzo near the American Express office on the cobblestoned Via dei Due Macelli (named for two *macelli*, or abattoirs, that once occupied the street). The rooftop terrazzo, reached by a caged elevator, offered a panorama from the dome of St. Peter's to the dramatic line of flat-topped umbrella pines atop Monte Mario. At the Villa Diana, Cox McCormack enjoyed long Sunday lunches in the company of their three married daughters: Eleonore, the youngest; Charis, then living in Milan; and the eldest, Virginia, the scholar of Arabic and Aramaic who so fascinated Thornton Wilder. She met the eldest son, the poetically named Percy, and handsome Vittorio, a promising medical student. With their palazzo in the historic heart of Rome, their rustic villa a streetcar's ride away in the *campagna*, the studio they'd inherited from Ezekiel in the Aurelian Walls, as well as the sixteenth-century tower near Ancona where the family summered overlooking the Adriatic Sea, the de Bosises seemed to live on a privileged, happy plane, far above the day-to-day turmoil of life in post-war Italy.

The First World War, though, had not left the family completely unscathed. As Cox McCormack sculpted his bust, Lauro told her the story of another brother, "*caro* Valente," who had risen to the rank of captain in a naval air squadron. At the age of twenty-three, this veteran of dozens of missions in the Venetian Apennines had encountered a heavy wind as he approached his base in Palermo. At one hundred metres, the engine of his seaplane suddenly failed, and it plunged into the sea.

When divers found his body, intact amidst the wires of the floating wreckage, Valente's corpse seemed to be wearing a grin.

"His usual smile!" Lauro recalled. "Perhaps he wasn't afraid to die."

Lauro, then eighteen, had begged to be allowed to enlist. His parents had convinced him that, with his two surviving brothers still in uniform, he was needed at home.

By the time the summer heat had begun, Cox McCormack's sculpture was complete. Unlike the full-size marble likeness of the archaeologist Boni, Lauro's was a desk-sized bust. The sculptor had modelled a wispy moustache, a furrowed brow, and other hints of maturity. But the skull was unlined, and so round and smooth it invited one to cup it in a palm. What Cox McCormack had cast, in weighty bronze, was the head of an infant.

By then, the headhunter from Nashville had decided on her next sculpture. This one, like its subject, would be larger-than-life. She had seen the man's likeness in newspapers, in posters in the *piazze*, and measured the jutting jaw and high temples while watching newsreels. She wouldn't have to go far to find him, for Il Duce and his blackshirts were already making plans for the day, in the very near future, when they would make Rome their headquarters.

Cox McCormack had already set about making the enquiries that would bring her into the presence of Benito Mussolini.

Thornton Wilder's sojourn in Rome had come to a sudden end, when—after seven months of freedom from his father's influence—a telegram arrived from New Haven, commanding him with capitalized concision: "HAVE JOB FOR YOU TEACHING NEXT YEAR LAWRENCEVILLE, LEARN FRENCH."

Wilder had dutifully cancelled plans to visit Florence and Venice, and taken a train to Paris, where he found a room in a Latin Quarter hotel. He knew no one in the city. Though he loved roaming the quais of the Seine, and sitting in the cheap seats of the Théâtre du Vieux-Colombier, mentally, he was still living in Rome. At night, he would return to his bed-bug ridden room, to work on a new prose manuscript he was calling *Memoirs of Charles Mallison:*

The Year in Rome, turning his tea-time conversations with elderly noblewomen into a fantasia about an aristocratic clique living in contemporary Rome who were actually immortal ancient gods. When the novel was published four years later as *The Cabala,* it bore the dedication: "To my friends at the American Academy in Rome, 1920–21, T.W."

In truth, Wilder had been ready to leave the American Academy. The appearance of an art history professor and his family had forced him, three months after his arrival, to move from his roomy suite in the Villino Bellacci into the dorm rooms on the upper floor of the Main Building, where he was forced to sleep in bunks and share a bathroom. By spring, he was looking for any excuse to get off the Academy grounds. Rolfe, the classical scholar with whom he'd shared a floor at the Villino, seemed to have taken a special dislike to Wilder. Roaming the halls restlessly, trailed by a trained nurse, Rolfe would pound manically on the piano, accuse the head-waiter of poisoning his coffee, or rave about a beautiful noblewoman with whom he was having an illusory affair. He was finally sent back to America, but not before threatening Wilder: "You're going into the Tiber this afternoon, see! This is no joke."

Leaving Rome was harder. The city had been an awakening, both political and aesthetic, for Wilder. He had witnessed the violence in the streets, the post-war poverty, all the ferment and turmoil of contemporary Italy. At the Teatro Valle, he had attended the second performance of *Six Characters in Search of an Author,* an astonishing play by a Sicilian dramatist named Luigi Pirandello.[*] Pirandello was undeniably a modern—it was well known the playwright identified himself with the new doctrine of Fascism—and so part of the world that his backwards-looking fellows at the Academy preferred to ignore.

---

[*] Sixteen years later, the meta-theatrical technique of opening the curtain on the Director, whose rehearsal is then interrupted by a family claiming to be play's author's unfinished characters, would find an echo in the Stage Manager of Wilder's *Our Town.*

Most of all, Rome had given Wilder the confidence to imagine what had until then been unimaginable: a life in writing.

His most vivid memories, though, were not of the cynical marchesas with whom he'd shared pastries, but of the de Bosises. The family lived, he would later recall "for books and conversation... the chief thing I remember about the family dinner was the *high-browism*, golly how learned they all were. But it was all so easy and joyous." In his last letter to his family from Rome, he confessed to a Platonic infatuation with their eldest daughter: "I am in love with an Italian lady, with Virginia de Bosis. With her amazing mind, I must add, so difficult and complex that to discover it all is ungallantly to have embarrassed her."

It was his friendship with their youngest son—that brilliant Italian youth with whom he'd taken long walks in parks and ruined palaces—that would prove the most enduring. Wilder was confident the world would hear more of Lauro. There was more to this young man than just high spirits and parlour tricks.

"There was something melancholy—no, searching, uneasy—in some bottom layer of his thought, life," Wilder later recalled. "I remember that he took me out to the tombs of the Appian Way one night with an American woman—he joking and playing all the time—but all was mask. He was unable to canalize the deep emotion that arises from the almost terrifying succession of mighty graves."

Before leaving Rome, Wilder handed the young man a handful of dollars. He told him they would come in handy, when—not if—Lauro crossed the ocean to discover America.

PART II

"I did not create Fascism. I drew it from the Italians'
unconscious minds. If that had not been so, they would not all have
followed me for twenty years—I repeat, *all* of them."
–Benito Mussolini

8 THE MARCH ON ROME

They came from the north, as the Visigoths had fifteen hundred years before them, trudging along the ancient roads that converge on Rome, their homemade shirts of black cotton and wool soaked through with the cold autumn rain.

Curious peasants who came out to watch the miserable columns marching along the Via Nomentana noticed that only a few of the men were armed, mostly with old hunting rifles. The rest carried clubs and daggers tucked into their belts. At crossroads, they stopped to ask directions, for the few maps they had were inadequate or outdated. When they reached the gates in the old city walls on the morning of October 28, 1922, they came to a complete halt, milling about under the sheets of drenching rain as they waited for news from their leader.

For months, Mussolini had been threatening to seize control of Rome, at the head of three hundred thousand disciplined Fascists whom he predicted would stream in from every corner of Italy.

"It is our intention to make Rome the city of our spirit," Il Duce had announced in a speech a month earlier, "purged and disinfected of all that have corrupted it and dragged it into the mire. We aim to make Rome the beating heart, the galvanizing spirit of the Italy we dream of."

Yet when the time came to march, only sixteen thousand Fascists, most from neighbouring Tuscany, gathered in the village of Monterotondo and the other main assembly points around Rome. Thousands had given up when their trains were stopped by police at three strategic rail stations along the way. Though subsequent myth-making would swell their numbers fivefold, as few as nine thousand men were present for the final march into Rome. Waiting for them within the walls was an entire garrison, reinforced by five battalions of crack Alpine troops, any one of which could have dispersed the poorly armed invaders.

Mussolini was not among the marchers. A week earlier, just before a party conference in Naples—the Fascists' first foray into the south, to a city within convenient striking distance of the capital—he had handed responsibility for the march over to the *ras* of Ferrara, Italo Balbo, and three other party leaders, and returned by train to his home in Milan, some five hundred kilometres north of Rome.

Edgar Mowrer, who happened to be passing through Milan, found Mussolini with his bags packed, ready to make a run north to the nearby Swiss border if the march failed. The night before he had made a public show of nonchalance by attending a performance of *The Merry Widow* at the Manzoni Theatre. Mowrer saw him just after a call had come from the king, summoning him to Rome. Mussolini crowed to the American newsman: "Now we shall have a government that will govern."

At 8:30 on the evening of October 29, Mussolini boarded a southbound *direttissimo*. The "express," which stopped along the way so he could address the crowds at Fascist-occupied stations, took fourteen hours to reach Rome. It was only then that the sodden marchers, who had been waiting without provisions for two days, were allowed to enter the city. Mussolini's "March on Rome," which began in the sleeping compartment of a train, ended in the back of the chauffeur-driven limousine that conducted him to the Quirinal Palace.

The King was waiting for him. Victor Emmanuel III, who had succeeded his father after Umberto was assassinated by an Italian-American anarchist in 1900, was an unlikely monarch. Little more than five feet tall, with watery blue eyes that darted around when he was nervous, he often seemed to be more interested in his collection of rare coins than in affairs of state. To the consternation of Luigi Facta, a Liberal who had only reluctantly accepted the post of prime minister, the king refused to declare a state of emergency. Some said he had been warned by the commander-in-chief of the army, General Diaz, that sympathetic soldiers might join the marchers. Others whispered he was worried his taller, more military-minded cousin, the Duke of Aosta—a Fascist sympathizer and second-in-line to the throne—was angling to usurp him. Mussolini, dressed in a bowler hat, spats, and wearing a formal morning coat over his tight-fitting black shirt, accepted the royal invitation to form a government. The king then implored him to send his followers, those feral-eyed ruffians who were parading in front of his palace chanting *"Eia, Eia, Eia, Alalà!"*, far away from Rome.

Italy's next prime minister, who had taken power with a show of violence against a faltering and disunited liberal state, magnanimously promised to disperse his men within twenty-four hours.

The place Mussolini had publicly scorned as parasitic and hopelessly debauched, the Eternal City that was secretly the focus of all his provincial ambitions, was now in his hands.

On October 31, 1922, Rome became a Fascist city. It would remain one for the next twenty years.

Nancy Cox McCormack could stand it no longer. All through that unusually rainy autumn, she had only adventured into the streets to walk around the corner from her studio, to dine at the Pensione Rocchi. There, welcomed at a table that included a Sicilian museum director, a captain in the cavalry, and an opera-singer in training, she tried to follow the dinner-time conversation on Italy's convoluted politics.

"I was in the midst of this group when Mussolini marched on Rome," she would later write. "Every artist I knew on the Via Margutta was enthusiastic about the *'stellone'* (great star) who had appeared in the sky 'to save Italy from utter ruin.'"

Finally, on the last day of October, she put on her best English tweeds, and walked towards the Via del Corso, where crowds had gathered in hopes of glimpsing Mussolini at his inauguration at the Chamber of Deputies. On walls along the way, people stopped to read typewritten notices announcing the triumphant entry of the Fascists.

"Driven by curiosity and the psychic pressure of it all," she would recall, "I ventured into the streets. I did not see another woman about. Fifty thousand armed men, in black-shirts, were taking posts inside and out of the city. The quiet of the streets was unbroken save by the marching of feet, the rushing by of machine guns and armed wagons. Several artists I knew passed among the spirited black-shirts. I learned later the parents were more surprised than I to know their sons formed a part of a practically secret army in full revolution. During the week that followed, I had reason to marvel at the lack of bloodshed."

In fact, the Fascists, their advance-guard swollen by new arrivals when it was clear the government was offering no resistance, were terrorizing the city's poorer neighbourhoods. They strutted through the working-class streets around the Basilica of

San Lorenzo, brandishing guns purloined from army barracks. The offices of left-wing newspapers, social clubs, and co-operatives were occupied and destroyed. Blackshirts burst into the home of former prime minister Francesco Nitti, hurling furniture out the windows to be burnt in a pyre on the cobblestones below. The violence was far worse in the provinces of northern Italy, where triumphant squadrists seized post offices, railway stations, and telegraph offices, and inflicted castor-oil purgatives on Socialists.

Nor did Cox McCormack witness Mussolini's performance when, at the age of thirty-nine, he entered the Chamber of Deputies as Italy's youngest prime minister. As Fascist ministers sang Gabriele d'Annunzio's battle-hymn, *"Giovinezza,"* he repeatedly lifted his right arm in a Roman salute, before making a hyperbolic speech in praise of his own self-restraint.

"With three hundred thousand young men armed from top to toe, determined for action come what may, ready, with almost mystical intensity, to respond to my command, I could have unleashed reprisals on all those who have slandered and blackened the Fascist movement."

True to his promise to the king, and determined to show that he was in complete command of his party, Mussolini ordered the marchers to leave Rome. The mobs who had expected to be given the run of the city roamed the streets like disoriented tourists, before boarding sixty specially commissioned trains waiting to whisk them away from Termini Station.

"This is indeed a step forward for civilization," Cox McCormack exulted at the seemingly orderly regime change. "A hope that the war had taught something and that there existed a mob psychology that ran towards construction instead of destruction."

From their rooftop *terrazzo*, the de Bosis family had a good view of the blackshirts in the Via del Corso. Lauro's father was initially philosophical about the success of the Fascists' bluff.

"Mussolini," Adolfo told Cox McCormack, "was the king's expedient for avoiding worse conditions. Italians needed strong leadership and discipline sufficient to strengthen the national morale." For all his freedom-loving romanticism, Adolfo remained a Conservative, deeply embedded in the established order.

His youngest son, for the time being, seemed to cautiously accept Mussolini's seizure of power. Since Lauro was a boy, one of his most intimate friends was Giorgio de Santillana. Handsome, scholarly, and arrogant, he was the son of a famous Jewish lawyer from Tunis, with whom Adolfo had attended university. Lauro and his friend shared a thorough disdain for the compromised Liberal elite, particularly Giolitti, the six-time prime minister whose self-serving machinations during the war they saw as a betrayal of the highest ideals of Italy's nineteenth-century Risorgimento.

"He had hopes in the new regime," de Santillana observed of Lauro. "His brother Valente had fallen while serving in the Air Force: love and reverence for the sacrifice of the army were a tradition in the family. He could not stand out against this movement which consisted mainly of ex-combatants." Lauro was gulled, like the journalist Edgar Mowrer and many observers at the time, by Mussolini's strategy of temporarily distancing himself from the worst excesses of his *squadristi*. Recalled de Santillana: "He used to say: 'I imagine we are all of one mind on the subject. We are for Mussolini and against the Fascists.'"

Lauro was more emphatic on the subject of the original *Duce*, his father's one-time friend Gabriele d'Annunzio. He admired the literary skill of the writer; for the man, he had nothing but contempt.

D'Annunzio, who in Fiume had also boasted he could lead three hundred thousand soldiers to Rome, was long considered the likeliest candidate to rule Italy. Party purists, disgusted when Mussolini had proposed a coalition with the Socialists and the

Catholic *Partito Popolare* that August, contacted the poet and implored him to seize the capital. But d'Annunzio, who by then was consuming large quantities of cocaine and sedatives, was indisposed. On a summer night, while reportedly fondling a cellist as her older sister played the piano, he had toppled headfirst from the windowsill of the Vittoriale, seriously fracturing his skull. D'Annunzio, style-setter and innovator of twentieth-century Fascism's death-worshipping aesthetic, had permanently fallen out of the picture. He would spend the rest of his life under genteel house-arrest, ensconced in *fin de siècle* decadence in his lakefront palazzo.

Lauro's family connection to d'Annunzio gave him intimate knowledge of the way the poet emotionally tortured the woman in his life. His father, who was an attorney to Eleonora Duse (with whom he was rumoured to have had an affair) had told him how d'Annunzio had cast aside the great actress.

"He is a pig," Lauro told de Santillana. "The man who never fell in love."

Lauro's disdain was rooted in what de Santillana saw as the key to his friend's personality: his chivalrous and open nature. But there was a Puritanical cast, perhaps passed on by his mother, to his gallantry. Once, after kissing a young woman he didn't truly love, he mortified his own flesh by pressing a lit cigarette into his forearm to impress the transgression on his memory. De Santillana was amazed when, after an admired friend confided that a cad had persisted with his unwanted advances, Lauro chose to become her avenger.

"I reproved him for letting himself in for a duel with a disreputable character for such a futile affair," recalled his friend. "Every time he was confronted with a serious issue, he analysed the situation from the point of view of universals. He reasoned out the case as Spinoza would have done. Then he went and dispassionately knocked down his man, for he had a heavy hand a well-trained fist." As much as he respected Lauro, de Santillana knew it was a dangerous time for chivalry.

At the time of the March on Rome, Lauro was at a crossroads. In an attempt to rid himself of what he called the family's "poetical whooping-cough," that summer he had completed a degree in chemistry at the University of Rome. But the job he found at a technological institute after graduating was unrewarding, and he turned his attention back to his real loves, philosophy and literature. He devoured Plato, William James, and Nietzsche, studied Heisenberg's physics, and began a translation of *The Golden Bough*, the anthropologist J.G. Frazer's comparative study of the founding myths of religions. Long confirmed in atheism, Lauro gravitated towards the philosophy of Hegel, Kant, and the Italian idealist Benedetto Croce.

De Santillana travelled with his friend to Sicily and the Aeolian Islands for the Easter vacations of 1922. In Syracuse, Lauro had watched ancient dramas being re-enacted in the Greek amphitheatre carved into a rocky hillside. On the island of Salina, which offered spectacular views of a Stromboli in constant eruption, Lauro was imprisoned after it was discovered thirty lire had been stolen from the post-office safe; the local police pinned the theft on the young strangers. In his cell, he asked to be given a volume of Sophocles to read. When he was released two days later—with apologies—he was well embarked on an Italian verse translation of *Oedipus Rex* from the original Greek.

Back in Rome, Lauro's literary projects were encouraged and fostered by the well-connected Cox McCormack. The sculptor gave him a letter of introduction to her friend Ezra Pound, whom Lauro visited in Paris on the way to sell some family prints in London. ("Afterwards," Cox McCormack observed dryly, "Pound wrote me that young de Bosis 'is my kind,' which he was not in reality.") On Lauro's return to Rome, she brought a man interested in producing a series of plays for the benefit of disabled veterans to the de Bosis's home. Lauro's translation of *Oedipus Rex* would fit the bill nicely, he thought. The performances were to take place that spring, in the vast first-century stadium atop the Palatine Hill overlooking the Forum.

It was there, within sight of Giacomo Boni's archaeological studio, on the evening of May 18, 1923, that Lauro was brought to the attention of the new *Duce* of Rome. Oedipus, played by a member of the same troupe Lauro had seen performing in Syracuse, struck out his own eyes with golden pins as the sun went down behind the Janiculum Hill. Watching from the front row, dressed in uniform to honour the gathered veterans, were the king and the Fascist prime minister he had brought to power.

Mussolini joined the applause of the enormous crowd when the gifted translator of Sophocles stepped forward to make a deep, gentlemanly bow of acknowledgment.

Lauro de Bosis, who had dared stage the story of a fate-doomed Greek tyrant on the greatest hill of ancient Rome, was a young man who would bear watching.

Lilian Mowrer was worried about her friends. She had chosen to stay indoors at their palazzo on the Via della Scrofa on the morning of the March on Rome. As curious as she was to witness the coming of the blackshirts, she was expecting her first child, and didn't want to risk her health by going out into the driving rain. In the weeks that followed, she was dismayed to observe the reaction in the household that had until recently seemed one of the happiest in Rome.

"With the de Bosis family it was though there were a corpse in our midst. Adolfo, the poet-businessman, aged ten years in a few weeks. He could hardly speak about what had happened to his country... the intense nationalism of Fascism was in sharp contrast to everything that they stood for. The de Bosises were among the few Italians who really kept 'open house' and put into practice their belief in the value of international co-operation."

As for Lauro, whom the Mowrers had first known as "a friendly inquisitive schoolboy," he "hoped at first that the bold promises of Fascism might really regenerate his country, but experience quickly disillusioned him."

Edgar had recently published *Immortal Italy*, which concluded by implying that Fascism was on the wane. But with Mussolini in power, life was getting more dangerous for an American newsman, particularly one who had predicted in print that the innately tolerant Italians would reject a reactionary government "that is somehow unnatural and comic."

Edgar made a trip to the United States. With the future of Diana Jane, their newborn daughter, in mind, he decided to accept a new posting from the *Chicago Daily News*.

"I returned to Rome in time for Christmas with my wife and fascinating baby daughter and to say farewell to the city which not even Mussolini could permanently spoil."

After eight years in Italy, Lilian was ready to leave. Daily life in Rome had become an endless spectacle of pompous parades, public speeches with military celebrations of First World War victories, and strutting blackshirt officers. They had found furnished rooms in a quiet neighbourhood in the west of Berlin, where Edgar was to begin work as a correspondent in the spring.

A well-ordered democracy like Weimar Germany promised to be a much better environment in which to raise a child.

9 TRAMPING THE CAMPAGNA

It never failed to amaze visitors, the way Rome simply *stopped*. One minute they were treading on cobblestones, surrounded by Baroque spires and Renaissance fountains. The next, they'd crossed one of the gates in the Aurelian Walls, and were tramping on pastureland, their only company shepherds and their flocks.

There was nowhere else in the world like the *campagna*. At the height of the Empire, the low-lying countryside outside Rome, bounded by the Tyrrhenian Sea to the southwest, the Alban and Sabine Hills to the southeast, and the Tiber to the north and west, was the playground of wealthy Romans. The emperor Hadrian built an immense villa, twice the size of the city of Pompeii, at Tivoli, and wealthy families turned the coast north of Ostia, ancient Rome's seaport, into a virtually uninterrupted line of noble residences. The roads and waterworks that starfished out from the city gates—among them the Via Appia Antica, the Via Tiburtina, the Via Nomentana, and the Via Salaria—made the metropolis and its hinterland into a single, continuous entity.

Then the water supply was cut off during the barbarian sieges, pirate attacks drove people back from the shores, and malarial mosquitoes depopulated the countryside. By the nineteen-twenties, what remained evoked Shelley's poem "Ozymandias": colossal wrecks scattered in verdant desolation, a landscape that haunted all who hiked through it.

"We went climbing," wrote Charles Dickens, when he visited half a century earlier, "over an unbroken succession of mounds, and heaps, and hills, of ruin. Tombs and temples, overthrown and prostrate; small fragments of columns, friezes, pediments; great blocks of granite and marble; mouldering arches, grass-grown and decayed. In the distance, ruined aqueducts went stalking on their giant course along the plain; and every breath of wind that swept towards us, stirred early flowers and grasses, springing up, spontaneously, on miles of ruin."

It was an atmosphere that had enchanted a young archaeologist named Gilbert Bagnani since he was a teenager. Though he was born in Rome, most of his boyhood had been spent elsewhere. As a young man, his father, the son of a pharmacist from Pisa, had joined the *bersaglieri*, the light infantry of the Italian army. Ugo Bagnani had risen to the rank of captain when he met Florence Ruby Dewar, who had grown up on the shores of Lake Ontario, the only child of a doctor in a small town a hundred kilometres east of Toronto. Just four years old when her father died, Florence was taken by her widowed mother to Scotland, where she was raised by relatives. The unlikely couple—a moustachioed Italian officer and his dour Canadian fiancée—were married at the chapel of the Trinity College School in Port Hope on September 14, 1897.

Their first and only child was born three years later. Gilbert had a privileged, if unsettled, childhood. Ugo's career kept his small family on the move, first to a posting in Verona, then to London, where he served as Italy's first appointed military attaché.

Gilbert learned to speak English, with impeccable diction and a slight lisp, at the Court of St. James. His playmates were the sons of the Duke of Aosta—King Victor Emmanuel's taller, more glamorous cousin—who had been sent abroad to be educated under Ugo's supervision. Since his earliest years, Gilbert was aware that a life awaited him overseas, should he choose to embrace it: in Scotland, one of his mother's uncles had left her his extensive property holdings in Canada. Gilbert would never lack for income.

He longed to be in Rome, but, throughout his youth, events conspired to keep him away from the city of his birth. After his father's sudden death from pneumonia, contracted while serving as an observer at the British front in France in 1917, Gilbert was able to embark on his dream of studying classical archaeology. But Italy was still at war, and he was forced to leave Rome for officer's training at the Royal Military Academy in Turin. In spite of the care packages from home containing woollen long underwear and maple syrup, he was miserable throughout the cold winter of 1918.

"Oh to think of the time," he wrote to his mother, "when I shall have no longer to be with people I detest, in a city I do not like, doing things that bore me to extinction." The days at the academy were long—the nights longer—the food execrable, the drills tedious. The only excitement came when the *Arditi*, black-shirted veterans, clashed with the Socialists who were occupying factories in the northern industrial city. Gilbert and his fellow trainees were often ordered to pick up their rifles and help the local police break up the demonstrations. Even though the war had ended the previous autumn, Gilbert's training was extended into the spring of 1919. "If they think of making me a soldier," he complained to his mother, "I shall desert to Canada." Any time he was granted leave, he would board a train to visit local archaeological sites. Sketching the triumphal arch and well-preserved Roman ruins in the Alpine city of Susa, he was stopped—and briefly arrested—by the local police under suspicion of being an Austrian spy.

After leaving Turin, Gilbert was able to resume his interrupted studies, obtaining a doctorate in letters at the University of Rome in 1921. His graduation coincided with archaeology's transition from Victorian antiquarianism to a more rigorous, scientific-minded undertaking. (The discipline would even become glamorous with the spectacular discovery, the following year, of King Tut's tomb in the Valley of Kings at Luxor. As Gilbert would later ironize: "Archaeologists, those harmless drudges, suddenly found themselves in the same popular estimation as murderers, footballers, and film stars.") Within the walls of Rome, Giacomo Boni had brought scientific methods, inherited from French and German colleagues, to bear on his excavations of the Forum. Boni's chief rival was Rodolfo Lanciani, the son of an engineer responsible for the Catholic church's waterworks. At the turn of the century, Lanciani became famous for the *Forma Urbis Romae*, a huge map of ancient Rome in the style of a modern municipal planning document. Fluent in English—his wife was American—Lanciani published articles in British journals about his excavations of the House of the Vestal Virgins, the Temple of Jupiter, and Hadrian's Villa at Tivoli.

Lanciani also had a passion for the Roman *campagna*, and he became a mentor to younger archaeologists keen to study it. One of his disciples was Thomas Ashby, the son of a Quaker brewer who had moved to Rome from Surrey in 1890 for his health. Ashby was a Victorian eccentric, a kind of perennial schoolboy who, after his father's death, cohabited with his mother in a Roman hotel, and spoke idiomatic Italian with an ineradicable British accent. Ashby's chief joy was exploring, photographing, and mapping the countryside around Rome. Described by a colleague as being "as pathetically tender-hearted as he was outspoken and blunt in manner," Ashby credited the awakening of his passion for archaeology to his long walks outside the gates of Rome in the company of Lanciani. Mapping the ruins of the *campagna* would become his life's work.

Ashby was most in his element breathing country air. He was less comfortable when confined in his official role as director of Britain's archaeological institute in Rome. The British School, a latecomer among the foreign academies, owed its existence in part to Lanciani, who was responsible for the 1911 exhibition commemorating the fiftieth anniversary of Italian unity. The celebrated architect Edwin Lutyens was called in to build a pavilion on the northern edge of the Borghese gardens to house artifacts, casts, and models that illustrated the Roman colonization of Britain. In spite of a grandiose facade that echoed the portal of St. Paul's Cathedral, Lutyens' pavilion was quickly and cheaply built, with fibrous plaster standing in for marble. Ashby, named director at the age of 31, became one of its first residents. He would spend much of his brief tenure at the British School struggling to scare up the funds to cover heating and basic maintenance.

In his walks through the *campagna*, Ashby was joined by the equally tireless Esther Van Deman. By the nineteen-twenties, the *"tufa* lady" of the American Academy, famous among her male peers for being able to date Roman masonry with a flick of her tongue, had been given a new nickname: "Aqueduct Annie." The focus of her research had shifted from the construction techniques of the Forum to the 500-kilometre network of waterworks that earned Rome the title *Regina Aquarum*, the "Queen of Waters."

Rome's aqueducts seemed to exert a magnetic pull on foreign scholars. The sight of the tiered structures of arched brickwork converging on the heart of the city, some from sources up to ninety kilometres distant, served as a vivid symbol of imperial glory and decline. They were also astonishing feats of engineering, which may have explained their appeal to pragmatic-minded British and American scholars. Constructed before the invention of pressure pumps, the aqueducts were gravity fed, which meant the water had to flow down a gradual slope—at an average incline of just 2.5 metres per kilometre—regardless of the topography.

By the fifth century, eleven major aqueducts supplied Rome's 1,800 fountains and eleven public baths with the equivalent of a million bathtubs of spring water a day. The greatest of these structures, the Aqua Marcia, ran through underground channels for eighty kilometres of its length. At the height of Imperial Rome, its waters flowed through lead pipes to the ground floors of the *insulae*, multi-floored apartment buildings, or was heated to soothe aching flesh in the *calidaria* of the sprawling Baths of Caracalla. The excess water—useful for cleansing the streets of trash and sewage—was expelled from the mouth of the Cloaca Maxima, the "Great Sewer," whose maw still gapes over the river south of the Tiber Island.

Before sacking the city in 537, the Ostrogoths, an east Germanic tribe, severed the aqueducts. By the Middle Ages, only one, the Aqua Virgo, remained in use. Starting in the sixteenth century, the papacy began to build new aqueducts on the ruins of the old, including the Aqua Traiana that feeds the *fontanone* near the American Academy. Over the centuries, though, the routes of many of the ancient aqueducts had been forgotten. "Aqueduct hunting" had been a genteel hobby among Romans since the Renaissance, but Ashby and Van Deman, encouraged by Lanciani, brought modern scientific rigour to the task. Scrambling over precipitous ridges in search of the telltale deposits of limestone that marked the *putei*, or shafts, of the waterworks, they made an unusual team. Ashby, who wore dark sunglasses over his flaming red beard, carried with him a flask of whisky and a green umbrella. The blue-eyed Van Deman, twelve years Ashby's senior, packed a seamstress's tape and a camera and tripod to record their discoveries.

Mocked for their unconventional ways by contemporaries, this unpretentious English brewer's son and single-minded

American, who grew up in a Kansas farmhouse without indoor plumbing, would end up publishing studies on Roman waterworks that are still considered major references in the field.

Ashby and Van Deman were often joined in their excursions by the young Gilbert Bagnani. In his early twenties, Gilbert wore a lush moustache and carried his slender frame with aristocratic insouciance. Witty, dapper, handsome, with a talent for languages (he would eventually master Latin, Greek, French, German, and Arabic), he moved in the same upper-class circles as the de Bosis family. He spent time with Lauro, who was a year his junior, at the Villa Diana, and knew him well enough to address him by his nickname of "Fofino." (When Gilbert learned that Lauro's sister Charis was engaged, to a man who would join the Fascist party, he wrote his mother: "I have met Cortese, Xaris's [sic] fiancé. What is more I think you have too. He was one of the... lieutenants who was always at the De Bosis'... always in the black and blue uniform, and with a stiff arm.")

Gilbert, who would never hold a salaried position in Italy, was wealthy enough to follow his passions where they led him. After graduating from the University of Rome, he'd spent three years touring archaeological sites in Libya, Turkey, and Armenia. In Athens, where he'd been accepted as a fellow at the Royal Italian School of Archaeology, he amused himself by contributing anonymous articles on the Greek political scene to London's *Morning Post*. As at ease riding on the back of a donkey through war zones to ruined Crusaders castles as he was taking tea in the salons of the Greek nobility, he penned well-informed dispatches on the Greco-Turkish War and the anti-monarchist coup that culminated in the 1924 establishment of the Second Hellenic Republic. He probably also engaged in espionage on behalf of his government. Under cover of seeking out the sources of the Styx River, he reported to the Italian embassy on political conditions and the state of the railways on the Peloponnese peninsula.

Back home in Rome, Gilbert revelled in living in a modern capital that also happened to be one of the world's great archaeological sites. Though he dismissed the British School and the American Academy as "marble sepulchres," he was intrigued by the work of Ashby and Van Deman, and shared their love for Rome's hinterland.

"The charm of the Campagna must be felt," he would later write, "for it cannot be described; it produces an intoxication of the spirit as potent as that of its own wine." Part of that charm lay in its accessibility. "Nearly all other great cities suffer from a kind of skin disease: the town is separated from the country by a wide, pimply band of objectionable suburbs. In Rome, however, a short drive is sufficient to carry one from the turmoil of the modern city into the silent, undulating plain, surrounded by its hills and mountains, and here and there relieved by ruin, castle, or pine."

But the *campagna* Gilbert and his colleagues knew and loved was under threat. The vast estates that for centuries had been used as seasonal pastures were being broken up and cultivated with plows pulled by noisy tractors. Alongside the ancient highways, new roads for motorized vehicles were being paved. Gilbert lamented the changes, but also profited from them. After joining the automobile club—which was run by a family friend, Prince Potenziani, soon to be named the Fascist Governor of Rome—he acquired a Fiat to facilitate his excursions. ("I find my pedestrian fellow-citizens extremely irritating," he wrote to his mother. "I am sure that Caligula was learning to drive when he said that he wished that all the Romans had but one neck!") Ashby invited the young archaeologist to collaborate on *A Topographical Dictionary of Rome*, to this day a much-consulted atlas to the ancient city's geography. At the same time, Gilbert was undertaking his own research and working on an English-language guidebook that would be published as *The Roman Campagna and Its Treasures.*

Gilbert, like many Italians of his class, professed a disdain for all things political. But social change was the order of the day, and even archaeologists were not immune. Ashby lamented that, as metropolitan Rome showed signs of overwhelming its *campagna*, nationalist elements in the government increasingly scorned foreign scholarship.

"Valuable information of all kinds has been irretrievably lost owing to its short-sighted policy of not inviting foreign cooperation in funds and supervision," he wrote in a 1924 memo to the trustees of the British School. "Of course I know there is no danger of my Italian colleagues becoming acquainted with my views, or otherwise I should be drowned in one of the volcanic lakes for which this part of Italy is so well known."

Ashby's real nemesis was the British School's assistant director. In her youth, the Cambridge-trained Eugénie Sellers Strong had been considered one of the great Victorian beauties; Oscar Wilde once rhapsodized about this "young Diana" who had to lecture from behind a screen, lest her sublime beauty distract the male students in the audience. A devout Catholic, Strong was known for championing the sculpture and painting of Rome, traditionally viewed as an uninspired imitation of the art of classical Greece. Unlike Ashby and Van Deman, she scorned "dirt archaeology," preferring to conduct her research in reading rooms. By the time she took over the management of the British School's library in 1909, she was a 49-year-old widow, known for her leonine mane of grey hair and her intimacy with Italy's minor aristocracy.

Strong was also a fervent admirer of the war-mongering Gabriele d'Annunzio, and fully approved what she saw as the salutary spirit of discipline and strong leadership emerging in Italy. When Ashby volunteered to serve with a British Red Cross unit on the Italian front in Trentino at the end of the First World War, Strong made it clear that she considered ambulance workers "shirkers," and that the proper place for a man was in the trenches. Writing to a young friend who had decided to join the blackshirts, she praised Fascism as "the best and healthiest thing for Italy."

"Mrs. Strong," observed Lutyens, the School's architect, with amusement, "is like a great big retriever and Ashby is a small wire-haired terrier that trots around after her." Being forced to share a residence with the imperious Strong proved a trial for the retiring Ashby. Serious problems arose when he decided to take a wife, choosing for his bride a short, round-face clergyman's daughter who worked under Strong in the School's library. Strong couldn't stand the new Mrs. Ashby. The real crisis arose with a dispute over sleeping quarters. Claiming her rights as the director's wife, Mrs. Ashby demanded that she, not Strong, should be given the warmer bedroom on the School's first floor.

By then, the committee had had enough. As much as they pitied Ashby's predicament—"placed as he is between a stupid wife and a domineering Assistant"—they decided it was best to make a clean slate of things. In 1924, both Ashby and Strong were dismissed, and a new director appointed. The School's general secretary would later write of Ashby that "his damnable silly wife's bickering with Mrs. Strong was the sole cause of his retirement."

Gilbert continued to tramp the *campagna* with Ashby as they collaborated on the topographical dictionary. At the same time, he was a frequent guest at the salon Strong established in an elegant apartment building on Via Balbo after being dismissed from the School. Impressed by Gilbert's erudition and aristocratic ways, Strong would even offer to leave him a collection of priceless pamphlets and miscellanea in her will. (Gilbert would later return the favour by dedicating a book on Rome's relationship with the papacy to her, "in gratitude for a long and inspiring friendship.")

For all the independence his background conferred on him,
Gilbert wasn't immune to the political changes that were overtak-
ing Italy. The March on Rome had taken place while he was
travelling in the Near East. He returned to find the city of his
birth taken over by Fascists, and his colleagues choosing sides.
Some, like Ashby, were skeptical about Mussolini, and worried
about the changes the progress-oriented regime was likely to
bring to the *campagna*. For Van Deman and Strong, Il Duce was
just the tonic the Italian people needed. Their field of study was
the Roman Empire, and Mussolini seemed intent on making himself into a twentieth-century Augustus. The risk, of course, was
that their scholarship would be commandeered to serve the purposes of furthering the ideology of Fascism, rather than advancing
human knowledge. In his war of ideas, Mussolini had every intention of laying claim to the ground of Rome. To that end,
scholars—even foreign ones—could be useful tools in promoting
the idea of *Romanità*.

Gilbert, like Lauro de Bosis and others in the upper echelons of
Roman society, was initially willing to reserve judgment on the new
regime. His youth had been spent among the nobility, and he
approved the fact that Mussolini's rise to power had taken place
with the sanction of the king, and without the intervention of the
military. The turmoil he had witnessed in Turin had been intolerable to him, and Mussolini—for the time being at least—seemed
to have restored order. In 1923, he put his thoughts to paper in an
unpublished essay titled "Dictators *versus* Parliaments."

"Signor Mussolini has now been in power for a year, an
unusual length of time for an Italian Premier, and any unpreju-
diced observer must admit that he has been on the whole
successful. Hardly any Italian, however much he may criticize
individual acts of the Dictator and especially of the Dictator's
friends, would appreciate a return to the chaos which preceded
the 'March on Rome.'" At the same time, he deplored the violence

of the new prime minister's Fascist subordinates. "Mussolini's chief difficulties have come from his own followers, many of whom think that a dictator should dictate much more and were disappointed at not enjoying a 'Roman holiday' with their opponents in the Colosseum. So far he has been able to keep these firebrands well in hand."

Yet violence, and the threat of it, was the very essence of Fascism. As was fear, from which, in the new Italy, not even the most aristocratic scholar was immune.

On a Tuesday afternoon, Gilbert drove out on the Via Appia Antica to photograph some ruins for his guidebook to the *campagna*. On his way home, he found his progress blocked by a quartet of horsemen, two of them in soldiers' uniforms.

"I thought they were a couple of horsemen and a couple of orderlies exercising their horses," he wrote in a letter. "I blew my horn but they did not budge, so I rather sat on the hooter. At last they got out of the way and I was putting my head out of the window to let them have few flowers of eloquence." Looking back, Gilbert immediately recognized one of the men in a soldier's uniform. The huge head was unmistakable.

"The leading horseman was Mussolini. I almost fainted!"

10 SCULPTING IL DUCE

Halfway up the Via Rasella, a quiet street of cobbles and sand-coloured apartment buildings that slopes up the Quirinal Hill to the imposing gates of the Barberini Palace, a plaque reads: "PALAZZO TITTONI SEC. XVI." A glance upwards will reveal the facades of the upper stories of the surrounding buildings are pockmarked with deep craters. It was here, on the anniversary of the founding of the Fascist Party during the Nazi occupation of Rome, that Italian partisans set off eighteen kilograms of dynamite, slaughtering most of a battalion of ss police. The explosives had been planted in a rubbish cart left outside the doors of the sixteenth-century palazzo, the former residence of Mussolini.

In the second week of May 1923, Nancy Cox McCormack walked up a broad marble staircase in a courtyard off the Via Rasella, and pressed the doorbell alongside the double doors on the apartment on the *piano nobile* of the Palazzo Tittoni. At her side was her calling card, Lidia Rismondo, the widow of a war hero who had been lauded for bravery by d'Annunzio after being executed by the Austrians in the First World War.

Mussolini was expecting them. For his first residence in Rome, he had chosen a curious location. When he'd left Milan, and with it his wife Rachele and their children, he'd revelled in his new-found power and freedom by staying on the second floor of the Grand Hotel, near the Piazza della Repubblica. In the weeks after the March on Rome, he'd turned heads at the Villa Borghese— where Cox McCormack had been serenaded with poetry by Lauro de Bosis—by cruising through the gardens with a full-grown lioness in the back seat of his noisy Alfa-Romeo Torpedo. Mussolini's public flamboyancy impelled Rome's chief of police to pay a visit to his suite, during which he implored him not to walk unaccompanied at night. (The new prime minister had been seen sneaking off to the Hotel Continentale to visit Margherita Sarfatti, his long-time Jewish mistress.) That spring, he'd moved into his new bachelor's quarters on the Via Rasella, a street that branches off an impressive tunnel leading directly to the Quirinal Palace. In the Palazzo Tittoni, the revolutionary Fascist had chosen the most respectable of addresses, at the threshold of the residence of the king who had brought him to power.

Cox McCormack and her companion were shown into the palazzo's large salon by Mussolini's housekeeper, a tall, matronly woman from a peasant family in Umbria who served as his trusted "guardian of the threshold." Her master, who had just returned from his morning gallop in the Borghese gardens, would join them shortly.

Mussolini, still dressed in riding boots, welcomed his guests in halting English: "I am glad to welcome you to my home." Switching to Italian, he broached the subject of the bust she proposed to sculpt with a standard Fascist maneuver: a veiled threat of violence.

"*Signora,*" he said, staring at her sternly from beneath a furrowed brow, "not long ago I began posing for a painter who made me so nervous I broke up the first sitting by nearly throwing him out the window!"

Cox McCormack gave as good as she got. "*Sua Eccelenza,* when I am nervous, I am so much more dangerous than you that it would not be I who would be tumbling out the window."

Turning to Rismondo, Mussolini said: "*Dio mio!* What have we here?"

Then he smiled and nodded his assent. He would allow Cox McCormack ten sittings to complete the bust. She tried not to show her relief. Getting to Mussolini—the head she had been hunting since she'd arrived in Italy—had taken her months of diligent work.

The de Bosis family had offered the first lead. Lauro's mother introduced her to Lilian Mowrer, who in turn presented her to Vittorio de Santo, Edgar's well-connected rival at the Rome bureau of the *Chicago Tribune.* In the first weeks of 1923, de Santo had written a letter conveying the American sculptor's request to Mussolini. When no reply was forthcoming, Cox McCormack began to cultivate Rismondo, who kept a salon frequented by prominent Fascists a few streets away from Mussolini's new residence. It was while working on a flattering terra cotta likeness of the young widow that she'd finagled an introduction to the residence of Rismondo's illustrious neighbour.

Cox McCormack returned to the palazzo the following day. A young fellow from the American Academy had already readied the plinth by trowelling clay over a wire armature. She fixed an appraising gaze on her subject, and liked what she saw.

"Mussolini's head is large and as much like Hadrian's as Hadrian's head was unlike some of the other Roman Emperors," she would write later. "His eyes in repose are the kindliest I have ever looked into... one instantly knows that he is all fearlessness and strength. He might well be vain because of his large, beautifully chiselled mouth, and because of his small but compact and useful-looking hands."

Mussolini, dressed for the occasion in a soft housecoat, took a seat at his desk in a high-backed chair draped with a satin matador's cape. He told her he would be forced to work while she sculpted, for in addition to being Prime Minister, he was also the Minister of Foreign Affairs, the Minister of the Interior, and the head of the army, navy, and air force. Cox McCormack had ample time to take in the decor of the sparsely furnished salon. On a table, a sculpted lion made ready to slash a coiled serpent with upraised claws. Over the mantel was an elaborate arrangement of the axe-headed bundles of wooden rods carried by a corps of lictors that preceded ancient Roman magistrates. These fasces, the official symbol of the Fascist party, had been devised by her friend from the Palatine Hill, the archaeologist Giacomo Boni, who had reconstructed them from artifacts excavated in the Forum. (For his service, the elderly Boni had been made a senator two months earlier.) From time to time, Mussolini would rise and cross the room to wind a Swiss-made music box which played a sprightly version of the Fascist marching song, *"Giovinezza."*

Cox McCormack never wavered in her admiration for her subject's physiognomy. She appreciated "the startling ivory pallor" of his skin, and thrilled to his "strangely modulated and mellifluous voice." She would later rhapsodize: "Mussolini is much of an artist, at heart a man of truth guided by tremendous will and admirable qualities of soul." But if she was swept off her feet, there is no indication she was seduced, which would be the fate of many female supplicants who dared call on him in his private chambers. Mussolini had good reasons for keeping a respectful distance from the formidable American. In the early years of Fascism, Italy still needed to cultivate its image abroad. Most of all, the war-weakened nation needed foreign money. For the time being, when an American came into his presence, he leavened intimidation with charm.

Cox McCormack, as it turned out, would become one of the most enthusiastic early propagandists for Fascism. When

Mussolini's self-aggrandizing First World War diaries were published in English, it was she who contributed a fulsome preface
likening the "honest dictator" to Cromwell and Hercules.

Her access to Mussolini didn't go unnoticed by her friend Ezra
Pound. When the poet came to Rome that winter, Cox McCormack
obliged him with an introduction to Boni; the archaeologist wrote
a letter of introduction that gave Pound entry to the Vatican Librar-
ies to do research for his *Cantos*. Pound hounded her with requests
for a meeting with Mussolini, writing her that Fascist Italy was
destined to be the intellectual centre of the world: "Germany is
busted, England is too stupid, France is too tired... America is too
far from civilization." To facilitate this renaissance, he suggested
Il Duce should subsidize a colony of the world's best writers and
artists. Failing that, perhaps Mussolini would consider writing an
essay on the Fascist restoration of Rome to its ancient glory for the
new literary journal Pound had helped found, the *Transatlantic
Review*. For the time being, Pound's requests went unanswered.

A young writer with whom Pound had sparred in Paris was
less impressed by Mussolini. Ernest Hemingway, one of the news-
men invited to a press conference in Lausanne in November, 1922,
had gone on record as calling Il Duce the "biggest bluff in Europe."

"Mussolini sat at his desk reading a book," Hemingway had
reported in a *Toronto Daily Star* dispatch. "Being an ex-newspaperman
himself he knew how many readers would be reached by the
accounts the men in the room would write of the interview he was
about to give." He wrote that he'd tiptoed up behind the statesman
to get a peek at the book he was reading: he claimed it was a
French-English dictionary, held upside down.

Hemingway concluded that Italy was more likely to find a
long-term leader in "that bold, bald-headed, perhaps a little insane
but thoroughly sincere, divinely brave swashbuckler, Gabriele
d'Annunzio." By then, of course, the prototypical *Duce* was already
out of the picture.

Hemingway fretted to Pound that such public mockery would prevent him from returning to Italy. In fact, he and his wife Hadley were able to join the Pounds in the seaside town of Rapallo a month later, where Hemingway led his hosts on a walking tour of First World War battle sites.

He needn't have worried. Early in 1923, the Fascist security state was not yet developed enough to stop all unwanted foreigners at the border. But things were changing, fast.

Six weeks after becoming prime minister, Mussolini had ordered Italo Balbo and the other architects of the March on Rome to attend the first meeting of the Grand Council of Fascism in his suite at the Grand Hotel. The Council's first act was to organize the unruly *squadristi* into the MVSN (Voluntary Militia for National Security), a revolutionary guard that would act as a Fascist army and police force. Setting up rival institutions to the Cabinet and the traditional forces of order—a move that would feature in the playbooks of authoritarian regimes for generations to come—was the initial step towards establishing a Fascist dictatorship.

In the meantime, Mussolini continued to mollify foreigners, assuring them he'd reigned in the violence that had brought him to power, and that his intentions on the world stage were peaceful. In her writing, Cox McCormack liked to quote one of his early parliamentary speeches: "Italy wants peace with honour, the peace with justice, the peace that does not commit violence to anyone."

Cox McCormack's sculpting sessions were interrupted by the eruption of Mount Etna. Mussolini rushed down to make an appearance at the scene of the disaster. Edgar Mowrer, on one of his last assignments in Italy, witnessed the explosions from the deck of the American cruiser *Pittsburgh*. Six tentacles of fresh lava flowed for up to eight kilometres from the crater, overwhelming and crumbling stone houses as they advanced. Mowrer was there when Mussolini appeared in a village menaced by the river of slag. Visibly paling even as he struck a defiant pose, Il Duce proclaimed to a group of desperate peasants: "We must stop this!" Then he'd turned on his heel, to be whisked away by his chauffeur.

On the first of July, 1923, Cox McCormack put the final touches on her portrait of the man that, more than ever, she saw as Italy's great star. The bronze she would cast from the clay set forth the idealized image of a mercenary-prince, streamlined for the machine-age: between massive, furrowed temples and full, compressed lips there gazed the watchful, determined eyes of a Renaissance *condottiere*. Unlike her infant-sized sculpture of Lauro de Bosis, fit for a desktop, Mussolini's bust was massive, at least one-and-a-half times life-size. It wouldn't have looked out of place among the images of the emperors in Boni's studio on the Palatine.

At the end of August, two months after Cox McCormack had been reassured of Il Duce's peaceful intentions, four members of an international boundary commission working in northern Greece died under mysterious circumstances. Mussolini ordered the Italian fleet to undertake the unilateral occupation of Corfu, a blatant contravention of the principles of the newly founded League of Nations. Before landing, the naval squadron shelled the island's fortress, then packed with Armenian refugees, many of them children. Sixteen were killed, hundreds wounded.

Mussolini hadn't taken long to reveal the scope of his ambitions. To be worthy of the name, his Third Rome would have to be the capital of much more than just Italy.

When Edgar and Lilian Mowrer left Rome with their baby daughter for Berlin in the spring of 1924, they still believed Italian Fascism would be a passing phenomenon.

Events in the weeks that followed proved them wrong. The Fascists had gained influence through legal and democratic means—as so many authoritarians would after them—abetted by the willingness of embattled Liberals and Conservatives to cut a deal with the far right in order to retain their power. In Mussolini's first eighteen months as prime minister, only 35 Fascists sat in the Chamber of Deputies. The existing system of proportional representation continued to give the Socialists and the Catholic Popular Party a strong presence in government. Hungry for a Fascist majority, the Grand Council devised the Acerbo Law, a "corrected" proportional system that would allow the party that received the most votes to automatically be given two-thirds of the seats in the Chamber.

The new law, it turned out, wasn't necessary. Against a background of assaults, attacks on opposition headquarters, and murders, the Fascists handily won the elections of April 1924, taking 374 of 535 seats in the Chamber. (Many of the new Fascist deputies were former Liberals, who had cynically signed on with the party of the future.) One of the few men to stand up to the ranks of blackshirts was the new leader of the reformist Socialists, a young lawyer from the Po Valley named Giacomo Matteotti. Braving Fascist guards who flashed daggers and guns at the Chamber's doors, he made a two-hour speech in which he accused the new government of using an armed militia at the service of the party "to hurl the country backwards, towards absolutism." Matteotti cited passages from his recently published book, which detailed two thousand assaults by blackshirts. Fascist deputies tried to silence him with cries of: "Hireling! Traitor! Demagogue!" When Matteotti finished speaking, he turned to a friend and said: "And now you can prepare my funeral oration."

A few days later, as Matteotti was walking along the banks of the Tiber towards Parliament, five men seized him, pushed him into a car, and, after a violent struggle, stabbed him to death. The killers drove around Rome for hours, before leaving his half-buried body in a grove twenty kilometres outside of the city, on the edge of the Sabine Hills. A doorman had noted the license plate number, which was traced to a car parked in the courtyard of the Ministry of the Interior the previous night.

It was quickly established that the lead killer was Amerigo Dumini, a 28-year-old born to emigrant parents in St. Louis, Missouri. Dumini was the head of a semi-official terror squad nick-named the *Ceka*—a nod to the formidable Soviet secret police—and controlled by the treasurer of the Fascist Party. The investigation was taken out of the hands of state magistrates and conducted by the Fascist police of chief. In spite of the fact that he had been in daily contact with Dumini's overseer, Mussolini stren-uously denied responsibility for the murder. Though the lead assassin eventually went to jail, he was rewarded by Mussolini with payments of over two million lire in the years that followed.

Matteotti was probably killed not for what he said, but for what he knew. For months the Socialists had been compiling a dossier on New York's Sinclair Exploration Company, which, with the connivance of the American *chargé d'affaires* in Rome, had bribed leading Fascists for exclusive rights to gas vaults and mineral oils in Emilia and Sicily. The revelation of secret negoti-ations with an American oil company would have been a public relations disaster for the Fascist regime.

There was one reporter in Rome brave enough to get the story out. George Seldes, who would later chronicle his experiences as a fearless muckraker in the book, *Tell the Truth and Run*, had interviewed Mussolini early in 1924 for the *Chicago Tribune*. Mus-solini had tried to ingratiate himself with American readers by recounting how, as a youth down on his luck in Switzerland, he had considered emigrating overseas.

"I was nineteen," he told Seldes. "I thought of trying my fortune in America. I tossed a coin. A dream! I wonder what would have become of me had I gone to America." Before Seldes left, Mussolini handed him a photograph of himself and his lion cub, dedicating it to his "Dear colleague, Giorgio Seldes."

Seldes knew a talented manipulator when he saw one. Before returning to Rome later that year, a colleague in Paris had urged him: "Try to get the facts on the assassination of Matteotti—go after this story: it will rock the world."

In Rome, Seldes was cleaning out the desk at the *Tribune* office in the Hotel Excelsior on the Via Veneto, when he discovered that his predecessor—Vittorio de Santo, who had provided Cox McCormack's letter of introduction to Mussolini—had, like many other foreign correspondents, accepted a bribe from the Fascists in the form of five thousand free words a month on the telegraph, a significant boon given the high cost of transatlantic cables. Seldes's interpreter had his own theory about why the Matteotti story hadn't got out of Italy. It turned out Salvatore Cortesi, who with his son Arnaldo worked as a stringer for the *New York Times*, was an arch-Fascist who would do anything to protect Mussolini's reputation. The foreign press corps, in short, was all too willing to whitewash Fascist crimes.

Seldes, meanwhile, had dug up new facts about Matteotti's murderer. Dumini, he wrote, was an "American gangster, and although his father had an Italian name, his mother was the American-born Jessie Williams... he was on friendly terms with Mussolini, visiting the *Duce* not only in his office, but in his home." He'd also found proof that Matteotti, on the day of his murder, was planning to give a speech exposing the Sinclair deal. Avoiding the Fascist-controlled telegraph, Seldes mailed the story to the Paris office of the *Tribune*, warning that if his story was published in the French edition with his name on it, he would almost certainly be killed.

In spite of Seldes's pleas, the following morning his world-rocking scoop was splashed over front pages across Europe. He was ordered to leave Italy immediately. Seldes was surprised when Mussolini's undersecretary of the interior Dino Grandi, responding to the protests of his colleagues, made a show of rescinding the order. Late that night, as Seldes and his friends toasted their apparent victory in his apartment, there was a knock on his door. Four men, two in police uniform, drove him to the train station. At the Italian-French border, where the Orient Express made a lengthy stop, blackshirts bearing clubs boarded the train, shouting: *"Dov'è* Seldes?" The reporter was saved from a beating, or worse, by three British naval officers from Malta, who invited him into their compartment and commanded the thugs: "Out! Get out, you *porco fascisti."*

The "Seldes Affair" sent a strong signal to the foreign press in Italy. The correspondents who stayed behind knew they would have to submit to censorship or face expulsion. Too many of them proved willing to accept the hospitality of the regime, which allowed not only the free use of a monitored telegraph, but also the run of the Foreign Press Club, near the Trevi Fountain, with its well-stocked bar and efficient long-distance phones, every one of them tapped. For years, the dispatches of the *New York Times's* Cortesis and other Fascist sympathizers painted a sunny picture of stability and prosperity reigning in the New Italy.

It took a decade for Seldes to get his revenge. When he did, his insider's knowledge of the Fascist regime would change the way the world thought about Mussolini.

Lauro de Bosis had made up his mind about Fascism. At the time of the Matteotti murder, he had taken on work writing brochures for the National Bureau for Tourism, and left for a working tour of the south. From a balcony in Palermo, Lauro and Cox McCormack had joined the crowds welcoming Mussolini, letting fall coloured ribbons that read *"Viva Il Fascismo!"* But his job with the tourist bureau, which called on him to arrange travel for Mussolini and his staff, had brought him in regular contact with the man. Back in Rome, Lauro told Cox McCormack he hadn't liked what he'd seen.

"When I asked if he had spoken to the *Duce*," the sculptress wrote, "he ruffed up like a fighting cock and replied that he had encountered him at one place along the tour and Mussolini was just an 'impossible ruffian.'" Cox McCormack surmised that Lauro's request for an interview had met with a rude refusal. "It was from the date of this *contretemps* that Lauro's personal feelings were 'set' in opposition to the 'Tyrant.'"

But Lauro already had a new plan, one that would completely remove him from Italy's troubled politics. Giuseppe Prezzolini, the opinionated editor of the literary journal *La Voce* and an old family friend, had put his name forward for a prestigious lecture series organized by a New York-based organization known as the Italy America Society. The society's secretary had come to Rome to interview candidates, and Lauro's erudition and knowledge of English made him a natural choice. After accepting, Lauro travelled to the family's summer home in Ancona, the stone tower that overlooked the black-hulled fishing boats with carved prow-figures bobbing on the Adriatic. He found his father, in the final stages of pancreatic cancer, "a skeleton under a single sheet," but serene and still capable of reciting Shelley. Lauro was there when Adolfo died, in the company of his family, on August 28, 1924.

Gabriele d'Annunzio made the trip from Lake Garda to attend his old friend's funeral. Adolfo de Bosis had embodied the highest ideals, now fast-vanishing, of nineteenth-century Liberalism: national unity, democracy, peace, universalism. For the occasion, Lauro hid his real feelings about d'Annunzio, the man he privately considered a "pig." D'Annunzio even consented to add his voice to Prezzolini's in recommending Lauro for his lecture tour, writing, in typically self-regarding style: "In him I see the realization of many of my cherished hopes."

The wealthy Borgheses, whose interests Adolfo had served for decades as the family's executor, invited Lauro to join them in mourning his father's death. He stayed on their private island in

Lake Garda with the beautiful Princess Santa Borghese, who shared her experience of America, where she had recently done a tour as the Italy America Society's first lecturer. When, shortly after, her mother committed suicide by casting herself into the lake on the anniversary of a lover's death, Lauro covered any private torment over mortality with a mask of rationalism.

"Why not die while one is still tingling with the enthusiasm of life?" he asked Cox McCormack. "Before the senses are dulled with the years? We should die *for* something, as she did, not just wear out with old age."

Lauro returned to find Rome still embroiled in the Matteotti crisis. The opposition parties had walked out on parliament in protest of the murder in the "Aventine Secession," named for the plebeian revolt on the Aventine Hill in the days of the Roman Republic. But boycotting parliament only served to protect Mussolini's government from being defeated in a confidence vote. A Fascist deputy had been gunned down in the streets of Rome, and *squadristi* were calling for a massacre of Socialists. Many in Rome thought that unless Mussolini dramatically asserted his authority, he risked being usurped by hard-liners.

On October 11, 1924, Lauro sailed for New York. In his wallet, he carried the dollars Thornton Wilder had given him three years earlier. His American friend had concluded his first novel *The Cabala* with his protagonist leaving the backward-looking city of Rome aboard a New York-bound ship that carried him "eagerly toward the new world and the last and greatest of all cities." Over the pounding of the engines, Wilder's hero seems to hear the spirit of Virgil enjoining him to "Seek out some city that is young. The secret is to make a city, not to rest in it."

Lauro, still only twenty-two years old, had no idea what the greatest city in the New World would make of him.

11 WOOING STEWART

Mary Augusta Stewart Houston—Stewart, or just plain "Stew" to her friends—was feeling like the very devil. When she'd presented herself at the door of the Neo-Renaissance palazzo off Rome's Via del Corso, she hadn't been sure what to expect. The doorman showed her into a vast room, formerly the private theatre of the noble Rospigliosi family, which was decorated with magnificent chandeliers and sixteenth-century frescos. After her dinner companion Gilbert Bagnani arrived, with apologies for his tardiness, knee-breached attendants brought them a meal of *vol-au-vent* and roast beef served with spinach and potatoes, followed by meringues and a snifter of Grand Marnier. Drinking liqueur, unchaperoned in public, with a handsome young Roman, in a private men's club. It was all a bit much for a twenty-one-year-old girl from Toronto.

Not that Stewart was unacquainted with the trappings of wealth. She was a fifth-generation Canadian, a descendant of the Family Compact that monopolized power in nineteenth-century

Upper Canada. Her maternal grandfather had been a Lieutenant-Governor of Ontario, her father, editor of the *Financial Post*. After his death, when Stewart was only seven, her mother decided to take her to England for her education. They'd returned to Toronto for the 1921 school year so Stewart could attend Bishop Strachan, Canada's oldest boarding school for girls, named after a relative who was the city's first Anglican bishop.

After graduating, Stewart had found herself at loose ends. Most of her former schoolmates were either married, or about to be. Throwing herself into Toronto's social swirl, she amused herself with ice-skating on Grenadier Pond in High Park, and playing the maid to Mrs. Malaprop in an amateur production of Sheridan's *The Rivals* at Hart House Theatre. Her mother, discovering that Stewart was being energetically courted by a young man named George, proposed a tour of the Continent, where she'd had a successful singing career in Europe in her youth. After renting out their house on Cluny Avenue, they took the morning train to Montreal, and boarded an ocean liner bound for Cherbourg. Nineteen-twenty-four, Stewart exulted in her journal, was to be her "Year of Experience."

They'd arrived in Rome shortly before Christmas. At first, Stewart hadn't known what to make of the city. Compared to the sun-dappled canals of Venice and the lively streets of Milan, Rome seemed melancholy, particularly in the early winter gloom. "I like it but I miss its charm," she wrote in her travel journal. "I don't think my previous incarnations extend beyond the Middle Ages. Certainly I was never Italian."

Gilbert was determined to make her change her mind about Italy. Their mothers were long-time friends, and saw no harm in the studious young archaeologist showing Stewart around the city. The two had much in common. Both, in spite of their Canadian parentage, had benefited from a European education. Both had lost their fathers at an early age. Of the two, Gilbert, three years Stewart's senior, was the more worldly. With his knowledge of Roman history, he promised to make an informative guide during her four-month sojourn. The two, though, would bear some watching. Gilbert found Stewart far more engaging company than the other visitors from the New World that he was sometimes called upon to guide around the city. Though he bridled when she teased him for his frequent displays of sententiousness, he was also charmed. She was, he thought, rather beautiful. As he showed her through the Forum and the Farnese Gardens, he found himself stealing glances at her long, gracile limbs, and noticing the way her wavy blonde hair shone in the pale sunlight. Stewart, for her part, was both amused and puzzled by her brilliant and tempera-mental companion.

"Such a queer mixture I never did know," she wrote in her journal. "Vague & extraordinarily decisive, irritable and very sweet natured, poseur and so unaffected and above all that extraordinary memory and brain. I really think he has never for-gotten anything he has ever read."

He was certainly an excellent guide. In spite of his impecca-ble English, and his preference for Savile Row tailoring, Gilbert was Roman to the core, and thoroughly at home in the city. He lived with his mother in the family palazzo in a five-storey Risorgimento-era apartment building, in a modern part of the city east of Termini Station. The club where they dined that evening, a half-hour walk away from their apartment, was the centre of his social life. The Nuovo Cercolo degli Scacchi, Gilbert explained, was founded in 1872 to welcome members of Rome's "black" and "white" nobility; *scacchi,* Italian for chess, being an allusion to the coexistence of the black-and-white squares on a chessboard. Though Gilbert wore his Catholicism lightly, he firmly identified with the Black Nobility, those who remained loyal to the Pope when Rome became part of the Kingdom of Italy under Victor Emmanuel II. Shortly after Stewart had arrived, he'd used his connections with the "Blacks" to get her a hard-to-come-by ticket to a ceremony in St. Peter's. She covered her head with black Spanish lace for the occasion, and marvelled at the sight of Pope Pius XI, wearing a brocaded robe and a crown studded with uncut emeralds, offering his benediction from a golden throne.

In the weeks that followed, Gilbert introduced her to his world, taking her to places other tourists seldom saw. They scaled the 350 steps to the dome of St. Peter's, from which height the Baldacchino looked like the canopy of a four-poster bed. He showed her newly excavated portions of Nero's Golden House, and took her to a talk, illustrated by slides, by Esther Van Deman, the American expert on the aqueducts. ("Worst delivered lecture I have ever heard," Stewart noted. "Woman with an untidy mind.") When Stewart suggested that most hoary of tourist experiences—a visit to the Coliseum by moonlight—Gilbert winced, but accompanied her nonetheless, yawning all the while. He was more keen on introducing her to the *campagna*, and took her on day trips to Hadrian's Villa, Castel Gandolfo, and the abbey at Grottaferrata in the Alban Mountains.

"As we drove home," Stewart wrote, "the most marvellous sunset made the whole Campagna covered with pink dust [sic] and the mountains were purple with the dust over them and the sky wonderfully red with wild woolly clouds whipped about." On one such excursion, Gilbert, tipsy from lunchtime wine, put his arm around her in the back seat of the chauffeured car, and playfully asked when they should announce their engagement.

By the time the wildflowers were blooming around the Temple of Castor and Pollux in the Forum, it was obvious that Gilbert was in love. Stewart warded off his advances, teasing him with limericks to puncture his self-seriousness. Went one:

There was a young doctor of Rome,
In St. Peter's he gazed at the dome,

When they said, "It's unique,"
He replied with some pique,
"I've a much better one of my own."

By then, Stewart's Roman spring was coming to an end. Thanks to Gilbert, she'd seen almost all of the city's major monuments. (In her travel journal, she would list more than three dozen churches she'd toured, most of them in his company.) Though Italy seemed to be in the grip of a crisis, politics had barely intruded on her visit. A week after her arrival, Mussolini had made his speech in the Chamber of Deputies declaring himself the personal dictator of Italy. For Stewart, the blackshirted youths she'd seen parading alongside the canals of Venice and in the streets of Rome were more picturesque than ominous. Indeed, she was delighted to witness a spectacle that had lately become an essential part of every tourist's visit: Il Duce addressing the masses from his balcony.

"As we were coming home this evening we saw crowds gathered round the Piazza Venezia waiting to see Mussolini. After about half an hour he came out. We didn't see much but I am glad to have seen him. He is an extraordinary man + something to have seen!"

At the beginning of May, her mother announced it was time to move on; it would not do, after all, if Stewart's "Year of Experience," was limited to Rome. By then, the city had won her over. "Rome has gotten into my blood now," she wrote in her journal. "I adore it. It eats into your heart. It seems truly the city of sorrows."

Gilbert had also found a place in her heart. George, the suitor she'd left behind in Toronto, was now long forgotten. On the eve of her departure, Gilbert took her to the Trevi Fountain and watched her toss in the coin said to ensure an eventual return to Rome. Accompanying her to the station the following day, he kissed her, and insisted on hanging from the door of her compartment as her Florence-bound train pulled away from the platform.

To Gilbert's delight, the coin tossed in the fountain worked. By the beginning of 1926, Stewart was back in Italy, studying art history at the University of Rome. Her timing, though, was not ideal. Gilbert had agreed to do a series of lectures in Toronto and Montreal. It would be his first voyage to the country of his mother's birth as an adult, and an opportunity to get to know Stewart's family and friends. He sailed from Naples on the Lloyd Sabaudo luxury-liner *ss Conte Biancomano*, arriving in New York in the second week of January.

"The first sight of N.Y. was very impressive," he wrote his mother. "The vast buildings rising from the sea in this slight mist. It reminded me very much of Constantinople at daybreak from the sea. But the illusion faded rapidly the moment one saw the buildings in length and not in depth." After checking into the City Club on West 44th Street, he rode the subway down to Wall Street. "The Subways here are amusing: you do not buy a ticket: there are turnstiles into which insert a nickel (5 cents) and it turns. The cars and trains are not half as nice as in London, but the trains go faster. I nearly got caught in one of the automatic doors." At the Dominion Bank, he was advised by a broker to hold on to the family's stocks in Canadian railways.

In the week that followed, between social engagements with friends of the family, Gilbert recorded his bemusement with New York and its inhabitants. He marvelled at Yankee efficiency, and how easy it was to get around the city. "No wonder the Americans are good at mathematics; they have got to be with the numeration of their streets." He found his interactions with the natives less interesting; they wanted to talk of nothing but "Fascism which, with prohibition, seems the staple piece of conversation on this continent, at least with the men. The women talk servants and rents."

He took in a Marx Brothers show with Lauro de Bosis, who was in New York as part of his own lecture tour, and visiting with Marie Harjes, the American heiress he was then courting. "Foffino there, quite amusing," wrote Gilbert, misspelling Lauro's nickname. "The show, the Coconuts, was a kind of musical comedy which I have never seen even paralleled for inanity. A thing as perfectly imbecile as that is almost a work of genius... entertainments of this sort develop an intoxicated feeling in one and we went out on Broadway feeling quite drunk... When we got to Marie's we simply invaded her flat and made some unsuccessful attempts at routing out a dinner."

For a few days, he stayed at the home of Gino Speranza, an Italian expatriate who had an estate in Irvington on the Hudson River. To Gilbert's Italian eyes, the North American countryside was delightfully untamed. "The scenery strikes me all over here as being very wild and savage," he wrote. "It looks as if man had only just made his appearance in the continent and that one is following in the wake of pioneers. The roads seem to have only now been cut through the woods... at the same time, the frame houses, a temporary kind of construction at the best, are just dumped down anywhere in a clearing and have nothing of the settled and civilized character of Europe." New York's great buildings all seemed to be mish-mashes of Greek and Roman styles, with the notable exception of Grand Central Station. "Really to my mind the finest building I have seen of the kind. It is very simple and effective: no imitation or adaptation of European styles but a straightforward piece of work, art nouveau at its best."

Gilbert found Toronto and its residents disappointing. "They are in a backwater and they think of it as a centre. They have the most hideous architecture that I have seen anywhere, and I am informed that 'Toronto has the finest public buildings of any city in this continent,' and they believe it!" His lecture at the University of Toronto, titled "Life in Ancient Rome under the Empire,"

was well received, though he feared his attempts at humour ruf-
fled local sensibilities. "When I showed my slide of the saloon at
Ostia I said 'but in the Province of Ontario I suppose I ought to
call it a cafeteria.' I got my laugh all right but they told me later
that... half the prohibition people were there."

He met Stewart's friends, among them George, her disappointed suitor, who eyed him with hostility. "It is quite amusing
to find myself a famous personage but sexually rather than intellectually. I am being scrutinized as if I were a curious specimen
of a prehistoric monster or rather a kind of Paris or Tristan or
Lancelot or one of the great famous lovers of antiquity."

Montreal, where Gilbert delivered his lectures at McGill University, was more to his taste. "It is all covered with snow, but not
a bit cold, at least one does not feel it." He stayed at the Mount
Royal Club, dined with the First World War general Sir Arthur
Currie, whom he'd met on the transatlantic crossing, and went
for a hike on the Mountain with members of the Molson brewing
family. As much as he credited Toronto for nurturing Stewart—a
city, he wrote, that "had the insuperable honour of producing you
and of which you are the fairest flower"—he had trouble imagin-
ing a life there. "I do not say Montreal is beautiful but it does not
give you a stomach ache." If their future together included a life
in Canada, he hoped she would consider making it anywhere but
Ontario. "Quebec and Montreal seem somehow to be so much
nearer. I suppose it is because they are so French but I feel that
Toronto is really the Wild and Woolly West."

On his return to Rome, Gilbert continued his research on the
campagna and began work on his book on Rome on the papacy.
He began to exchange passionate letters with Stewart, who had
returned to Canada after completing her studies. Writing with a
fountain pen on baby blue stationery, she signed her letters with
a circle, to indicate the exact spot her lips had touched the paper.
Gilbert, writing on the coffee-and-cigarette-ash stained letterhead

of his men's club, reminded her of how he'd kissed her shoulders the night she'd donned a long black evening dress. When he teased her by sending her postcards of Classical nudes locked in embrace, inscribed on the back with punning inscriptions in Greek and Latin, a terse note arrived in the mail asking him to desist.

"There are certain things which people of a certain class do and do not," he was frostily informed by Stewart's mother. "Your judgment on this point needs cultivating."

By then, it was too late. In spite of the objections of their mothers, both of whom had reservations about the suitability of the match, in March, 1927, Gilbert and Stewart announced their engagement. It was agreed, to the groom's chagrin, that the wedding was to take place not in civilized Rome—nor even in the more palatable Montreal—but in the backwater that was prohibition-era Toronto.

Gilbert still saw their future together in Italy, not Canada. Fascism was changing the nation, but in the aristocratic circles in which he moved, politics intruded only tangentially. When Dino Alfieri, the political undersecretary of the Fascist Party, was proposed for membership at Gilbert's club—after being nominated by another prominent Fascist, Prince Potenziani, the Governor of Rome—the members voted to exclude him, provoking a minor scandal.

"A most frightful row!" he wrote his mother. "On about 86 votes there were 20 black balls. I do not know how far it is political or personal dislike or whether, as others think, it was done to spite Potenziani. The worst of it is that now no one talks of anything else." Gilbert's was almost certainly one of the dissenting votes. (He would later write to his mother: "On principle I black-balled all politicians.")

In totalitarian Italy, where the state aspired to occupy all aspects of private and public life, lofty indifference was becoming less of an option. Gilbert was aware that his fellow scholars were being pressed into the service of ideology. Some, like Strong and Van Deman, enthusiastically endorsed the regime's vision of reviving the glories of ancient Rome in the name of building a new empire. As a student of history, Gilbert had little time for such distortions. He made his opinions clear in the preface of his book on Rome and the papacy.

"It was natural," he wrote, "that the new Italian nationalism should adopt as its own the traditions and glories of ancient Rome, of which it considered itself to be the legitimate heir. This idea, though natural, is completely false. Modern Italy has no more to do with ancient Rome than modern France with Charlemagne or modern England with King Arthur. The Roman Empire was Roman, not Italian; its last most serious war was against its revolted Italian allies, and when it ceased to be Roman it became international and universal. Let no one read my references to the Roman Empire as allusions to the present Italian state."

When *Rome and the Papacy* was published in England in 1929, the year the Fascist state signed the Lateran Accords with the Vatican, such words would be read as heretical. Mussolini's rhetoric in his rise to power had stressed the continuity between ancient Rome and modern Italy. As Il Duce's attention turned to building a new Mediterranean empire, anyone—even the most dilettantish archaeologist—who questioned the legitimacy of that vision implicitly made himself an enemy of the state.

While Gilbert hoped his principles could keep him aloof from politics, there was one principle he held dear: that of speaking the scholarly truth. As he planned his future with his bride-to-be in Italy, he was still unaware that such a commitment would make pursuing a career—or even a life—in Mussolini's Third Rome a dangerous proposition.

12 A GILT-EDGED TRAP

In upper Manhattan, in the middle of the busy stretch of Amsterdam Avenue between 116th and 117th streets, there is an apparition straight out of fifteenth-century Florence. A Renaissance palazzo—or a very convincing replica of one—rises from amidst the Brutalist monoliths of Columbia University's uptown campus. Cut into the stone beneath the dentil frieze that runs the length of its facade is the Romantic homage to Italy from Lord Byron's poem *Childe Harold's Pilgrimage*: "MOTHER OF ARTS—THY HAND WAS ONCE OUR GUARDIAN—AND IS STILL OUR GUIDE."

Compared to the American Academy in Rome's setting on the Janiculum Hill, the Casa Italiana's setting is inauspicious. Despite being located on the relative eminence of Morningside Heights, the seven-storey structure's main view is of the water-stained concrete of the neighbouring international affairs building. Yet the Casa Italiana was once Italy's leading cultural outpost in America. It was designed, like the American Academy's Main Building, by the architectural firm of McKim, Mead & White, and decorated with exquisite Baroque furniture donated by Mussolini himself. Within a few years of opening, it would also become the home of the Italy America Society, the leading conduit for the dissemination of Fascist propaganda in the New World.

When Lauro de Bosis arrived in Manhattan on November 6, 1924, the Society had yet to relocate to its new headquarters uptown. He instead reported to a commercial building a block north of the New York Public Library. There he was warmly greeted by Irene di Robilant, a countess from Turin, just four years his senior. The daughter of a First World War general who fought off the Austro-German advance at Mount Grappa, di Robilant was uniquely suited to be the Society's manager. Decorated for her work with the Red Cross during the war, she spoke excellent English. As charming and forceful as she was well-connected, di Robilant had cultivated a relationship with Prince Gelasio Caetani, the Italian ambassador in Washington, and helped oversee the establishment of the Society's twenty-two branch offices in major American cities.

In the Society's 43rd Street office, di Robilant showed Lauro copies of a handsomely printed brochure promoting his tour. The cover featured a photo of Lauro, his wispy teenage moustache now full and black, dressed in a black three-piece suit, his white collar cinched by a bow tie from his late father's closet. The following page was filled with words of praise from the archaeologist Giacomo Boni, Gabriele d'Annunzio, and the Fascist Minister of Public Instruction. A program of twenty lectures was outlined, with themes ranging from "Recent Archeological Discoveries in Italy" to "The Woman in the Italian Conception." Only one of them explicitly focussed on contemporary politics, a talk, "illustrated with moving pictures," titled "Benito Mussolini and his Spiritual Ancestry."

Lauro had at first hesitated to sign on to the tour, which would see him crossing the country from Baltimore to Berkeley, and heading north to Canada. At issue was not the gruelling schedule, nor the money—the fee was a handsome four thousand dollars—but his own sense of integrity. Lauro feared that, despite the Society's claims to be strictly non-political, he would be called upon to discuss, or even justify, the Fascist takeover of Italy. His qualms had been assuaged by Chester Aldrich, the Society's president. Aldrich was an architect trained at Paris's Beaux-Arts, a trustee of the American Academy in Rome, and a lover of Italy with the reputation for being a staunch Liberal. He assured Lauro that the tour was intended to make Americans aware that "Italy belongs to the civilization of the whole world, which existed before Mussolini and will continue to exist when Mussolini has disappeared from the scene."

When the Society was founded by an Italian banker at the end of the First World War, its mandate had been strictly commercial and cultural. Six years later, it was quietly remaking itself into a vehicle for political influence. Di Robilant was a keen supporter of Mussolini, and she would work hand-in-hand with Ambassador Caetani's successor, the arch-Fascist Giacomo de Martino, to further the regime's fortunes abroad. The man whose recommendation had brought Lauro to the United States, his father's old friend Giuseppe Prezzolini, would soon turn the Casa Italiana into America's most prestigious showcase for Fascism, a place where visiting officials were feted with the blackshirt marching song *"Giovinezza."*

When Lauro entered the office on 43rd Street that day, he was walking into a perfect trap for a man of conscience. By associating his name with the Society, he was not only becoming complicit in the whitewashing of the blackshirts, but also the grandest of the Fascists' projects: the remaking of Rome in the image of Il Duce.

In the 1920s, North Americans were of two minds about Italy.

For those wealthy enough to enjoy foreign travel, it was a nation that evoked sultry and serene Venice, the atmospheric hill towns of Tuscany, the sun-dappled beauty of Naples and Palermo, and all the glory that was Rome. For the great majority of Americans, Italy was something quite different: a benighted backwater that had sent Sicilians and other southerners flooding down gangplanks and turned San Francisco's North Beach, Manhattan's Little Italy, The Ward in Toronto, and Boston's North End into teeming ghettoes. For many, these peasants, bomb-throwers and organ-grinders brought only crime, political extremism, and a superstition-ridden version of Catholicism. The long-running case of Sacco and Vanzetti, anarchists accused of a double murder in an armed robbery, stoked anti-Italian sentiment throughout the twenties. Rum-runners and crime bosses, who had grasped the opportunity to graft the codes of Sicily's Mafia and Calabria's 'Ndràngheta on the underworld created by Prohibition, became the bogeymen of upright teetotallers.

The Johnson-Reed Act, enacted five months before Lauro de Bosis arrived in New York, specifically targeted immigrants from eastern and southern Europe. In the first fifteen years of the century, close to one million Italians a year chose to seek their fortunes abroad, a mass emigration that eventually drained the nation of a third of its population. As many as a quarter million a year had settled in the United States. In response to a rising tide of Nativism, which played on fears that white Protestant Americans were in danger of being overwhelmed by swarthy Catholic newcomers, the Immigration Act of 1924 set the annual quota at a mere six thousand.

Because he seemed to be keeping Italians where they belonged—in Italy—Mussolini became the idol of American Nativists. One of their key texts was *Black Magic*, a celebration of the blackshirt revolution by the novelist Kenneth Roberts, serialized in the *Saturday Evening Post*, then the highest-circulation magazine in the United States. Before the Fascists came along, the Mediterranean races, wrote Roberts, were turning Americans into a "hybrid race of people as worthless and futile as the good-for-nothing mongrels of Central America and Southeastern Europe." For Roberts, Fascism "was the opposite of wild ideas, of lawlessness, of injustice, of cowardice, of treason, of crime, of class warfare, of special privilege; and it represented square-dealing, patriotism and common sense." Mussolini, himself a "gluttonous worker," was finally putting the Italian people to work. Il Duce, readers were told, had singlehandedly warded off the threat of Bolshevik revolution. According to the Nativists, dictatorship, not democracy, was the only system fit for unruly Latins.

In the years that followed, a more sophisticated class of writers would help buffer Il Duce's image. George Bernard Shaw and the philosopher George Santayana approved his program, and the best-selling author Emil Ludwig deemed Mussolini as fit a subject for one of his hagiographic biographies as Napoleon and Lincoln. Ida Minerva Tarbell, whose diligent turn-of-the-century muckraking had helped bust Standard Oil's monopoly, was offered $25,000 by *McCall's* Magazine to "look into" Fascist Italy. Though she possessed only a few words of Italian, Tarbell returned with a series titled "The Greatest Story in the World Today," filled with glowing reports of a leader who "worked and made people work." A private interview with the prime minister confirmed all her preconceptions. Though Mussolini was no doubt "a fearful despot," Tarbell wrote, "he had a dimple."

Richard Washburn Child had been so impressed by what he had seen of Fascism during his time as American ambassador in Rome that he agreed to ghost write Il Duce's English-language "autobiography," compiled from notes by Mussolini's brother Arnaldo, which was then serialized in the *Saturday Evening Post*. Will Rogers, the most popular American humourist of the day, met Mussolini and reassured his readers in his syndicated column that he was a regular guy. "Dictator form of government," wrote Rogers, in his folksy, telegraphic style, "is the greatest form of government; that is, if you have the right Dictator."

The blackshirts were by then making their presence felt on the streets of New York. The Italian Library of Information on Madison Avenue distributed the latest books and pamphlets by Fascist publishers. (Gabriele d'Annunzio's third son Ugo Veniero, born while the poet was sailing the Adriatic with Lauro's father, managed the Library, when he could spare time from his real job of selling high-end Italian racing cars to millionaires and movie stars.) In 1924, the Fascist League of North America, an attempt to amalgamate the far-flung pro-Mussolini groups that had sprung up across the continent, was organized by Count Thaon di Revel. League members, following the lead of their brothers in Italy, specialized in wrecking the offices of the few anti-Fascist publications in New York, and made headlines when they crashed a rally in Newark, leaving six attendees with knife wounds. When 75,000 mourners filled Broadway for the funeral procession for the silent-screen idol Rudolph Valentino, blackshirts attempted to form an honour guard around his flower-wreathed casket before being driven off by anti-Fascists.

Matteotti's murder, and the international outrage that followed, briefly put Fascism on the defensive. At a protest rally at Carnegie Hall sponsored by the Italian Chamber of Labor, the respected anti-Fascist diplomat Count Carlo Sforza accused Mussolini of being directly responsible for the killing. In Italy, a besieged Mussolini had initially responded to demands to broaden the administration by naming prominent nationalists to key ministries, a compromise that enraged Fascist hard-liners. As armed *squadristi* in Tuscany and the Romagna broke into prisons to liberate fellow blackshirts, Mussolini ended all doubts about who really held power by making a dramatic speech in the Chamber of Deputies.

"In front of the entire Italian nation, I declare that I, and I alone, assume political, moral and historical responsibility for all that has happened." Silencing the prolonged applause that greeted his words, he continued: "If Fascism has been simply castor oil and clubs, and not the magnificent passion of the very flower of Italian youth, the fault is mine! If Fascism has been a criminal association, I am the head of that criminal association!" It was a blatant acceptance of culpability, and further proof—if any were needed—of Balzac's dictum that every great fortune begins with a crime. The crime that ensured all of Fascism's subsequent fortunes was the cowardly kidnap and murder of Matteotti. The enduring moral indignation over that same crime would launch and sustain the anti-Fascist resistance that would ultimately topple Mussolini's regime.

On January 3, 1925, three months after Lauro de Bosis left Rome, Mussolini declared himself personal dictator of Italy. In so doing, he assumed the role the young poet had already assigned to him: The Tyrant.

The Italy America Society was also undergoing a radical change. At the beginning of 1925, its president, Chester Aldrich, the gentlemanly Liberal who had reassured Lauro that the Society's goals were strictly non-political, was replaced by another prominent American Italophile.

Thomas W. Lamont possessed style, beautiful manners, and a circle of friends that included H.G. Wells and the poet Robert Frost. Like Lauro's mother, he was the son of a scholarly Methodist pastor, and was known for bringing a measure of evangelical certainty to business dealings. After graduating from Harvard, Lamont had worked the city beat for the *New York Tribune* as a reporter covering Tammany Hall. A key designer of the First World War reparations at the Paris Peace Conference, he was, like Aldrich, generally considered a Liberal. But above the handsome Italian refectory table in Lamont's New York office, there hung a signed photo of Benito Mussolini.

Lamont became a partner at J.P. Morgan & Co. in 1911, two years before Morgan *père* died in Rome while overseeing the construction of the American Academy. J.P. Morgan, Jr. was often conflated in the public mind with his father: in middle age, both were bald, portly, and bulbous-nosed—living caricatures of the top-hatted tycoon. Over forty years, father and son had built the House of Morgan into what one biographer has called "the most formidable financial combine in history," an institution, in a time before multinationals and foreign-aid programs, whose command of vast pools of capital could determine the fate of nations. Its critics viewed the House of Morgan as a sinister monopoly responsible for coaxing America into the First World War for profit.

In contrast to the boorish, gruff Morgans, Lamont was cultured and easygoing, and his love of foreign travel made him a natural ambassador for the firm. On his Italian trips, he liked to visit the scholars at the Morgan-funded American Academy, picnic among ruins in the Roman *campagna*, and take tea with Bernard Berenson at *I Tatti*, the Bostonian collector's art-filled villa in the hills outside Florence. His first meeting with Mussolini, six months after the March on Rome, was arranged by Ambassador Child, Il Duce's future ghostwriter. Lamont was deeply impressed by the prime minister, whom he saw as just the kind of strongman needed to stabilize the economy. The Morgan Bank, Lamont pointed out, had always supported Italy. But he also warned Mussolini that the world was watching the nation. Once the issue of her $2 billion in war debts to Washington could be settled, Italy would make an ideal candidate for future Morgan loans—provided the Fascists didn't do anything rash on the international stage. The regime's shelling and occupation of Corfu later that year, a blatant challenge to the authority of the League of Nations, deeply jolted Lamont. Nonetheless, he continued to praise Il Duce, referring to him in public as "that impressive figure."

In March, 1925, Lamont and his wife were ready for another trip abroad. On the dock in New York, as he boarded a Naples-bound ocean liner, he told reporters that he was indeed making a trip to Italy, but strictly for his "health."

Lauro's North American tour, meanwhile, was running into problems. Accommodations had been found for him in the Greenwich Village apartment of Arthur Livingston, a Columbia Italian professor who was grooming the young poet as a potential translator. The first lecture, titled "Italy's Contribution to World Democracy," had taken place in Lamont's palatial upper east side townhouse. But then Lauro left Manhattan, and began to address larger audiences at prestigious venues: at Amherst, he spoke on archaeology; at a meeting of the Dante League, on poetry; at Yale, on the contemporary theatre.

On the day Mussolini declared himself dictator in Rome's Chamber of Deputies, Lauro was delivering a lecture on Italian poetry in New Haven. The organizations that had invited him suddenly loss interest in genteel talks on the arts. As a visiting Italian intellectual, Lauro was called upon to offer his opinion on one pressing subject: Mussolini, and what his seizure of power meant for the world.

Cox McCormack, who had returned to Chicago from Rome in 1924, was there when Lauro addressed a large luncheon crowd at the city's Fortnightly Club. The sculptress was impressed by her young friend's new-found polish and self-assurance: with his black suit and pale skin, Lauro looked like a "very attractive *signorino*" who had stepped out of the frame of a painting in a Florentine art gallery.

"All was going splendidly with the lecture and lecturer when from the right hand corner table an exiled enemy of Mussolini and Fascism raised his voice to heckle the speaker," recalled Cox McCormack. "Lauro, flushed, responded to the challenge and acquitted himself well in defense of Mussolini."

By then, Lauro was walking a fine line. Being in the United States under the aegis of the Italy America Society meant he felt compelled to moderate his opinion of Mussolini, the man he privately considered an "impossible ruffian." But America also exposed him to critics of the regime he wouldn't have heard back home. One was the principled Walter Lippmann, who had met Mussolini, but—unlike his friend Lamont—refused to be charmed. In the editorial pages of the *New York World*, Lippmann called out the Fascists for election thuggery, the invasion of Corfu, and their abrogation of democracy in Italy. Another critic was Giorgio La Piana, a former Catholic priest who welcomed Lauro into his home on the Boston leg of his lecture tour. A naturalized American who taught at the Harvard Divinity School, La Piana shared Lauro's suspicion of leftist ideologies, but impressed the young man by rejecting Fascism as an affront to every standard of social justice. As the tour progressed, Lauro's respect for the intellectual integrity of La Piana and Lippmann deepened his doubts about Mussolini.

In April, Lauro travelled by train from Cleveland to Toronto. An appreciative crowd of six hundred politely applauded Lauro's speech on Benedetto Croce, Italy's most famous living philosopher. But then he was surrounded by reporters demanding to know where he stood on Mussolini.

"I am not a *fascisto*," he told one of them. "At times in my lectures I make some severe criticism of the *fascisti*. But I am compelled to admire Mussolini in many respects. There is no doubt that he saved Italy a few years ago. There were twelve parties. None could secure power. Yet Italy had to have a strong, stable government to avert a financial debacle." Asked if Mussolini was a dictator, Lauro pointed out that, for the time being, Italy's leader enjoyed a strong parliamentary majority and broad popular support. America's president, by contrast, was technically irremovable. The following day's headlines, though, told another story:

"'He Saved Italy,' Says Bosis of Mussolini," read the front page of the *Toronto Daily Star* on April 22. For all the nuance he had tried to deliver, most readers would come away concluding he was an apologist for the Fascist regime.

Despite his growing misgivings, there were some aspects of the cross-country tour that appealed to Lauro. He spent a total of a month in California, and the long train trips that took him deep into the south, and across the Midwest to Seattle, gave him his first sustained exposure to the land of his mother's birth. Taking the stage in his well-tailored black suit in places like Urbana, Illinois, and Lincoln, Nebraska, Lauro was aware that many of the young women in the audience saw him as a dapper and cultivated European, a charming exotic. He found the free-spirited women of Jazz Age America equally fascinating.

"American girls definitely seemed a different breed," observed Luigi Barzini, another young Italian who had arrived in the United States at the same time as Lauro. For Barzini, whose dashing foreign correspondent father had come to New York to start an Italian-language newspaper, they were "as different from the average Italian girls as prancing circus horses were from the weary animals harnessed to country carts... They were radiantly healthy, with porcelain skins, clean, delicately shaped, and always well groomed. They were free as cattle on the range. Nobody seemed to keep watch over them.".

The unattached poet didn't hesitate to flirt. Cox McCormack records how, in Chicago, a friend was astonished by the Latin ardour of Lauro's campaign to woo her dark-eyed niece. Other women he'd met in Berkeley and Oakland would find Lauro's passionate letters and poems in their mailboxes. Soon, though, he would renew a more serious relationship, the beginnings of which Thornton Wilder had witnessed on the moonlit Rome's Via Appia Antica five years earlier.

By the time Lauro had finished his first North American tour, he had delivered ninety-nine lectures, at least a third of them about Mussolini. Back in New York, he was shaken by the latest news from Italy. The Fascist education minister, Giovanni Gentile, had succeeded in convincing four hundred leading artists, among them the playwright Luigi Pirandello and the futurist Filippo Marinetti, to sign an oath of loyalty to the regime. On the first of May, 1925, forty-one of the nation's leading cultural figures responded with a "Manifesto of Anti-Fascist Intellectuals." The document was issued by the philosopher Croce—who had until then reserved judgment on the regime—and Giovanni Amendola, the leader of the Aventine Secession. (The Liberal deputy would die in exile in Cannes, succumbing to internal bleeding nine months after being severely beaten by Tuscan blackshirts.) Among the signatories were several friends of Lauro's father, and the philosopher Gaetano Salvemini. For Lauro, a clear line had been drawn: as an intellectual, you were either for Fascism, or against it. From that point on, as he would later write, he "refused to utter one single word in public in its favour."

Di Robilant, unaware of Lauro's decision, declared the tour a success. The speaker had excelled in presenting a positive picture of life in Fascist Italy. "As a result of his journey the Society received hundreds of letters requesting information about Italian books, travel, and the present status of the Italian people," the Society's manager wrote to Lamont and other members of the board.

As Lauro prepared to sail back to Italy, he sent a letter to Lamont at his Wall Street office thanking him for arranging the successful tour: "I wish to avail myself of this opportunity to thank you for the admirable work you are doing in cementing and furthering the cultural ties between this great nation and Italy."

Lamont, as it happened, had just returned from his own successful tour. After visiting Capri and Pompeii, and attending a Good Friday service at St. Peter's, Lamont had found his health improved enough to see to some business for the House of Morgan. In Rome, he called on the chief officers of the leading banks and the Fascist Minister of Finance, and paid a repeat visit to

Mussolini's offices in the Palazzo Chigi on the Via del Corso. Impressed by the dictator's determination to stabilize the lire, he agreed to do what he could to smooth the way for an emergency loan, and told him he would authorize a credit line of $50 million.

"The Italy through which I travelled seemed to be industrious and prosperous," Lamont reported on his return to the United States. "The newspaper headlines in the New York and even London papers seemed to me exaggerated. Everybody, both in and out of the Government, laughed at these stories of street fights, [of] unrest upsetting the Government."

From New York, Lamont rode the Morgans' private railway car to Washington. There he informed the Secretary of Commerce that Mussolini had asked J.P. Morgan & Co. to organize a substantial bond issue. The bank was willing, provided something was done about Italy's war debt. In the next meeting of the Italian Debt Commission, the interest on the debt was reduced to four-tenths of one percent, and Italy was given 62 years to pay, terms more favourable than those extended to any other European nation.

In the final weeks of 1925, the House of Morgan announced it was floating a $100-million bond issue to the Kingdom of Italy. The news provoked no public outcry. For the time being, elite opinion, in part informed by Lauro's headline-making tour, seemed to favour giving the new dictator a chance. American money began flowing into Fascist Italy.

For Mussolini, the timing was propitious: the building of the Third Rome had already begun.

13 I PICCONI DI ROMA

On the afternoon of New Year's Eve, 1925, the sidewalks around the Piazza Venezia were thronged with spectators. In spite of the low temperatures and the overcast sky, thousands of Italians and foreigners had turned out for a glimpse of Il Duce, the man who had lately become Rome's single greatest tourist attraction. Shortly before four o'clock, a long black Lancia Lambda turned off the Corso Vittorio and proceeded slowly up the sloping Via d'Aracoeli. Shouts of *"Viva Mussolini! Evviva il fascismo!"* mingled with the clangs emanating from the bell towers that encircled the Campidoglio.

The limousine pulled onto the piazza atop the Capitoline Hill, and parked beside the imposing bronze statue of the emperor Marcus Aurelius mounted on horseback. For the occasion, Michelangelo's oval piazza, bounded on three sides by peach-coloured buildings, had been cleared of crowds. Mussolini, in a conscious display of virility, trotted up the great staircase of the Palazzo dei Conservatori, covered that day with a crimson velvet canopy dripping with golden fringes. He was flanked by the *Moschettieri del Duce*, his personal bodyguards, whose uniform included a double-edged dagger and black fezzes emblazoned with white skulls. Turning back to the piazza, where a detachment of Fascist militia waited on horseback, he was rewarded with tribute in the form of cries of *"Du-chay!"* and stiff-armed Roman salutes.

Entering the palazzo, Mussolini strode down a broad corridor, boots clattering on the marble floors, and walked through the exquisitely carved wooden doors of the Sala degli Orazi e Curiazi. The high-ceiling room, famous for its seventeenth-century frescos showing Romulus and Remus being suckled by a she-wolf, the rape of the Sabine women, and other episodes from the city's founding, had been adorned with three-coloured national flags emblazoned with Fascist rods-and-axes. Every seat was filled. Among the ranks of senators, deputies, and undersecretaries was Guglielmo Marconi, the inventor of radio, General Badoglio, the army's chief of staff, and the fearsome Roberto Farinacci, secretary of the Fascist party and the second most powerful man in Italy. Mussolini mounted a stage, on which the new Governor of Rome and his vice-governors sat in gilded armchairs. Taking his place at a podium, beneath the raised right hand of the statue of Pope Innocent X, he delivered a short, emphatic speech which would have crucial implications for the future of Rome.

"Within five years Rome must become a marvel to the entire world; vast, ordered, powerful, as it was during the empire of Augustus." The allusion to the greatest of the Caesars provoked deafening applause. Mussolini turned to the pro-Fascist banker who had been appointed Governor of Rome and addressed him directly. "*Governatore!* You must continue to liberate the trunk of the great oak from everything that still binds it. Create space around the Mausoleum of Augustus, the Theatre of Marcellus, the Capitoline, the Pantheon; all that has grown up over the centuries of decadence must disappear... then the Third Rome will spread over other hills, along the banks of the sacred Tiber, out to the beaches of the Tyrrhenian Sea." He concluded: "*Governatore!* To work, without further procrastination. The Fatherland and the world await the fulfillment of the omen."

Il Duce had chosen an auspicious site for his proclamation. The Capitoline Hill was the political, religious, and administrative epicentre of ancient and modern Rome. It was here that Mussolini—who as a provincial newspaper editor had professed scorn for Rome—was made an honorary citizen of the Eternal City in 1924. (The date was April 21, the putative anniversary of the city's founding, which had supplanted the traditional workers' day of May 1 as a national holiday.) Now, as dictator, he set out a vision of a future rooted in the imperial past, rooted in another concept borrowed from d'Annunzio: *Romanità*, the militaristic essence of "Roman-ness," transplanted to the machine age. The template for the new city would be first-century Rome, under Caesar Augustus, when the empire had reached its greatest extent. Everything that stood in the way—the medieval city, the Renaissance city, the Baroque city, and most of all the decadent Risorgimento city, built by the detested Liberals—was liable to be swept away.

The work of *sventramento*, or disembowelling, began the following day. On New Year's Day, 1926, the governor, hand-picked by Mussolini and directly answerable to the Minister of the Interior, officially replaced the mayor and his democratically elected municipal council. The *manganello*, the lead-tipped stave with which the *squadristi* had clubbed their way to power, was now supplanted by the *piccone*, the pick-axe, as the symbol of the transformative power of Fascism. Hand-held *picconi* began to crash down on the roofs of apartment buildings and ancient Christian churches and anything that stood in the way of Imperial ruins selected for elevation into Fascist monuments. Mussolini, shadowed by the cameramen of the state screen propaganda unit, was often recorded striking the first blow. Newsreels produced by the

Istituto Luce would show him, dressed in immaculate labourer's clothes, clambering atop a roof to smash the tiles on the rooftop of a liberal-era theatre, kicking off work that would evict families from 120 tenements around the Mausoleum of Augustus.

The Rome that Shelley and other Romantic travellers had celebrated, the Rome the de Bosis family inhabited, the Rome that enchanted Thornton Wilder—this was exactly the Rome the Fascists wanted to wipe off the map. The futurist Marinetti had fantasized about driving into Rome "on a speeding sixty-horsepower... the steering wheel aimed directly at the Arch of Constantine." Early in his career, Mussolini fulminated against how the "foreigners—especially those *boches* [Germans] with their accursed Baedekers—went from Venice to Taormina, rubbing themselves against Italy's glorious, ancient patrimony."

Insisted Mussolini: "The Coliseum and the Roman Forum are glories of the past, but we must build the glories of the future."

But by the time Lauro was back in Rome after his American lecture tour, Mussolini had come around to embracing the symbolic power of the past, provided it was cleansed of any hint of backwardness. The man responsible for overseeing the purge was Antonio Muñoz, the head of the Fine Arts and Antiquities administration within the offices of the Governatorato. Though his expertise lay in restoring medieval churches, Muñoz endorsed Mussolini's plans for reviving the Rome of Augustus, and proved an enthusiastic promoter of the growing cult of an all-seeing, all-powerful Duce.

"Nothing escapes his watchful eye," Muñoz wrote in a booklet titled *The Rome of Mussolini*, "from the restoration of famous buildings... to the most modest issues of civic aesthetics, from an illuminated sign that enlivens a modern street to a billboard defacing an old piazza, from a lamp-post out of place to a withered tree in a garden. He observes, supervises, corrects all."

Under Muñoz, the arches of the Theatre of Marcellus were cleared of the stables and warehouses that had grown up over the centuries. The public scribes, day-labourers, and open-air barbers who had so charmed Goethe were forced out of the adjacent square, formerly the centre of the Jewish ghetto. The neighbourhood around the Theater, the site of an ancient olive oil market where ships on the Tiber unloaded their amphorae, was cleared of working-class tenements to make way for the broad new Via del Mare, which would link the centre of the city to the Tyrrhenian Sea. Hanging laundry was banished from the Capitoline Hill, and lesser structures of antiquity demolished to free the view of the Tarpeian Rock. Excavation work now focussed on uncovering such monuments of Imperial Rome as Trajan's Market and the Fora of Julius Caesar and Augustus. Construction began on the Via dell'Impero—a ruthlessly straight processional route from the Piazza Venezia to the Coliseum paralleling the Forum's ancient Via Sacra—that would eventually entail the demolition of 5,500 residences, as well as the base of the twelve-storey-tall bronze of Nero that had given the Coliseum its name. New developments were plotted out, in the streamlined Neoclassical style that would become the architectural signature of the regime, among them the Foro Mussolini, a vast sporting complex for Fascist youth on a northern bend of the Tiber.

In a progress-oriented era of radio waves, fast planes, and mighty ocean liners, archaeologists had until recently been derided by Fascists for their backward-looking *passatismo* ("past-ism"). With the building of the Third Rome, Mussolini's embrace of *Romanità* gave classicists new-found legitimacy. On the first anniversary of the March on Rome, the de Bosis family's elderly friend Giacomo Boni, whose excavations of the Forum provided the artifacts used as models for the party's official *fasces* symbol, conferred legitimacy to the regime by standing alongside Mussolini at the Tomb of Julius Caesar. After Boni's death in 1925, his disciple Giulio Giglioli became the most powerful archaeologist in Fascist Italy. Giglioli was the director of the Museo del Impero, devoted to glorifying Italy's ancient and modern imperial adventures, and a teacher at the state-funded Istituto di Studi Romani. The Istituto became a brain trust for archaeologists, architects, and urban planners working in the service of *Romanità*, and maintained close relationships with scholars at foreign academies, whose papers were regularly published in the Istituto's journal, *Roma*.

At the American Academy, Esther Van Deman's work on ancient aqueducts served the regime's purposes well by spotlighting the grandeur of Imperial Rome's public works. It didn't hurt that Van Deman herself was an enthusiastic supporter of Fascism. Marion Blake, the Academy's expert on Roman mosaics, observed of Van Deman: "She conceived an ardent admiration for Mussolini, from which she never wavered." (Years later, when Italy invaded Ethiopia, the never-married Van Deman would throw her engagement ring into the pot on the "Day of Faith," joining a quarter million Italian women who offered up their gold to be melted down to fund the war effort.)

More often, though, the pace of change caused foreign scholars consternation. One of Fascism's most publicized projects was the draining of the Pontine Marshes, long the breeding grounds for the malarial mosquitoes that left the Roman *campagna* so romantically depopulated. On the newly habitable wetlands, sterile new towns rose, centred on Neoclassical and Art Deco youth centres, post offices, Fascist Party headquarters. (Two similar new towns that rose on former swamps in Sicily and Sardinia were christened "Mussolinia.") Rome itself, whose population within five years would reach one million—surpassing its maximum in the Augustan era—was sprawling at a rate that alarmed preservationists.

"The city is spreading rapidly on every side beyond the walls," observed the British School's Thomas Ashby. "We have already lost most of the picturesqueness of the narrow lanes shut in by high walls, of the vineyards and gardens within the city, of churches half-forgotten... there is no doubt that the medieval feeling, which, to so many lovers of Rome, was not the least of its attractions, is disappearing fast."

Ashby, as it happened, had time on his hands to observe these changes. In 1925, the British School announced he would be replaced by a relatively undistinguished, and much younger, director. Eugénie Sellers Strong was dismissed as assistant director, on the grounds of "cataloguing errors." Strong was convinced that the School's administrators in London fired her for her devout Catholicism; others believed she was let go for her squabbling with Ashby's wife. Whatever Ashby's shortcomings as director, his Italian colleagues considered him an eminent topographer, and would soon acclaim his classic study *The Roman Campagna in Classical Times*. With Ashby and Strong out of the picture, the British School, which would shutter its doors after Italy's invasion of Ethiopia, was sidelined as a force in Roman archaeology for the rest of the Fascist era.

For all her approval of Fascism, Strong occasionally took exception when the regime ran roughshod over the old to build the new. The demolition of two churches and the remains of the Meta Sudans, a first-century fountain, to make way for the Via dell'Impero caused widespread distress among foreign scholars. A year after her dismissal, Strong founded a society which, she hoped, would "be of use in controlling public opinion as regards building Vandals." In the years that followed, the "Friends of Rome" and concerned archaeologists managed to save only a few buildings from the Fascists' pick-axes. Dozens of churches, palaces, villas, and towers were reduced to rubble.

Added to the fifty thousand or so poor Romans already living in *baracche*, or huts, outside the city walls was a new population driven out of their homes by the Fascist disembowelling. Many were relocated to the *borgate*, "scraps of city" fifteen kilometres or more outside the city walls. The largest of them would be

Primavalle, where displaced Romans were transported by truck, with their few possessions, and deposited in a muddy field northwest of the Vatican on which a few makeshift buildings had been erected; it would later become a hotbed of left-wing and anti-Fascist resistance. The regime tried to justify the relocation with claims that shifting the population to the healthful countryside would encourage larger families. (Mussolini believed that, in order for Italy to compete with France and Germany, the nation's population would have to increase by twenty million by mid-century; to achieve that goal, families of twelve would be necessary.) A step up from the *borgate* were the *case popolari*, up to ten storeys high, where large families were crowded into small apartments, cooking was done on coal or wood stoves, and shared bathrooms were located in the corridors.

For the regime, the complaints of foreign scholars concerned about the loss of Rome's historic charm were but minor irritants. If the archaeologists of the American Academy, and foreigners such as the Jewish-Bostonian connoisseur Bernard Berenson, were tolerated in Fascist Italy, it was largely for their propaganda value. Italian archaeologists, who had long suffered an inferiority complex in relation to the enterprising French and disciplined Germans, valued the implicit stamp of approval. Many, like Van Deman and Strong, supported the regime, and their international reputations helped confer lustre and legitimacy to the project of *Romanità*. Those who didn't, like Berenson, knew to keep their opinions to themselves.

Three months after his speech ordering the Governor to embark on building the Third Rome, Mussolini returned to the Capitoline Hill to give the inaugural address at a congress of surgeons. On this occasion, the public had been allowed into the piazza, and the Campidoglio was overrun with spectators. Emerging from the Palazzo, Mussolini paused to acknowledge a group of students singing *Giovinezza*. New and bellicose lyrics had recently been added to the Fascist marching song that explicitly honoured a new Caesar by name.

Within Italy's borders,
Italians have been remade
Mussolini has remade them
For tomorrow's war,
For labour's glory,
For peace and for the laurel
For the shame of those
Who repudiated our Fatherland...

Before the verse was finished, an emaciated, grey-haired woman in a black dress stepped out of the crowd and levelled a pistol, from a distance of less than a foot, and began firing at Mussolini just as he lifted his arm in a salute. The first bullet clipped a divot off the bridge of his nose. The second shot was a misfire; the bullet stuck in the chamber. As blood spurted from Il Duce's face, the would-be assassin was knocked to the ground by a policeman and pummelled by the crowd. Violet Gibson, a troubled Irish aristocrat who had conceived a violent dislike for Mussolini, and also intended to shoot the Pope, would spend the rest of her life in prisons and mental institutions.

Another assassination attempt would come in October of that year, in the form of a grenade lobbed by an anarchist marble-cutter, which bounced off Mussolini's chauffeur-driven Lancia and injured four bystanders. In all, four attempts on Mussolini's life were made in two years, providing the pretext for the implementation of the next, and most sinister, phase of Fascism: the establishment of a new public security state. The spectre of an imminent menace to Il Duce's life became, in the words of his press officer, "the cornerstone of a strategy for the totalitarian conquest of Italian life."

To the policy of *Romanità*, brought to life atop the Capitoline Hill, was added a philosophy justified by the flesh-wound inflicted on the piazza of the Campidoglio: *totalitarismo*. From now on, "All would be for the state, nothing outside the state, and nobody against the state."

For anybody who valued freedom, life in Italy was about to become intolerable.

When Lauro returned to Rome in the summer of 1925, the changes had already begun.

On the old stone walls around the family's palazzo on the Via dei Due Macelli, new slogans of totalitarianism were daubed in glossy black varnish: "Believe, fight, obey"—"We shall shoot straight"—*Libro e moschetto—fascista perfetto*. ("Book and rifle—perfect Fascist.") Fascism, true to its promise, was invading every aspect, and every age, of life. In the display windows of photo studios, babies were shown posing in tiny, perfectly tailored black shirts. For grown-ups, a national network of *dopolavoro* (after-work) clubs organized sports activities and leisure outings for workers. The sons of Lauro's sister Elena, Paolo and Arturo Vivante, told him the Roman salute was now compulsory in schools (handshakes had been banned as an unhygienic foreign import). He was disgusted to learn that his young nephews had been forced to join the *Balilla*, the scouting movement—named for a Genoese street urchin who started a riot when he threw a stone at an Austrian official—intended to inculcate enthusiasm for Fascism in boys aged six to twenty-one.

These were just the most obvious signs of change. Opposition parties, whose members had long since vacated parliament in protest of the Matteotti murder, were formally banned. Associations and trade unions would soon be outlawed. Mussolini, naming himself head of six ministerial departments—in addition to the cabinet, the Fascist Grand Council, and the National Fascist Party—became the supreme dictator of a one-party state. As a former newspaperman, Mussolini was aware of the power of the media. Half of his ministers were recruited from the press corps, and he promulgated a law giving the government supervisory power over all publications. Mussolini regularly inspected the front-page layout of national newspapers to make sure the wording was to his liking. Printers were made liable for all fines incurred by the newspapers—turning typesetters into the censors of the editors—and forced to print the word "DUCE" in capitals. Many opposition newspapers were so heavily censored they printed pages that were entirely blank except for advertisements; even then, entire editions were often confiscated at the printing press. By the end of 1926, the liberal editor of *Il Corriere della Sera* was forced to step down, and the newspaper joined the other leading national daily, *La Stampa*, in becoming an organ of the Fascist state. Henceforth, all of Italy's 81 daily newspapers would fill their pages with news from a single Fascist-controlled agency, the Agenzia Stefani.

State propaganda presented Mussolini as omniscient, invulnerable, omnipresent. His image was everywhere visible on postcards, in newspapers, on posters. He could be seen posing with his pet lion, wearing shorts and boxing gloves, playing the violin, swimming, driving a sports car, fencing, or working a scythe, shirtless, in a wheat field surrounded by happy peasants. With thirty million pictures in 2,500 different poses in circulation, he was believed to be the most photographed man in history. Like the Caesars, who had given their names to the months of July and August, Mussolini even changed the calendar. Henceforth, years would be indicated by Roman numerals, starting with Anno I in 1922, numbered not from Christ's birth but the year of the March on Rome. A new slogan, devised by a journalist, began to appear on walls: *Mussolini ha sempre ragione.*

"Mussolini is always right" was the official message, but Fascism's main policies came from the *gerarchi*, the officials who occupied the upper ranks of the party. Alfredo Rocco, a former Marxist and Nationalist, transformed d'Annunzio's constitution for Fiume into the basis for the Fascist corporative state. Workers and factory owners were made to sit together in "corporations" devoted to furthering the fortunes of the Fascist state; the head of the new Ministry of Corporations, naturally, would be Mussolini himself. *Totalitarismo*, first used as an expression of scorn by the Liberal deputy Amendola, was adapted by Rocco and the education minister Giovanni Gentile into a vision of total subordination to the state, in which individuals existed only to serve a nation united under Fascism.

For the English-born writer Iris Origo, who witnessed the rise of Fascism from her Tuscan estate, the *gerarchi* were as energetic as they were intellectually bankrupt. "Arrogant, half-educated (most of them self-made men), unscrupulous and sometimes corrupt, they represent the worst element in the country, and are regarded with contempt and disgust by the older men they have superseded and whose ideals they are betraying."

Lauro's frenetic movements, however, spared him sustained exposure to the true impact the *gerarchi* were having on Italy. In 1926, he agreed to chaperone over a hundred paintings and sculptures to New York and Chicago, as part of a touring exhibition of modern Italian art organized by the Italy America Society. His duties, which called on him to cross and re-cross the Atlantic, allowed him to pay three visits to Paris. There, he made a final attempt to win the woman whom he'd first courted by moonlight on the Via Appia Antica. Marie Harjes was the daughter of the senior partner at the J.P. Morgan & Co. affiliate in Paris, and a close friend of Thomas Lamont's. Lauro's long campaign to wed an American—as his father had before him—almost ended in marriage. (It was at this time that Lauro enjoyed an evening on

Broadway at a raucous Marx Brothers show, with fellow Roman Gilbert Bagnani, who was passing through New York to deliver his lectures in Canada.) In the end, Harjes may have turned down the impecunious poet as a risky prospect. Lauro was able to laugh off the rejection as a narrow miss.

"For eight months, I was on the point of becoming a millionaire," he wrote to his friend Giorgio La Piana at Harvard. "I was in very grave danger of marriage, but now I am free forever." Lauro would stay with La Piana in the summer of 1926, when he taught two summer courses at Harvard, an experience remembered fondly by both Lauro and his students.

Yet each time Lauro returned to Rome, it became clearer that the cult of Mussolini, and with it Fascism's hold on society, had planted its roots deeper into the nation. The de Bosis family's place in the upper echelons of society meant that he moved easily in elite Fascist circles. His brother Vittorio had even helped save Mussolini's life. Early in 1925, just five weeks after proclaiming himself dictator, Mussolini began to vomit blood in his Via Rasella apartment. Rumours spread that he was dying. (Walter Lippmann's *New York World* published the headline: "Mussolini Faces Lingering Death From Cancer; Stroke Has Paralyzed Duce's Face.") A duodenal ulcer was diagnosed, which Mussolini blamed on the tinned meat he ate during the war. Vittorio was called in to act as surgeon's assistant to Mussolini's physician. The operation was a success, and Mussolini swore off meat, wine, and coffee and became a keen proponent of yogourt with lunch. It was a near miss, however, and Il Duce was grateful to Lauro's older brother for keeping quiet about the operation.

Lauro knew many of the most prominent Fascists personally, including Rocco and Gentile, the architects of totalitarianism, and Italo Balbo, the intelligent but cynical *ras* of Ferrara, who was serving as the undersecretary of aviation. Intimate contact with Mussolini's henchmen further soured him on the regime.

"While keeping on friendly terms with Mussolini himself, he had occasion to meet several of the 'hierarchs' and watch them at work," Lauro's old friend Giorgio de Santillana would recall. "It was obvious to him that these people, despite a certain mental suppleness and practical ability, were howling fools. He had watched them at close quarters... he saw through their shallow convictions, their thinly disguised craft, their loud and tactless echoing of cheap phraseology, their perpetual declamations and meaningless jingoism." De Santillana remembered his friend despairing aloud: "My God, I can't understand how the damn bounders *can* go on and on with the same old bag of tricks. I suppose they've got the stomach for that."

Even more sinister developments were taking place behind the scenes. The 1926 Emergency Law for the Defence of the State, hastily rolled out after the fourth attempt on Mussolini's life, empowered the regime to confiscate passports, shut down newspapers, and exile dissidents without trial. A new institution, the Special Tribunal for the Defence of the State, allowed judges drawn from the ranks of the Fascist militia to pass sentence on political prisoners. Jails, where torture and prolonged solitary confinement were common, could no longer contain the ranks of "criminals." The death penalty, abolished by the Liberal regime in 1889, was reinstated for political crimes, and police were ordered to shoot all clandestine border-crossers.

Internal exile, known as *confino*, became a common punishment. Thousands were shipped away from their hometowns, chained and handcuffed, in cattle cars attached to third-class trains. In all, Fascism would send fifteen thousand Italians into internal exile, mostly in internment colonies on Lampedusa, Ponza, Ustica, and other barren, poverty-stricken islands, far off the tracks beaten by tourists. One of the first figures hauled up before the Special Tribunal was the leader of the Communist Party, Antonio Gramsci. (At his trial, the prosecutor declared:

"We must prevent his mind working for at least twenty years.")
Another high-profile victim was the philosopher Benedetto Croce,
who had been under house arrest since signing the Manifesto of
Anti-Fascist Intellectuals.

Lauro went to visit Croce in his family's palace in Naples. The
philosopher advised him not to join the exiles who had started to
flee Italy to form nuclei of resistance in France, Switzerland, and
the United States. Croce believed it was better to work within the
system, preserving "tradition, civility, and Italian culture, preparing for the country's recovery, and a not-so-distant better future."

For the time being, Lauro agreed with Croce about the best
way to deal with the Fascists. "They are our own people," he told
de Santillana, "whatever they do, and must be fought from within
the nation. Foreign help under any form could not be thought of."

Lauro began to realize that he was in a remarkable position.
Unlike the great majority of Italians, his work in America allowed
him to cross the border at will. According to de Santillana, "He
was not only free, he was favourably looked upon among the
Inner Circle of the Party. The Duce knew him and liked him, and
so did many of the chiefs." None of them suspected how much
Lauro's attitude to Fascism had changed. In his friend's view,
Lauro was, first and foremost, "a believer in liberty as the ultimate
creator of truth." The regime's attacks on freedom of thought, the
press, and speech horrified him.

"The outcome of his meditations," recalled de Santillana, "was
a very simple plan of action: keep quiet and unobtrusive, on good
terms with official circles, collaborating if advisable. Meanwhile,
get in touch with the scattered and disillusioned elements of liberalism, call back the so-called cultivated people to a sense of
decency and proportion, and show them that the ideas they had
been taught in their youth were not as obsolete as they believed."

For the time being, he would pursue various literary projects,
and continue to travel. He had time, on his crossings of the

Atlantic in ocean liners, to finish his version of *Antigone* and a translation of *Hamlet*. (The Danish prince's lament would come to have a particular resonance for Lauro: "The time is out of joint. O cursèd spite,/That ever I was born to set it right!") He had his first experience of flying, boarding an airplane to cross the English Channel to London. He was in Paris, visiting Marie Harjes, when Charles Lindbergh was greeted by a crowd of one hundred thousand after making the first successful solo crossing of the Atlantic. For Lauro, who had been sketching Pegasus, the winged horse of Greek mythology, since he was a child, the new aircraft were irresistible. Flight was a heady combination of freedom from earthly bounds, combined with the projection of human will in the conquest of distance, space, and time.

Mussolini's pursuit of *Romanità* had one very direct impact on Lauro. The rebuilding of the city had cost him his studio in the brick tower in the city walls, which his parents had inherited from the sculptor Moses Ezekiel; it was lost, he wrote a friend in New York, to "wicked and powerful hands." In the summer of 1927 he retreated to the Torre di Portonovo, the family's tower near Ancona. Inspired by his recent flights, he succumbed to a "terrible 'writing fever.'" Secluding himself in one of the sixteenth-century tower's small rooms, as austerely furnished as a monk's cell, he wrote an entire classical tragedy of 1,750 verses, in the highest Sophoclean style, in just two weeks.

It was called *Icaro*, and it was a retelling of the venerable Greek myth. Daedulus, a brilliant Athenian inventor, crafts a pair of wings out of wax and feathers which allows his son, Icarus, representing the poetic élan, to defy the tyrant Minos and escape captivity on Crete. In Ovid's version of the story, Icarus points out to his father Daedalus, the inventor of the wings: "Though he may possess everything, Minos does not possess the air." For Lauro, the symbolism was clear. If Mussolini was setting his sights on the earth of Rome, using ancient ruins to legitimize his imperial projects, he would turn his gaze to the sky, and all the freedom that it promised.

When he'd finished, Lauro knew exactly what he'd do with *Icaro*. The following May, he planned to submit the tragedy to a new literary competition. Winning would be a kind of poetic justice, for the contest was organized by the Governatorato—the administration responsible for the building of the Third Rome.

14 APPARITION IN ROME

Almost every citizen of Rome can point out the balcony, high up on the facade of the Palazzo Venezia, where Mussolini made his most important wartime speeches. Fewer know the location of Il Duce's original balcony. It is found two blocks to the north, on the southeast corner of the Palazzo Chigi, a sixteenth-century palace that has long served as the official residence of Italian prime ministers. The stone landing is L-shaped, and the three flagpoles that tilt outwards from its iron railings resemble the spars of an ocean-going vessel. For a decade after the March on Rome, this was considered the "prow of Italy," from which Il Duce delivered "oceanic" rallies that steered the nation. One side of the balcony looks out over Marcus Aurelius's spiralling column in the Piazza Colonna. The other side is three metres—barely a cobblestone's throw—over the heads of the shoppers strolling on the Via del Corso.

In the early years of Fascism, the exercise of power was this intimate and direct. Very little distance separated the dictator and the mob.

On the afternoon of March 14, 1928, a performance by a foreign visitor was scheduled to take place in the oldest part of the Palazzo Chigi, rooms that were once the residence of a counter-reformation cardinal. Mussolini had agreed reluctantly, for the string of attempts on his life had made him wary about allowing new-comers into his second-floor offices. His secret police had recently broken into a hotel room across the street, just as a would-be assassin, an ex-Socialist deputy, was aiming a sniper's rifle through the slats of a window at the famous balcony. In spite of his con-cerns, Mussolini instructed a black-coated usher to fetch the visitors. They were shown into a high-ceilinged room, frescoed with scenes from Genesis, whose centrepiece was a one-metre-high bronze of the Victory of Samothrace.

A middle-aged actress entered, followed by an attendant car-rying a bundle under her arms. She was a veteran of command performances at Windsor Castle and the White House, and her identity had been verified by the current American ambassador. Yet when her maid began to unbundle the shawls needed for changes of costume and character, Mussolini began to show signs of extreme agitation. Perhaps he was recalling the English-speaking woman who had come close to putting a bullet in his head on the Capitoline.

"I saw for a moment what lay behind that facade of grandeur and bellicose power," the actress would later tell a friend. "The great ruler suddenly seemed petrified. He flung up his arms in front of his face. 'Via! Via!' he cried ('Take it away!'). As the maid spread out the shawls and the expected explosion did not occur, his efforts to recover his dignity were so pathetic that I couldn't help feeling sorry for the poor little man."

Fortunately, the actress was skilled at improvisation. As she unfastened her handbag, she contrived to let its contents spill on the floor. Mussolini stooped to retrieve a fallen lipstick, and handed it to her with a gallant bow, a face-saving gesture executed with enough aplomb to provoke a burst of relieved laughter from the senior Fascists in attendance. The performance was allowed to continue. The following day, as the actress noted in her journal, her suite at the Hotel de la Ville was filled with "Flowers from Mussolini."

Within a few days, Ruth Draper, considered by some to be the greatest actress the world had seen since Sarah Bernhardt, and the only plausible successor to Italy's recently deceased Eleonora Duse, would be exposed to another, more sincere, show of Italian gallantry. On the same day she performed for Mussolini, she attended a lunch at the Palazzo Borghese given by the Marchesa Presbitero, an American painter who had married an Italian nobleman. There, she'd been introduced to a handsome young Italian-American poet, Lauro de Bosis. Three days later she ran into him again at an evening party at the Contessa Pasolini's.

Lauro, tapping his significant reserves of charm, launched an energetic courtship. He invited her for a drive to the town of Frascati—being sure to show her the family's villa in the *campagna* along the way—then took her for butter-and-parmesan drenched fettuccine at Alfredo's, down the Via della Scrofa from the Mowrers' old address, before finishing the day at a performance of Pirandello's latest play.

Less than a week after they met, Lauro took a seat in the theatre of the Palazzo Odescalchi, on the other side of the Via del Corso from Mussolini's offices, and watched in wonder as Draper revealed her talent.

Lauro would later say that, on that day, he witnessed a "miracle."

A young woman wearing a smock and a broad-brimmed Panama hat bustles into a church, and, choosing a spot in the nave, unfolds an easel. She is spending her morning in Rome with a friend copying an early Renaissance Madonna hidden away in a side-altar.

"I just love squeezin' paint," she tells her companion, in a no-nonsense English accent. As they work their brushes with broad, energetic strokes, they complain about the trickiness of mixing colours, the mounting heat of the day, and the overly flirtatious waiter at the *albergo*. It's clear she thinks she's a better painter than her friend, whose workmanship she surveys with a conde-. scending air.

Their brushes pause in mid-stroke as the day's first group of tourists bursts into the church. Suddenly, the air is filled to the clerestory with unmistakably American voices. Out of the corner of an eye, the English girl notes that the tourists are trailed by a bent crone, shawled in black, who works her way from group to group, begging for coins.

"*Un soldino,*" the old woman wheezes, raising fatigue-hooded eyes towards the Madonna. "*Per l'amor di Dio, prego.*" A lira in her hand earns a warm "*tante grazie,*" a refusal muttering and dark looks. To avoid embarrassment, the English girls hastily pack up their painting gear and exit out the side door. As they leave, a young Italian woman appears, skipping light-footed over the antique marble, carrying a red rose in one hand. She turns an avid gaze to the pews. A man rises to meet her, and, in hushed voices, they arrange a tryst in the piazza the following day, when her mother will be at the market. Blowing her *inamorato* a kiss, she seems to dance out of the church, but not before pausing beneath the gaze of the Madonna and crossing herself.

Her place is taken by a tall German woman in a green loden cape and a hat of Bavarian felt, who carries a red Baedeker's guide, a cane, and a large purse. Imperiously, she directs the gaze of her party—"*Gretl, Frieda, und Willy!*"—towards the Madonna. Their countryman Goethe has visited this church, she informs them, as well as the Kaiser himself. They express their approval, and turn their attention to where they will eat lunch. *"Macaroni, macaroni, macaroni! Nein!"* She will lead them to a place that serves bratwurst and good Munich beer.

When the noisy tourists leave, a white-haired woman wrapped in a black cape rises from a pew, and then slowly drops to her knees, eyes closed, before the Madonna della Misericordia. In the sudden stillness, her silent praying restores the church to its intended vocation. The anguish that has led her to implore grace from the Virgin Mary is legible on her tense features. Ever so slowly, a look of peace suffuses her features, and the church—a moment ago a destination for lovers and tourists—is made numinous by the intensity of her feeling.

Then—the curtain went down. The audience, spellbound, remained silent. There was a vast exhalation, a kind of collective sigh, and a beaming Ruth Draper reappeared to take a bow. Lauro, ecstatic, joined the applause, which was prolonged and thunderous.

There had never been any paintbrushes or easels; no Madonna in a side-altar; no chattering tourists, nor a lovestruck ingenue. Just one plain-featured, diminutive woman, well into middle age, who somehow conjured an entire Italian church, and all who entered it, out of thin air.

Ruth Draper had performed "The Italian Church" in London for the first time eighteen years earlier. She would always insist she was a monologuist rather than an actress. She played alone, and created—never wrote—her own material, perfecting it over the course of years. (When an adoring Henry James crafted a monologue for her, she politely refused to perform it.) Eventually, she would carry within her slight frame a repertoire of fifty-two individuals—among them "the Lady of the Manor," "the little Jewish tailor," "the Southern girl at a dance"—each painstakingly developed over the course of eight to ten years. Through an instantaneous metempsychosis, she could make any one of them live through a tiny movement of a hand, the dart of an eye, or a change in her posture. George Bernard Shaw, asked for his opinion of her acting, responded: "That's not acting. That's life."

Or, as an old doorman at the Aeolian Hall in London, watching an audience mesmerized into utter stillness by one small woman, would put it: "It is mass hypnotism, night after night."

The New York-born Ruth Draper was already thirty-five when she made her debut. Arriving in Rome, after eight years of incessant touring, she was still looking for *"la grande passion,"* a love equal to, or exceeding, her powers of imagination. Lauro was all that she had been waiting for. The fact that she was seventeen years his senior didn't seem to bother her, or him. After their first motor excursion into the *campagna*, they spent at least part of each day together, for twenty days in a row. He showed her the Rome he loved, and they "walked miles thru the streets and along the river," the ancient ruins on the Palatine, the churches on the Pincio, the bathing beach in Fregene. Before she boarded the train to Florence for her next engagement, Lauro serenaded her with lines from Shelley beside the lake in Villa Borghese. Six years earlier, he had walked with Nancy Cox McCormack in the same gardens, reciting the same poems.

Ardent, aching letters followed, addressed to his "archangel," and his *"leoncino,"* or "baby-lion." They suggested that, in the beginning at least, he saw Ruth not as an individual, but an ideal—and thus an ideal object of his romantic attention.

"I have drunk the milk of Paradise and will never more be the same as before," he wrote, two days after her departure. "I kiss your hand with worship and adoration." He signed it *"Lauro di Ruth,"* binding his first name to his lover's with a possessive preposition, a technique he'd practised on Cox McCormack and other women. Ruth fit a pattern: she was American—like his mother—as almost all the women Lauro had seriously courted had been, and older than he. Within days of their meeting, he took her to the top-floor apartment on the Via dei Due Macelli to meet his mother. Ruth and Lillian shared a New England upbringing and Bohemian proclivities, and sympathized immediately. A long-lasting friendship was born.

If there was something of the performance to the beginning of their affair—with Lauro a natural in the role of the Mediterranean swain—they soon established the basis for a genuine, long-lasting love. Ruth had bloomed into her career relatively late in life, and her demanding tour schedule meant she didn't have the time to cultivate relationships. Lauro, whose ardour in love may have alarmed Marie Harjes and earlier objects of his affection, had remained his mother's adored last-born. His father's death had only strengthened their bond. When Lauro showered Ruth with attention in the Roman spring, she had neither the will nor the inclination to resist. Together, they were able to indulge the playful, creative, and childlike sides of their natures. Lauro and Ruth shared a measure of innocence, one that made them anomalies in the wised-up, materialistic Jazz Age.

Their relationship promised to be a long-lasting one. At a time when only the lucky few had the means or freedom to see the world, Lauro and Ruth were experienced transatlantic travellers, with footholds in both North America and Europe. When they were apart, they could afford to maintain their connection with telegrams, long-distance calls, and even by mailing vinyl discs etched with recorded messages of endearment.

By the spring of 1928, Lauro was trying to decide on his next move. Not surprisingly, his play *Icaro* had been passed over by the awards panel of Rome's Governatorato. He then submitted the tragedy to the Olympiad in Amsterdam (at the time, the Olympics offered prizes for literature). Though Giuseppe Prezzolini, who happened to be on the jury, would later write that he viewed the play as the best of a mediocre lot, this old friend of the de Bosis family saw to it *Icaro* won the silver award (no gold was awarded that year). At a time when Pirandello and his fellow modernists were breaking new aesthetic ground in drama, *Icaro*, written in a classical, Sophoclean style, seemed old-fashioned. Its subversive underlying theme—the need to challenge tyranny with science, reason, and poetry—wouldn't be recognized until years later.

Lauro looked for work that would keep him as close as possible to Ruth. Early in June, Irene di Robilant suggested to Thomas Lamont of the Morgan Bank that Lauro replace her as manager of the Italy America Society. The job had the advantage of putting him in New York, close to Ruth. Lauro accepted the title of the Society's executive secretary, on the understanding that he would stay on for two years at most, and that his duties would be strictly non-political.

For the second time, the Society was luring Lauro into a trap. Behind the scenes, di Robilant had been working on a pet project since 1921. In Italy, Fascism had established effective control over the entire Italian press corps, and all but the bravest foreign correspondents. However, in spite of the best efforts of Mussolini's ghost writer, Richard Washburn Child, and such wide-eyed sycophants as the *New York Times*'s Anne O'Hare McCormick, critical news of life under Fascism continued to appear in outlets like *Harper's*, *The Atlantic*, and Walter Lippmann's *New York World*. Mussolini was determined to establish a pro-Fascist press service, headquartered in Rome, that would censor all negative commentary and transmit only good news about Fascism to America. Italy must be known as the land where trains now ran on time, where new towns were rising on once-malarial swamps, where a super-competent Strong Man had reined in the Mafia. Lamont, who needed public opinion in America to remain favourable to the regime in order to arrange future Morgan loans, approved the plan, and worked with Ambassador de Martino in Washington and a fixer in Rome, to find someone to man the Rome press bureau. Their choice for the job, approved by Mussolini, was a friend of Lauro's, Percy Winner of the *Associated Press*. Winner's chances were scuttled, however, by the untimely publication of a profile in *Current History* in which he called Mussolini "Italy's uncrowned autocrat."

News of these machinations leaked to Lauro. In a forceful letter to di Robilant, he pointed out that if American reporters asked him about censorship or the end of free elections, he couldn't be expected to reply by handing out official Fascist bulletins. "How could either you or I have the *face* to go through with such hypocrisy?" He continued: "You told Lamont that I was not a Fascist. Try to tell that to [Ambassador] de Martino or to the Fascist party, local or central." He acknowledged that he had a cordial relationship with Mussolini, who had always been "benevolent" to him. Nonetheless, his conclusion was: "I cannot accept without compromising my conscience." By going on the record as a Liberal, even an anti-Fascist, Lauro thought he had washed his hands of the Society.

But di Robilant and Lamont were apparently desperate enough to resort to trickery. Di Robilant, for her part, had little to lose by lying. She'd made the mistake of voicing her displeasure at the founding of the Casa Italiana, which she saw as rival Italian cultural centre. When an Italian-American professor at Columbia accused her of being "not Fascist enough," word got back to Rome, and Lamont was asked to dismiss her; as a golden handshake, she was awarded a lucrative Westinghouse speaking tour of Italy. Lamont, too, was about to be replaced as the Society's president by Paul Cravath, a friend of Lauro's. Di Robilant cabled Lauro in Lamont's name, and begged him to reconsider. He would have no involvement with the press service; his duties would involve editing the Society's bulletin, and boosting cultural ties between the two nations. On such terms, Lauro was willing to accept.

It wasn't long after arriving in New York, early in October 1928, that Lauro realized what he'd gotten himself into. The cover of the latest issue of the Society's bulletin—bearing his name on the masthead as editor—featured a translation of Mussolini's speech on the sixth anniversary of the March on Rome. One of his first duties was to oversee the Society's relocation from 43rd Street to the newly completed Casa Italiana building on the uptown campus of Columbia, a university considered a hotbed of Fascist sympathizers. Nicholas Murray Butler, its Republican, pro-Mussolini president, had been publicly criticized for supporting a lecture series on Fascism in Italy held at the Casa. Butler had also enthusiastically accepted the gifts of expensive furniture from Mussolini that adorned the Casa's auditorium, and allowed Il Duce's portrait to be hung next to his own on its walls. By association, Lauro would be seen as an abettor, if not an accomplice, in whitewashing the blackshirts' image in America.

Making matters worse, Ruth's tour schedule meant she was rarely in New York. Lauro's own duties frequently had him riding trains to Washington and the Society's offices in other east coast cities. Writing to Ruth in Boston, he lamented: "I adore you. But I am a wreck. Everything pouring on me at once: the Bulletin, the Ambassador... the Casa Italiana, Butler... My!!! What a life!! And tomorrow to New Haven. I need you *ferociously*."

Lauro's work in Manhattan was indeed draining. His role at the Society put him at the heart of the city's social life. One night, he would be at a small gathering in an uptown apartment, coaxing a smile out of visiting conductor Toscanini with his parlour tricks. The next, he might be wearing black tie at a hotel ball; one such Society fundraiser at the Ritz-Carlton went on until six-thirty in the morning. At the Ethel Barrymore Theater, he produced a benefit for the Eleonora Duse Fellowship, in which Ruth recreated one of the late actress's most famous parts: the role of Francesca of Rimini, written for La Duse by her lover Gabriele d'Annunzio. (The play was directed by Stark Young, the Italophile whose vignettes in *The New Republic* had first lured Thornton Wilder to Rome.) Though Lauro and Ruth were photographed together at the event, she still thought it impolitic to reveal to her public that she had a lover.

Lauro tried to minimize the Casa's pro-Fascist reputation by organizing as many non-political events as he could. He talked Thornton Wilder into accepting his invitation to present a series of talks. (His old friend had won the Pulitzer Prize for his novel *The Bridge of San Luis Rey*, which Lauro somehow found the time to translate into Italian. He wrote to Wilder on Society letterhead: "*The Bridge* has been for me a real school of style.") He arranged for Prezzolini to be invited as a resident-professor at the Casa, returning the favour done for him when his older friend had put his name forward for his first lecture tour of America. Soon he was sharing rooms with Prezzolini in an apartment on the building's fifth floor.

Lauro was compelled to accept an invitation to the headquarters of the Women's Fascist Association on Fifth Avenue, where he spoke on Italian poetry to an attentive crowd of one hundred. He took charge of organizing a lunch for Italo Balbo, one of the architects of the March on Rome, who later that year would become minister of the Air Force. Lauro's role compelled him to smile and shake hands with the brutal *ras* of Ferrara. It was increasingly evident to him, though, that his activities in New York were helping to put a public stamp of respectability on Fascist violence.

In private, he was already looking at his work at the Society as a cover—a potentially very useful cover—for activities more in line with his true convictions. Within a few months, Lauro quietly contacted a man increasingly seen as the philosophical leader of the global anti-Fascist resistance, and asked him for a private interview.

At first, the esteemed historian found excuses to refuse. The man knew Lamont—who had recently infuriated him by defending Mussolini's handling of the economy at a public debate on Fascism—and suspected that as executive secretary of the Morgan-sponsored Italy America Society, Lauro was merely another complacent apologist for the regime. But Lauro had a habit of never taking "no" for an answer.

Late in the summer of 1929, just one month before Wall Street would crash, Lauro finally met Italy's most notorious exile, Gaetano Salvemini.

Salvemini preferred the word *fuoruscito* to "exile" or "refugee." The latter terms suggested a reluctant flight from one's homeland. The former, first used by Machiavelli, implied that leaving was a matter of individual will, rooted in conscience. In lighter moments, Salvemini referred to himself as the "wandering Jew of anti-Fascism."

In reality, escaping Fascist Italy had been a matter of life or death for Salvemini. Born one of nine children to a poor family in Apulia, on the heel of the Italian peninsula, he was intelligent and dedicated enough to win a scholarship to study at a college in Tuscany. After being starved of reading for five years in a southern Italian high school, Salvemini found Florence an awakening. He became an enthusiastic Marxist, and made friends with Carlo and Nello Rosselli—the learned Jewish brothers who would soon join the community of anti-Fascists in exile—as well as Bernard Berenson, becoming a frequent guest at the American expatriate's art-filled villa in the city's foothills.

Salvemini's life, and philosophical outlook, was changed forever by one of the twentieth century's most dramatic natural disasters. After finishing college in Tuscany, he'd moved to Sicily to teach school. In 1908, the island was struck by a 7.1-magnitude earthquake, followed by a tidal wave, which killed more than one hundred thousand people and wiped out the city of Messina. Salvemini was thrown from a window, and watched from beneath the architrave that broke his fall as his wife, sister, and five young children vanished in a cloud of plaster. After days of groping through the rubble, he found all but the bodies of his wife and his youngest son.

"I am a miserable wretch," he wrote to Carlo Rosselli, "who has seen the happiness of eleven years destroyed in two minutes."

After the Messina earthquake, Salvemini acted with the courage of someone with nothing left to lose. He returned to the University of Florence, where he brought an intensely pragmatic approach to the study of history, coupled with an Enlightenment-born reverence for science and a heroically Socratic duty to the truth. He was a severe critic of the philosopher Benedetto Croce and the elderly prime minister Giovanni Giolitti, both of whom he thought addicted to what he saw as the distinctly Italian vices of idealism and empty rhetoric. He became the elder statesman to an influential magazine, *La Voce*, started by Prezzolini, whose early contributors included both Mussolini and his Liberal foe Giovanni Amendola. His political convictions brought him to Rome in 1919, where after being elected as an independent deputy, he stood up in the Chamber and accused Mussolini of embezzling half a million lire collected from the United States to fund Gabriele d'Annunzio's adventure in Fiume. The embattled Mussolini challenged Salvemini to a duel. It was only called off when the injured party's seconds refused to investigate the truth of the accusations.

Salvemini had picked the wrong enemy. Il Duce's rise to power made the historian a marked man. In 1923, Mussolini refused to grant him a passport to lecture at King's College in London. Salvemini went anyway, securing papers from the Italian consul in Paris that got him across the Channel. He returned to Tuscany—at a time the region was home to one in four of all Italy's Fascists—where thugs with truncheons awaited him in his lecture hall. His reputation for bravery made him the leader of Florence's anti-Fascist resistance, and he helped the Rosselli brothers publish the newsletter *Non Mollare* ("Don't Give Up"), providing them with damning documents on Matteotti's murder. After being arrested and imprisoned in Rome, Salvemini was brought to trial in Florence. The judge, anticipating international condemnation if the historian were imprisoned, granted him provisional liberty, as long as he was accompanied at all times by two "bodyguards." Salvemini, seeing the writing on the wall, decided to join the growing ranks of the *fuorusciti*. (Berenson— who also wore a pointed beard—apparently laughed off a suggestion that Salvemini borrow his passport to cross the border.) Zigzagging across northern Italy in a series of trains, Salvemini threw off his guards and reached the south of France in the summer of 1925.

He quickly established a reputation as the voice of conscience of the anti-Fascist exile communities in Paris and London. Salvemini hated the Socialists and Communists, referring to himself as a "democrat of the antediluvian school." His life was constantly in peril. The regime's newspapers had proclaimed a vendetta against the disloyal professor. "Go ahead, you Fascists who love the Duce with passion and dedication! Cross the frontiers," one urged its readers, "go ahead, Fascists, and kill." A year after Lauro completed his last lecture in the United States, Salvemini crossed the ocean to embark on his own four-month tour of America.

Unlike Lauro, Salvemini had nothing to lose by openly attacking Mussolini. The evening after his ship docked in New York, he attended a debate at the Knickerbocker Club, moderated by *World* editor Walter Lippmann, who, with Berenson, had helped Salvemini obtain a U.S. visa. His opponent was Thomas Lamont, who had just returned from negotiating the $100 million Morgan Bank loan to Italy. Salvemini won points by shooting down Lamont's sunny assessment of Fascism's impact on productivity, arguing the Italian economy had already begun to improve in 1920, well before Mussolini's seizure of power. He argued that the only success the dictator had achieved was swindling the American people into granting him loans. In spite of his thickly accented English, Salvemini emerged as the clear victor in the debate.

At a debate in Boston, Salvemini, paunchy, wearing a pointed goatee, and dressed in an ill-fitting, travel-worn suit, was confronted with dapper Fascist propaganda agents who had been approved and dispatched by de Martino, the pro-Mussolini Italian ambassador in Washington. For the rest of his tour, he was shadowed by two men: James P. Roe—inevitably introduced as a New York lawyer, but in fact a supporter of the Fascist League of North America—and the impressive Bruno Roselli, whose excellent Oxford-accented English won him favour with audiences. After going north to Montreal, Salvemini faced off with Roselli at the Foreign Policy Association in New York. "Italy no longer has free, representative institutions, but a dictatorship!" he charged. A voice from the crowd interrupted: "You're a liar!" The accuser was the founder of the Fascist League, Count Thaon di Revel, who held up a book that he claimed included the name of "Fascists assassinated by Bolsheviks—your friends."

Salvemini, through his incessant lecturing, and the publication of such works as 1927's *The Fascist Dictatorship in Italy*, became an incisive analyst of the causes of the Fascist malaise, and so a thorn in the side of Fascists in Italy and abroad. Italian-Americans, he realized, had long suffered an inferiority complex in the country of their adoption.

"Now they heard everyone say, even Americans, that Mussolini had turned Italy into a great country, that there were no unemployed, that everyone had a bathroom in his house, that trains ran on time, and that Italy was now respected and feared. Whoever contradicted this not only destroyed their ideal country, but insulted their personal dignity."

Salvemini's definition of Fascism was succinct, and remains cogent. "Italians felt the need to get rid of their free institutions," he wrote, at the very moment when they "should step forward to a more advanced democracy." Fascism, for Salvemini, was a malady of sick or failed democracies, whose people consented to abandoning hard-won liberties in return for the promise of national unity, purity, and strength. As Salvemini saw it, Mussolini had discovered a winning formula, one that future would-be autocrats would adopt freely. The modern strongman triumphed by promising to make the nation great again. In Italy's case, as great as it had been in the time of Augustus's empire.

Salvemini was in New York preparing to return to Europe when another request for a meeting with the executive secretary of the Italy America Society reached him.

When he finally agreed, the young man quickly won Salvemini over with his charm and directness. It helped, as the historian later told the *New Yorker*, that Lauro was "a beautiful boy with black eyes—tall, slim elegant, a perfect example of manly beauty." Lauro explained the evolution of his attitude towards Fascism, and how he was striving to eliminate pro-regime propaganda from the Society's program. It was the beginning of a dialogue that would continue, in person and via letters, for several years. Lauro, Salvemini realized, was a Liberal, and closer to Benedetto Croce than Marx: he recoiled from Communism and Socialism, and supported the Constitution, but thought that for Italy to become a modern republic, power would have to revert—temporarily at least—from Mussolini to the king.

Before leaving, Lauro asked Salvemini for his opinion on a plan he'd been contemplating. What if an airplane flew over Rome, and the pilot dropped books and leaflets exhorting the Italian people to end their slavery and shame? The older man replied that, were it indeed possible, he would applaud such a deed with all his heart.

"It is possible," Lauro muttered. "An English aviator, my friend, assures me that it is possible."

Salvemini was the first person Lauro had mentioned the idea to. Even Ruth, who'd settled into an apartment on East 79th Street, a block and a half from Central Park, was unaware of what her lover was contemplating.

Thoughts, once turned into speech, have a way of becoming things in the world. And events in the final months of 1929 made the plan Lauro had suggested to Salvemini seem like an increasingly plausible course of action.

It had been a year of triumph for Mussolini's Italy. October had brought the collapse of the stock market in America. Capitalism appeared to be in crisis, and many economists were willing to entertain the idea that Fascism had inoculated Italy against unemployment and the collapse of prices and production gutting the industrialized nations. Turning his back on the anti-clerical railing of his youth, Il Duce signed the Lateran Pacts with Pope Pius XI, laying the groundwork for a temporary accord between the secular power of the Fascist government and the spiritual dominion of the Catholic Church.

Nancy Cox McCormack, who was renting a studio in Greenwich Village, was one of the first to notice that something was preoccupying Lauro. He dropped by one evening for a Christmas-season party and, as he had done in the old days in Rome, delighted her guests by sending sheets of paper, intricately folded into birds, flapping over their heads.

When he was alone with Cox McCormack in her study, Lauro's "gaiety slipped off as a tired actor's cloak following a masquerade. He, only twenty-eight years old, seemed years older. Fine little wrinkles were gathering around his eyes and across his forehead... I felt that Lauro was perhaps beginning to mature in that he was for some reason displeased with himself. But I knew that the melancholic mood mooted some challenging new horizon."

Cox McCormack was partially right. In his own mind, Lauro *was* turning his sights on the horizon. The horizon in question, though, was a very old one. As ancient, in fact, as the skyline of Rome.

PART III

Facade of the Palazzo Braschi, Corso Vittorio Emanuele, on the eve of
Italy's 1934 national "elections."

15 THE BROADSIDES OF CONSPIRACY

A twenty-five-minute metro ride south of the Piazza Venezia is a vision of what Italy, and the world, might look like had Fascism triumphed.

The district known as EUR was built for the Esposizione Universale Roma, or E42, the world's fair planned—though never held—to celebrate the twentieth year of Fascism in Italy. Starting in the mid-thirties, kilometre-long axial boulevards were laid out alongside the ancient Via Ostiense, vast piazzas were studded with obelisks pillaged from Italy's new African colonies, and a cubic version of the Coliseum—the Palace of Italian Civilization— was erected where, until recently, sheep had grazed. Orderly, monumental, and sterile, the district has become a favoured location for corporate headquarters, executive villas, and movie shoots. On a sunny summer day, EUR is all sun-bleached colonnades and long shadows, as eerie and barren of human life as a Giorgio de Chirico canvas.

At the eastern end of Viale Europa, broad marble steps rise to a portico of unadorned Tuscan columns that mark the entrance to Italy's Central State Archives. The building, originally meant to house the palace of the Armed Forces, is capacious enough to warehouse the staggering number of documents that were necessary to keep Fascist Italy running. Hidden behind fireproof iron doors, they repose in tightly serried cardboard boxes on ranks of closely spaced, floor-to-ceiling shelves.

A disproportionate number of the boxes are devoted to the files of the Political Police, a division of the Directorate of Public Security within the Ministry of the Interior. Beginning in 1926, after the series of attempts on Mussolini's life, the chief of police Arturo Bocchini was empowered to recruit a network of undercover agents. Within years, nine thousand spies would work for his shadowy organization, which kept a watch on subversive, dangerous, or simply insufficiently nationalistic citizens. The operating branch of the Political Police was known as "OVRA," a name selected by Mussolini himself, reportedly for its sinister consonance with *piovra* (Italian for octopus). Bocchini, who would come to be known as the Himmler of Italy, was a lukewarm Fascist but a zealous bureaucrat with a prodigious memory. Notorious for his appetite for fine wine and pretty women, he held court, his ample belly cloaked in a brocade dressing gown, at a villa outside Rome furnished with statues of naked girls that squirted streams of coloured water from their nipples.

Bocchini's tentacles crept into every sector of daily life. His spies listened to and reported conversations overheard in cinemas, restaurants, and classrooms; there was even a paid informant in the Vatican, a monsignor on the Pope's staff. (Bocchini had Mussolini's phone tapped, and his knowledge of his boss's personal life eventually earned him the title the "Dictator of the Dictator.") Obsessed with ensuring Mussolini's safety, Bocchini had steel bars welded over all the basement entrances of the Palazzo

Venezia, and formed a *"squadra di sottosuolo"* to patrol the sewers. OVRA eventually created files on 130,000 Italians, thousands of whom would endure torture, solitary confinement, and the prolonged internal exile of *confino.*

The records on individual citizens compiled by the Political Police are filed in thousands of cardboard boxes in the State Archives. Each record is topped by an ornately calligraphied name, and an indication of the subject's "political orientation"; most include mug shots, newspaper clippings, and details of known aliases, activities, and recent movements. Some bear a stylized capital "M" in the margins, indicating the file was read, and initialled, by Mussolini. Lauro de Bosis's record is filed, in alphabetical order, in box 1,643, following the folders of Carlo de Boni *(SOCIAL-ISTA / "*Naturalized—Swiss") and Emilio de Bortoli (*ANARCHICO /* "DANGEROUS—SOUTH AMERICA"). It lists his mother, siblings and lover ("Ruth Draper, American Actress"), and includes three black-and-white photos and a description of his appearance (hair and moustache—chestnut; complexion—pallid; special markings— scar on chin). The word "ANTIFASCISTA" is stamped, in blue block capitals over two inches tall, on the front of the manila folder. The file was opened, according to the first of three dozen handwritten entries, on December 19, 1930.

It took less than a year for Lauro to go from being a trusted representative of Italy, a friend of the regime whose impeccable connections with the Fascist *gerarchi* went all the way up to Mussolini, to an enemy of the state, condemned by the Special Tribunal for "inciting rebellion through the diffusion of clandestine publications," and sought by OVRA agents working in Italy and abroad.

This was no case of mistaken identity; Bocchini and his agents had done their work well. Lauro's name belonged in the files. He had finally chosen sides, publicly assuming the one identity that— for Italy's all-encompassing totalitarian regime—excelled all others in infamy: the role of anti-Fascist.

In the spring of 1930 Lauro was preparing to conclude his tenure as executive secretary of the Italy America Society. The New York financial world's honeymoon with Mussolini was over, and American bankers had refused Italy a second $100 million loan. Fascism, it was becoming clear, had not inoculated Italy from the worst effects of the Depression. State finances were a shambles, and unemployment was on the rise; within two years a million Italians would be out of work.* Lauro agreed to take a four-month leave without pay. Looking forward to another summer with Ruth in the family's seaside tower on the Adriatic, he sailed for Italy on the eighteenth of May.

Lauro was already leading—and revelling in—a double life. In Italy the previous summer, he'd met with an old friend of the family. The meeting needed to be face-to-face, as OVRA spies made communicating by mail or telephone dangerous. Mario Vinciguerra was a historian, fourteen years Lauro's senior, with impeccable anti-regime credentials: he had run the newspaper *Il Mondo* with Giovanni Amendola, the Liberal deputy who died after being beaten by Fascist thugs. Vinciguerra listened in astonishment as Lauro, the son of a Romantic poet whose conversation had always tended to the high-flown and intellectual, laid out a very practical scheme for regime change. At its heart would be an *Alleanza Nazionale*—a National Alliance—uniting Socialists, moderate Fascists, Catholics, and Liberals; all major parties, in fact, except the Communists. It would operate in the name of, as Vinciguerra put it, "the only entity of right and of fact: the Constitution itself" and seek to rouse the people to use the king's

---

* Though it was reported abroad that Mussolini had made the trains run on time, this was true of only a few prestigious routes, frequented by tourists and businesspeople, in northern Italy. Most working Italians could count on the usual delays and cancellations.

powers to overthrow Mussolini's regime without violence. The Alliance would be a "second Risorgimento," a continuation of the work of Mazzini, Cavour, Garibaldi—all the patriots who had fought to unite nineteenth-century Italy. Vinciguerra, entranced at how Lauro's charisma created an "atmosphere part hymn, part romantic adventure," agreed to support his plans.

En route from the United States to Italy, Lauro began to put his plan in motion. In London he called on one of the most prominent of the political exiles, Don Luigi Sturzo, the anti-Fascist founder of the Popular Party, the precursor to Italy's modern-day Christian Democrat Party. The high-minded priest was forced out of Italy in 1924, after being betrayed by the Vatican, which had already started the secret negotiations with Mussolini that would end in the Lateran Accords. Sturzo was still respected in his homeland, and Lauro thought he would make a useful ally. He also met with old friends, *Manchester Guardian* journalists Sylvia and Cecil Sprigge, who had introduced him to Vinciguerra when they'd been stationed in Rome four years earlier.

After arriving in Rome, Lauro took a stroll with his friend Giorgio de Santillana. In the piazza beside the Spanish Steps, a few hundred yards from the family's apartment on the Via dei Due Macelli, he began to root around in his pockets.

"Got fifty lire?" Lauro asked his friend. When de Santillana asked what he needed the money for, he replied: "To buy the substances necessary to free these countrymen of ours."

Lauro went to a store and bought a large quantity of paper and ink. Later, he would acquire a second-hand mimeograph machine. He wrote to Ruth, then performing in London, that he was having an agreeable time in Rome; he'd visited Alfredo's for fettuccine, where he'd been sure to sneak a peek at the guest book where they'd signed their names after they'd first met, and was delighted to report that somebody had broken a bookstore window to steal a copy of his play, *Icaro*. On a more serious note, he'd spent two hours in the Senate listening to Fascist speeches and studying "the Boss," as he'd taken to calling Mussolini. He added: "I had a delightful talk with Croce and with other philosophers and they all think the plan of my book is very good."

"The book" in question was an anti-regime newsletter, an acid critique of Mussolini and a call to overthrow the Fascist regime by peaceful means, which he'd already started work on. Croce in Rome, Salvemini in New York, and Sturzo in London—Italy's three most respected anti-Fascists—had all signalled their approval for the National Alliance.

Lauro began work at the family's tower in Ancona, where the first verses of *Icaro* had come to him in a flash of inspiration. In another letter to Ruth, then in Geneva, he wrote: "I have been doing some good work but not about Dante. More actual. And am very satisfied." The first issue of the newsletter addressed the reader in familiar, winning tones: "We know you. You are intelligent and honest, which means you can't be a Fascist." (An allusion to a joke popular at the time: while you may be two of the following—"honest," "intelligent," and "Fascist"—it was impossible to be all three at once.) He typed the two-page newsletter, the first of eleven issues, on a stencil, dated it the first of July, and signed it "The Directorate."

De Santillana and another boyhood friend helped Lauro to address envelopes with the names of six hundred prominent Italians. Acting quickly to thwart OVRA spies, they made a lighting tour of northern cities, casually dropping the envelopes into as many unattended mailboxes as they could find. A friend of Vinciguerra's, a Roman literary critic name Renzo Rendi, was soon recruited to type up stencils on onion-skin paper. Lauro's mother agreed to help him copy the letters, and keep the mimeograph machine hidden in the family's apartment.

Recipients were told that a new newsletter would arrive every two weeks, and were asked to make at least six copies of each, to be mailed to as many acquaintances as possible—including, if possible, two Fascists. The mailings were greeted with either disgust or exultation, depending on the political leanings of the recipient, but always with amazement. In the eighth year of Fascism, Mussolini had purged all criticism of the regime from public discourse. Intellectuals had been jailed or exiled, foreign newspapers banned, Italian journals made organs of the state. In a totalitarian state, where information from the outside world came in the form of propaganda newsreels and censored newspapers, the National Alliance's modest little newsletters were snowballs—growing ever bigger as they rolled from city to city— that exploded like bombshells.

Lauro, with the most limited of resources, was doing to Italy what Mussolini had tried, and failed, to do in the United States. The press office managed by the Italy America Society had been meant to channel only the most positive news about life under Fascism to the outside world. With a mimeograph machine and a supply of ink, Lauro was flooding Italians with news on the regime's failures, showing them that many in the outside world viewed the omnipotent Mussolini as a laughable failure. The fact that he wasn't calling for violent revolution—Lauro acknowledged the king and the church as "the two greatest forces in Italy that exist outside of Fascism"—may have enraged many Communists, but it also won over vast numbers of moderate Italians.

In an article that would later be published, in highly edited form, in the *New York World*, Lauro set forth the Alliance's goals. "It would be completely inconceivable to think that a Ku Klux Klan-style secret police in the service of the Republican Party could arrest the editors of the *Times* and the *World* and try them to see if they should be banished to a savage island or sent to Sing Sing for a certain number of years. But that is exactly what is happening in Italy. The National Alliance is an editorial group that, given the impossibility of publishing a newspaper, each week sends private letters containing editorials that could easily pass for those published in the *Times*: objective facts and proposals of a program for a coalition of all the constitutional parties."

Recalled de Santillana, "The country was literally flooded with his little papers. I happened to hear of people, quite harmless and unpolitical to all outward appearance, who sat up all night to type hundreds of copies."

The technique was the venerable system of the chain letter, in Italy known as the *Catena di Sant'Antonio*, which promised the sender a saint's blessings for keeping up the chain. (During the First World War, chain letters that included a prayer for peace were seized by the police as enemy propaganda.) Lauro ended his letters by an appeal not to superstition, but to decency: "If...you let the chain fall, you will assume a grave responsibility in the face of Italy and of your own conscience."

Many were eager to help. Alliance newsletters were sent to Tunisia, Switzerland, England, Germany, France, and the United States; Ezra Pound and H.L. Mencken were among the recipients. A total of 40,000 Italians received them, including senators, counts, generals, editors, the leading Fascist *gerarchi*, and even Mussolini's Jewish mistress Margherita Sarfatti—a significant proportion of Italy's most influential minds. For many, the newsletters, signed by a "Directorate" that hinted at a vast, organized resistance, offered a direct refutation to the slogan painted on so many walls: "Mussolini is always right." Hundreds of Italians were disseminating Lauro's call to action, and tens of thousands more were reading his words. The very fact of their existence was proof that totalitarianism had failed to monopolize all thought, action, and expression. The revolutions that had toppled China's Manchu dynasty and Russia's czars had begun with much less.

Lauro did most of his National Alliance work ensconced in Ancona—an idyllic setting for fomenting a revolution. The family's stone tower was reached by a steep path down a hillside and stood so close to the waterfront that at high tide it seemed to rise straight out of the Adriatic. He sent Ruth, then performing in Switzerland, dozens of letters urging her to join him, and she finally drove down to join him for six weeks of swimming and sailing. (She also took to the easel, completing a landscape, her only known oil painting, of the hill rising over the tower.)

Once the mailings began, OVRA's agents seemed powerless to stop them. Returning to Rome, Lauro was delighted to hear that the chief of police, Bocchini, had taken the news to the top.

"The success of his snowballs," wrote de Santillana, "was enormous. Everyone I knew got dozens of them from different sides. 'I have the Boss on toast,' [Lauro] said grinning. 'I guess I've got him where it hurts most. I've been told that when the papers were shown him by the Chief Police, he thumped both his fists on the table and shouted 'Give another turn of the screw.'"

The news that Mussolini not only took the Alliance seriously, but was maddened by its publications, was exactly what Lauro wanted to hear. Despite his relative obscurity in the hierarchy of the Italian state, he had come to see himself as Mussolini's nemesis. In his mind, his convictions and moral purpose gave him the right—and duty—to confront and defeat Il Duce. As long as he could keep his identity, and his true intentions, hidden, he would keep up the fight. De Santillana, who had witnessed how thoroughly liberty had been curtailed in Italy, was less sure.

"To check individual action the State had provided automobiles, tanks, machine guns, gas and wireless. To check individual opinion there were literally hundreds of thousands of spies." He suspected that OVRA agents were already closing in on Lauro and his friends. He warned Lauro: "If they find you out killing you won't be enough for them. You know they are venomous journalists at heart... the more they fear, the greater their cruelty. They will tear your name in shreds after you are dead, they will call you a double-crosser and a traitor, they will heap derision on your family and your memories, they will not leave one spot of your life or your name undefiled."

On October 3, de Santillana accompanied his friend to the train station. Lauro was bound for Naples, where he and Ruth would sail for New York. De Santillana warned him that returning to Rome would almost certainly mean imprisonment or death.

"Let them do what they like," Lauro replied. "I'm here to do what's got to be done." De Santillana looked at Lauro as he gazed fixedly at the red lights stretching down the tracks into the distance. "I know quite well that I'm risking not only my life, but my reputation. But I'm serving an absolute principle, and that's something more than my reputation."

As the train began to move, Lauro reached out the window and shook his old friend's hand. It was the last time de Santillana saw him.

Lauro, who had promised to train his successor at the Italy America Society, returned to New York for six weeks. Reports of his newsletters had reached the United States—in fact, he had been sure to mail some of them himself—and were causing consternation in Washington and at the Casa Italiana. Shortly after his return, an October 26 headline in the *New York Herald Tribune* read "Fascist Control in Italy Fought by Chains [sic] Letters." Desperate to control the damage, Ambassador de Martino contacted Lauro and asked him to go to the newspaper's offices and pry as much information as he could from the editor-in-chief about who was responsible. Lauro, happy to muddy the waters, reported to the ambassador that the newsletters had originated in Paris, the city that had become European headquarters of Italy's exiled anti-Fascist community. The following day, Lauro confided to Prezzolini that he was responsible for the National Alliance's newsletter. The bitter Prezzolini, who had always considered the younger man an unfocussed, well-to-do dilettante, claimed not to be impressed. He dismissed the chain letters as just another "little game," like the origami birds Lauro concocted at parties.

Then bad news came from home. OVRA agents had caught four people in Verona mailing Alliance newsletters, and there were reports that Bocchini's men were in the process of tracing the plot to Rome. To make matters worse, with the end of his tenure at the Italy America Society, Lauro had lost his cover. He'd been seeking nomination as the Italian representative for the League for International Education, an uncontroversial posting that would allow him to continue to travel freely in Europe and North America. Receiving de Martino's endorsement was crucial, but the ambassador had begun to suspect that many at the Italy America Society were insufficiently fervent about the regime, and asked for a frank declaration of loyalty from its staff. Lauro, with his eyes on the new posting, obliged.

On November 15, he wrote a letter to de Martino that would come to haunt him. "Permit me to address to His Excellency a warm request: that I may be able to be used in Italy to serve the country and Fascism. This particular experience that I hope to have acquired in four years of propaganda in America (70 lectures on Fascism in a little more than four months) and this very faith of which I am certain to have given proof, makes me hope that this request will not be made in vain." He concluded: "I only want to continue being useful to Fascism in one way or another."

The Ambassador accepted Lauro's profession of faith at face value, and praised his "noble desire to be useful to your country and the Régime." Lauro quickly forgot the letter. In his mind, it was a petty lie to achieve a nobler end. The Ambassador sent a copy to Rome, where it made its way to the appropriate desks, to be filed away for later use.

Lauro, accompanied by Ruth, made his way to the West 14th Street docks on November 26, 1930, for the five o'clock sailing of the RMS *Mauretania*. He was so confident that his double-life had gone undetected that he was doing exactly what his friend de Santillana had warned him against: returning to Italy.

The Cunard Line's *Mauretania*, nicknamed "The Maury," was best known for being a past winner of the Blue Riband prize for the fastest transatlantic crossing, averaging 24 knots in 1909, a record she'd defended for twenty years. Like her running mate, the *Lusitania*, which would be torpedoed by German U-boats, she was named for one of ancient Rome's Mediterranean provinces.

By the time Lauro boarded the *Mauretania*, she was known as "The Old Lady of the Atlantic," and decidedly past her prime. The liner had been fitted out in the highest Edwardian style, with twenty-eight kinds of wood, including the walnut of the grand staircase, but the decor already looked fusty and out-of-date. The crossing started out rough—one big wave sent Lauro's armchair flying twenty feet down the deck—but fortunately he wasn't prone to seasickness. He was amused to note Giuseppe Volpi's name on the passenger list. The former Italian Finance Minister had been instrumental in helping to arrange Morgan Bank loans to Mussolini.

"He is really very nice," Lauro wrote to Ruth, who was then in Boston, "and not very Fascist." They had long talks over meals, and the elder statesman read, and claimed to enjoy, Lauro's play *Icaro*. "There are otherwise very few people, all very bored, boring and stiff." In spite of the tedium, Lauro's tone was insouciant, and he was delighted with the impact of his National Alliance plans.

"Darling Angel," he wrote, "remember that the best thing you can do for me and for the success of my 'Enterprise beyond the Sea' is to be gay. It is quite a big thing to ask but a big thing to give too."

He would stop in England, where he would have another meeting with Don Luigi Sturzo, then continue on to Italy.

Just before the *Mauretania* docked in Plymouth, on November 30, his mother, along with his eldest brother Percy and his sister Charis, were arrested in their apartment by OVRA agents. The following day, Lauro's Harvard friend Giorgio La Piana told Ruth about the arrests, just as she was sitting down to a dinner party before the opening night of a performance in Boston.

"She was stunned," recalled a friend. "She turned dead white, I thought she would faint. But she said 'I can't talk of it now but immediately after the performance I must go to a cable office to wire Lauro not to cross the frontier.'" With the sang-froid of the professional, Ruth made it through her monologues, and then rushed off to dispatch the telegram.

But Lauro had already heard the news. The radio room of the *Mauretania* had received a cable from a friend, probably de Santillana. Not only had his mother been arrested, Vinciguerra and Rendi had been seized by OVRA and were already in prison.

In the five days it had taken the *Mauretania* to cross the Atlantic, Lauro's existence was overturned. The National Alliance was finished, his ability to act and travel without suspicion permanently destroyed. The aristocratic de Bosis name, once above suspicion, would now join those of the hated anti-Fascists in the files of the secret police.

For Lauro, obeying his strongest impulse—to rush to Rome and his family—would almost certainly mean imprisonment, or even death.

16 40,000,000 SHEEP

In February 1930, Stewart and Gilbert—the "Bagnani brothers" as some of their friends had taken to calling them in jest—moved into a rented apartment in Rome. Located on Via Pompeo Magno, half a block from the right bank of the Tiber, where Gilbert liked to go rowing in the summer, it seemed a world away from the frigid shores of Lake Ontario. They turned the third-floor apartment into a cozy haven, decorating it with prints by Dürer and Rembrandt, Byzantine icons, and other treasures Gilbert had acquired in his travels. Throwing open their shutters, the view was not of migrating geese flying over an ice-rimmed lake, but of the storks that nested atop St. Peter's, the outline of whose dome was picked out by oil lamps on feast days.

The Bagnanis had become husband and wife the previous summer in the Presbytery of St. Peter's Church, Toronto's somewhat less grandiose version of the Roman basilica. The reception was held in the Rosedale house where Stewart spent much of her childhood. "The bride," reported the *Mail and Empire*, "who received with the groom in front of the fireplace which was banked with ferns and masses of pink peonies and delphinium, looked charming in a graceful chanel gown of white satin. She wore a picturesque headdress of pearls, a copy of the famous picture of Beatrice d'Este, which admirably suited her fair hair." Stewart's mother, who had approved the union with reluctance, allowed them to use the family's cottage in Muskoka for their honeymoon. Gilbert's mother, who couldn't be present, was informed of the happy event with a telegram that read: "LOVE FROM BOTH CHILDREN: STEW AND GIL." After a month puttering around Lake Huron in a second-hand motorboat purchased for the occasion, they boarded an ocean-liner to begin their new life in Italy.

The Rome they returned to was a different city than the one Gilbert had introduced to Stewart six years earlier. Gilbert thought Mussolini's *sventramento*, or disembowelling, of the city had had mixed results.

"The changes in Rome are amazing," he wrote to his mother, who was then in England. "All the houses in front of Trajan's Forum are down... and will make it a very handsome square. Also all the houses along the Capitol side of the Tor de' Specchi. That I do not like so much. It was one of the most characteristic streets in Rome, and now it has all gone."

He also noticed the effects the previous fall's Stock Market crash in New York was having on Rome's upper classes. "Any number of cars have already been turned in... and the tailors have had any numbers of orders for suits and fur coats cancelled." The value of Gilbert's shares in Canadian mines and railways had plummeted, and he now had reason to fret about his professional future in Italy. Though his books on the papacy and the *campagna* had been published in 1929, to good reviews, he felt his chances of securing an academic position in Italy were slim. Scholars who embraced Fascism, such as Strong and Van Deman, were thriving, but those who refused to endorse the regime found their careers sidelined. Gilbert had thus far managed to avoid getting a Fascist *tessera*, the card that proved one's membership in the party and was key to securing an academic post. Given the political climate, he didn't know how much longer he'd be able to put it off.

He was also concerned about Thomas Ashby, with whom he had spent so many agreeable days wandering the *campagna*. There were rumours that his former mentor's eyesight was failing, and that he'd undergone a nervous breakdown after exhausting himself with his work on his topographical dictionary. Even Eugénie Sellers Strong, whose quarrels with Ashby's wife had been responsible for his firing from the British School, was concerned.

"Mrs. S," recorded Gilbert, "suggests that he is now just the age that his father was when he committed suicide and that it may be preying on his mind."

Fortunately, a solution to Gilbert's professional problems had recently presented itself. Two years earlier, the Bagnanis had visited Egypt with Stewart's mother, taking a leisurely cruise down the Nile River from Aswan to Cairo. After the trip, Gilbert began to visit the Egyptian collections in major museums in the Netherlands, Germany, Belgium, and France, and set about mastering hieroglyphics, a task aided by his excellent memory. Egypt, with its sixty-thousand-strong Italian expatriate community, was seen as an important component of a policy the Fascists had taken to calling the "peaceful penetration of the Mediterranean." The Foreign Ministry had allocated a half million lire to the Egyptian mission. Archaeological digs could provide evidence of early Roman presence, at the same time telegraphing to the international community that Italy was claiming its perceived rights in Egypt.

Gilbert knew, of course, that such claims were a sham. Any serious archaeological activity would show that Egyptian, not

Roman, civilization was the force that had shaped the land of the Pharaohs. A few months after the Bagnanis arrived in Rome, Carlo Anti, the archaeologist Gilbert had first met in Athens, wrote to inform him about the discovery of the ruins of Tebtunis, a town of temples and multi-storeyed houses in the desert southwest of Cairo. Anti, a convinced Fascist, was interested in the laying out of new towns in Italian-colonized Libya. He thought the Tebtunis site might provide information on Graeco-Roman urban planning, which could have immense propaganda value for Fascist plans for dominance in North Africa.

Anti was unaware, when he invited Gilbert to join him, that he had provided a resolution to the young archaeologist's dilemma. Gilbert had no intention of allowing his research to be made into an instrument of the Fascist glorification of *Romanità*. Working on the site in Egypt was more likely to contradict the claims of the Italian peninsula's uninterrupted domination of the Mediterranean: Egyptian civilization, after all, had predated the Roman Empire by three millennia. If finding work in his field meant leaving his beloved Rome for a few years, so be it.

Gilbert accepted Anti's invitation in the summer of 1930. Only one challenge remained: convincing Stewart, his new bride, to join him in the Egyptian desert.

By the beginning of Anno viii of the Fascist Era—the end of the year known as 1930 outside Italy—the historic centre of Rome was a vast construction site. In the Forum legions of workers were using pick-axes and wheelbarrows to raze one of the ancient hills of Rome. The Velia, on whose flank the fourth-century Basilica of Constantine rose, was being eliminated to allow an unimpeded view of the Coliseum from the Piazza di Venezia, where Mussolini had recently relocated his offices from the Palazzo Chigi. Key to the project was the new thoroughfare being cut, in a remorseless diagonal, between the Republican and Imperial Fora. Upon completion, the Via dell'Impero would be at once a viewing platform for Rome's ruins—best seen from an Alfa-Romeo or Fiat, moving at speed—and a parade route for the victorious armies of Fascism. The Coliseum, once revealed abruptly to the view of visitors only after they'd navigated a maze of narrow lanes, stood alone, "liberated" from the now-demolished medieval buildings. Soon, it would be surrounded by cars and trucks, and the greatest amphitheatre of antiquity would be reduced to the hub of a vast traffic roundabout.

In other parts of Italy, Fascist progress meant the construction of modernist new towns, chromed city halls, and streamlined sports complexes. In the heart of Rome, it meant the destruction of the old—especially anything suggestive of "local colour"—to make way not for new buildings, but new roads. Two years earlier, the inauguration of the Via del Mare had fulfilled Mussolini's dream of linking the Third Rome to *Mare Nostrum*, as the Mediterranean was once again being styled.

From its start at the base of the Capitoline Hill, the Via del Mare swept drivers past the arches of the Theatre of Marcellus, sped them along the banks of the Tiber, and ejected them from the city gates next to the sun-bleached pyramid of Caius Cestius. From there, it paralleled the Via Ostiense, arriving, after twenty-three kilometres of straightaways and high-speed curves, at a pier in Ostia, Rome's long-neglected outlet to the sea. There, a new *idroscalo*, or seaport, had been built to accommodate the most up-to-date Italian-made seaplanes. The Via del Mare, which turned the monuments of ancient Rome into highlights in a Fascist theme park, became a favourite speedway for the *gerarchi*, many of whom had fond memories of late-night truck rides through the countryside to terrorize Socialist rivals. (Engineered without shoulders, the Via del Mare is now infamous as the "killer road," Italy's most lethal stretch of highway.) Late some nights,

Mussolini would jump on a motorcycle parked outside his office in the Piazza Venezia, and try to beat his bodyguards by racing along the Via del Mare to his beach house north of Ostia.

The new roads satisfied the Fascists' desire for speed, but they also had another function. When the time came for a major public announcement, trucks with loudspeakers would fan out through the city, proclaiming the next rally. From the new *borgate*—the "scraps of city" on the urban fringe—an audience for Mussolini's speeches could be swiftly marshalled to the centre on well-paved roads, all of which led to the balcony above the Palazzo Venezia.

On the opposite bank of the Tiber, two nineteenth-century structures had been deemed useful enough to remain untouched by Fascist modernization. One was the city-block-sized Palazzo di Giustizia, a legacy of the Risorgimento, now used to stage the show trials of enemies of the state.

The other, located a few hundred yards to the south, was Regina Coeli, whose blackened facade crowds a long stretch of Trastevere riverbank. It was in the "Queen of the Heavens" prison, on the night of the first of December 1930, that two members of the National Alliance—Lauro de Bosis's most faithful "lieutenants"—were being tortured by the agents of OVRA.

In normal times, approaching a mailbox, dropping a few letters through the slot, then turning around and continuing with one's business would have been the most straightforward of gestures.

But these were not normal times. For Mario Vinciguerra, mailing a letter had become an act fraught with peril. The dozen stamped envelopes he was carrying in an inside pocket contained mimeographed copies of the eleventh Alliance National newsletter, with another of Lauro's impassioned appeals for the rejection of Mussolini and Fascism. He knew that in Verona, four people had been jailed simply for mailing on typed copies of a previous newsletter. Vinciguerra was familiar with the methods of the Fascists, and had no doubt that, should he be determined to be one of the originators of such a "libel," he would be imprisoned. He was a widower, and he dreaded what would become of his daughter if he were caught.

On a Friday afternoon, Vinciguerra called to seven-year-old Claudia to wait for him in their apartment while he ran an errand. Walking out onto the Via Sant'Onofrio in Trastevere, Vinciguerra crossed a bridge over the Tiber that led to the labyrinthine streets of Ponti, one of the most densely populated districts in the old city. In an effort to throw off any potential tails, he turned several sharp corners, before doubling back to the tiny rectangular Piazza del Fico, where he knew he would find a discreetly located mailbox. He would post a handful of letters—just enough to make it look like he was paying some bills—and turn towards home, dispatching the rest at other mailboxes in the bustling lanes of Trastevere.

He was unaware that, by trying to distance himself from his apartment, he had walked into a zone of heightened surveillance. Bocchini's secret police had tracked the postmarks of previous National Alliance newsletters to an approximately two-square kilometre zone of the old city. Within this perimeter, plainclothes agents were lurking near every mailbox. The Piazza del Fico happened to fall just within the western edge of that zone. As he walked away from the mailbox, Vinciguerra was approached by two men, who flashed badges and demanded his identity papers.

What happened next is recorded in a report in the Central State Archives. "Stopped and searched, he was found in possession of a small pack of envelopes containing the aforementioned circulars, already stamped and ready to be mailed. Subjected to the most stringent interrogations, Vinciguerra retreated into the most obstinate silence."

The interrogations were beyond stringent; they were brutal. Vinciguerra was taken to a nearby police station, where he was beaten, stripped naked, and left on the roof on a night when temperatures dropped to within a few degrees of freezing. The following morning, he was transferred to Regina Coeli, which happened to be located just a few hundred yards from where he'd left his daughter waiting for him. An OVRA torturer drove tiny spikes under his fingernails and into his legs. When he refused to talk, he was boxed so hard on the side of his head that his eardrum ruptured, leaving him permanently deaf in the right ear.

The Fascist tortures, which would continue with repeated lashings with a cat-o'-nine-tails, failed to break Vinciguerra. He refused to implicate Lauro or any other collaborators, and insisted he bore sole responsibility for the National Alliance. (It was only days later, when other arrests were made, that he gave the police the names they already had.) But OVRA already had a file on Vinciguerra, and in it his friendship with Renzo Rendi was noted. The latter—also a father, of twins—was arrested while he was watching a movie at the Cinema Imperiale. A search of Rendi's apartment turned up an Underwood and a Remington whose keystrokes corresponded to the typewriting on two of the newsletters. Rendi was also brought to Regina Coeli, where, after being beaten and tortured, he "offered vague indications about where the family who supplied the copy machine lived."

These were enough to lead OVRA's agents to the top floor of Via dei Due Macelli, 66, where Lillian and two of her children were sitting down to enjoy a meal of risotto. Lauro's brother Percy politely invited the men into the apartment, but his sister Charis received them icily, ordering the agents to remove their hats. Both of the de Bosis children were shocked when the agents found the mimeograph machine—with a stencil of the seventh issue of the newsletter still in its drum—beneath their mother's mattress. Hidden in the bathroom were a thousand copies of the newsletter, a mailing list identical to the one found in Rendi's apartment, and the Corona typewriter on which Lauro had typed the first six issues of the National Alliance newsletter. Lillian had been caught red-handed.

As he led her out of the apartment, one of the young agents asked: "But why did you do it, Signora?"

Straightening her back, she replied: "Because I am not a sheep."

The reference—probably lost on the agent—was to one of Mussolini's recent speeches, in which he referred to the Italian people as "forty million good sheep, ready to give their wool to the regime." After spending a night with their mother at a police station, the de Bosis children were released. The following day, Lillian was transferred to the women's wing of Regina Coeli.

When, a few days later, Lauro learned of his mother's arrest—and her defiant reply—he professed to be delighted.

"Everybody's admiration for mother is boundless," he wrote to Ruth in a letter dated December 13. "If young Italian liberals do not get shaken, what can they expect more?" Of the arrest of Vinciguerra, he wrote: "His child 9 years old [sic] waited for him for 9 hours without even crying." His only regret was that he couldn't share the glory with his friends. "If I were not sure that I could wage a good war from here, I would take the first train and join them. You know it is no bluff." Lauro believed that even if Vinciguerra and Rendi were given thirty-year sentences, it would make no difference, since "this Regime·cannot possibly last more than two years."

Ruth was more alarmed by the immediate consequences of her lover's actions. She took steps to make sure that Vinciguerra's daughter and Rendi's twins would receive enough money to be taken care of.

But Lauro was merely putting on a brave face. In reality, news of the arrests had sent him into a panic. He'd immediately left England, determined to join his family in Rome. Across the

Channel in Paris, he'd borrowed a Cadillac from his former fiancée Marie Harjes, and driven down the Rhine alone to Switzerland,
within reach of the Italian border.

In Bern, he was met by his old friend Sylvia Sprigge, the *Manchester Guardian* journalist, who had hurried up from Rome to
try to convince him not to enter Italy. The Italian consul, whom
he knew, gave him the same advice, as did Salvemini. Lauro told
Sprigge he was upset by the way the international press was
portraying the National Alliance; the headline in the *New York
Times* read "ARREST OF 27 NIPS ANTI-FASCIST PLOT." The article,
signed by Arnaldo Cortesi, the arch-Fascist journalist who fed
regime-approved bulletins to the foreign press from Rome,
reported that those arrested were "members of a clandestine anti-
Fascist organization which had plotted various criminal acts
against the Fascist regime on the eighth anniversary of the Fascist
revolution." Sprigge made sure an interview with Lauro appeared
in the *Guardian*, in which he took credit for writing most of the
newsletters, and argued the chain letters were justified by the
Fascists' complete monopoly on the news.

"How can a man know his duty as a citizen," asked Lauro, "if
he has not the faintest idea whether it is true, as the press implies,
that neighbouring countries are arming against Italy and that the
overthrow of the Fascist Government is being planned by foreigners who want a weak Italy at their mercy?"

In his hotel room in Bern, where he was staying under the
alias "James Jackson," Lauro wrote his own side of the story, a
much-edited version of which was published, without a byline, in
Walter Lippmann's *New York World*. The financial crisis, he
argued, meant that the Fascists in Italy were cornered and
"desperate."

"The only chance of Fascism depends on a dictatorship by Hitler," he wrote, while conceding that foreign financial support
from American bankers might "prolong its life considerably. In

their hands lies, in great measure, the fate of Italian Liberty."
Without naming names, he was pointing a finger at his former
boss at the Italy America Society, Thomas Lamont, and the House
of Morgan loans that had bailed out Mussolini. Back in New York,
the Society hastily issued a statement declaring that Lauro
de Bosis was no longer in their employ.

The day after the *Guardian* interview, a short retort from Mussolini, titled "The Worm," appeared in a Roman newspaper,
stating Lauro's mother had "transformed her residence into a
clandestine printing office engaged in the publication of repugnant libels." Such was Fascist clemency, the article concluded, that
Signora de Bosis, being in ill health, had been transferred to a
private clinic of her own choice.

Lillian, in fact, was in a bed in a three-by-five-metre room at
the Clinica Villa Luisa, shared night and day with three plainclothes detectives seated behind a screen. She was not permitted
to speak to anyone but the family lawyer. The four de Bosis children in Rome, choosing to distance themselves from their brother,
had the lawyer compose a grovelling letter of apology to Mussolini, in which they "solemnly reconfirmed their sincere and
fervid devotion." Then they sent a cable to Lauro in Bern, reacting
to the *Guardian* interview: "Refuse to believe unbelievable
betrayal requiring telegraphed denial."

In a letter to Ruth, Lauro tried to laugh it off. "No de Bosis
would have written such a telegram... I wanted to answer 'Police—
Rome—your false telegram doesn't fool me. Regards de Bosis.'
But I let it go."

In fact, the de Bosis family, thrown into crisis by the arrests,
had drafted the telegram. Immediately after the arrests, his sister
Charis's husband had been dismissed as a centurion in the Fascist
militia. Charis instructed the family lawyer to mislead their
mother into believing she and her brother were still imprisoned,
in the hopes she would be pressured into a public recantation that

would save the family's fortunes. When Sprigge brought a bunch of flowers to the clinic, she found Lillian "unexplainably laconic and unresponsive." The journalist would only realize later that, to spare her other children, Lauro's mother had already taken a decisive step to distance herself from anti-Fascist politics.

Convinced he would be more help to the cause outside the country, Lauro headed for Paris, a city that had become the headquarters of the Italian anti-Fascist community in exile. From a ground-floor room on Rue Seveste, on the edge of Montmartre, he waited for news from Italy, and professed to be in good spirits.

"Of course ousting tyrants is not as simple as opening an egg and it is long, but still it must be done," he wrote to Ruth. "You cannot deny that it is thrilling and the best is yet to come."

Things, in fact, were about to get worse than Lauro could ever imagine.

The Special Tribunal for the Defense of the State, the highest court for trying the enemies of Fascism, was held in the vast Palazzo di Giustizia, just north of the Castel Sant'Angelo on the right bank of the Tiber.

The trial began at precisely three o'clock in the afternoon, on December 22, 1930, only three weeks after the arrests. The vaulted main chamber, filled with blackshirted guards with their bayonets at the ready, was overlooked by galleries filled with party functionaries and secret police. Journalists, among them Sylvia Sprigge of *The Guardian* and Arnaldo Cortesi of *The New York Times*, were placed next to the semi-circular table where the judges were seated. It was the first time members of the foreign press had attended one of the regime's kangaroo courts in significant numbers. Six of the seven presiding judges were senior members of the Fascist militia. The president of the tribunal, Lieutenant-General

Cristini, in his mid-thirties, wore a blue sash over his black shirt. There was no jury.

Vinciguerra and Rendi, newly arrived from Regina Coeli, were brought into the chamber chained together by the manacles around their wrists. Along with three of the men who had been caught mailing National Alliance newsletters in Verona, they were locked into an iron-barred cage, where five *carabinieri* kept guard. Outside the cage, Lillian de Bosis, dressed in a black hat and dress, a grey coat, and white gloves, was seated next to the lone female defendant from Verona. The court heard the charges: the accused had conspired to incite armed insurrection and civil war through the distribution of clandestine publications.

On the stand, Vinciguerra admitted to writing the newsletters with Rendi. "But these writings had a polemical character," he insisted, "and were not intended to incite violence, something I've always opposed."

"I would say that they were writing lies," interjected Cristini.

When it was Rendi's turn, he admitted to the court that after Lauro left Italy, he'd helped write and print some of the newsletters and address the envelopes.

The prosecutor then read Lillian's tortuous letter of apology to Mussolini, which had been drafted with the family attorney's help. "I want to declare to you that I deeply and sincerely regret the sad errors in which I have fallen by my incredible naivete and absolute ignorance of the interpretation that could legitimately be given to thoughtless expressions of ideology that were not intended to hamper or disregard and so much less offend the marvellous reconstructive work that Your Excellency undertook with titanic vigor for the benefit of Italy, and that I have always admired and verbally exalted my chosen country that is the sole country of my heart!" In the prisoners' dock, Lillian silently wept as the family attorney made the case that his client had sincerely repented of her transgressions.

Another document was entered into evidence. It was the letter Lauro had written before leaving New York, responding to Ambassador de Martino's request for a declaration of fidelity to the Fascist regime. The prosecutor read it aloud: "Permit me to direct a warm prayer to Your Excellencies: that I will continue to be of use in Italy to serve the Nation and Fascism."

For Sprigge, seated at the press table, it was "one of the worst moments in that court." In absentia, Lauro seemed not an intrepid freedom fighter, but a self-serving hypocrite. While anti-Fascists in Italy had suffered torture and imprisonment for refusing to beg Mussolini for clemency, Lauro, safe and prosperous in New York, seemed all too willing to betray his ideals in exchange for continued favour. "Coming almost immediately after the reading of his mother's letter, it certainly achieved the desired effect among the foreign correspondents gathered there: were not all these conspirators double-crossing each other?"

"Do not think I am defending Lauro de Bosis," concluded the public prosecutor. "I feel no sympathy for a man who delivered pro-Fascist lectures in America at the same time he was publishing anti-Fascist pamphlets in Rome." Noting that he could have asked for the death penalty, he demanded that the ringleaders be imprisoned.

Cristini, echoing Mussolini's characterization of Lauro, made his position clear: "You are no conspirators. You are just political worms who tried to poison the minds of others, thinking yourselves perfectly safe. Abroad you pass as conspirators, but you do not deserve that honour." His words were reported in Cortesi's article, which was published on the front page of the *New York Times*.

At sentencing, the tribunal's president dismissed the National Alliance as made up of "weak, colourless pseudo-intellectuals, representatives not of a significant current in the country but an individual aberration, blind to the overwhelming movement of

Italy's rebirth through the Fascist regime." Lillian, judged suffi-
ciently penitent, was freed, and only one of the Verona group was
punished, with a relatively light sentence of three years' imprisonment. Rendi and Vinciguerra were given the maximum:
fifteen years. They would serve the first two-and-a-half years of
their terms in solitary confinement, allowed only forty minutes
of exercise a day in a high-walled courtyard.

In Paris, Lauro awaited news of the trial in his small room,
which he'd decorated with photos of Ruth, turning it into a shrine
to his lover. When her cable arrived, he was incredulous. Not only
had the court dropped his name from the list of the accused; they
had not even deigned to sentence him.

"I am awfully disappointed at not having received a death punishment," he wrote to Ruth, "not even a tiny bit of condemnation.
I don't understand why: if my 2 lieutenants got 15 years, I should
have got 25. Probably they felt that it was better not to try me in
order not to give me publicity... it is a terrible anticlimax and am
deeply humiliated at the too secondary role that I am going to
have for years... my fate still continues to get others in trouble
and I always remain untouched."

In fact, Mussolini had managed the trial with the flair of a
master propagandist. Refusing to sentence Lauro meant denying
him the publicity he craved. An impression had also been created
in anti-Fascist circles that the National Alliance's ringleader was
cowardly, ignoble, and self-serving. Wasn't it suspicious that he'd
left Italy just when his associates needed him most?

Lauro was able to reach his mother by telephone in Rome
after the trial. "She says she is in perfect health," he wrote Ruth,
"but her nerves have been quite shaken. I don't wonder and understand how at the trail she weakened from her former position,
though of course I am sad that that should prove necessary as
that is the only part that found place in the Italian papers." He
refused to worry about the rest of the family, who had turned

their back on the cause. "At the maximum I can bring more incon-
venience to my brother. But this really cannot be taken in
consideration."

It would take Lauro some time to realize all of the consequences of the trial. A mysterious underground of Liberals,
Socialists, and Catholics, with the potential to form a broad-based
anti-Fascist resistance, had been successfully portrayed by the
Fascist court as the work of a trio of bumbling discontents, aided
by a white-haired old lady with a mimeograph hidden under her
mattress. In New York, one of Lauro's former allies, Walter Lippmann of the *New York World*, told the Italy America Society's
former manager Irene di Robilant that he considered Lauro "a
scoundrel" for leaving Rome and "the whole thing" to his mother.
The *Herald Tribune*, meanwhile, reported that Lillian, because she
had been living in Italy since childhood, was no longer considered an American citizen. Many in the anti-Fascist movement's
left wing now thought it credible that Lauro was a double agent.

The leader of the shadowy National Alliance had joined the
ranks of the powerless and disconnected Italian exiles in France.
Ruth worried that Fascist agents would be dispatched to Paris to
assassinate him. Lauro assured her that he was safe, but urged
her not to join him before she began her next European tour in
London.

Lauro took up a solitary existence in Paris. Though isolated
and tormented by guilt, his natural high spirits would soon
reassert themselves. His thoughts returned to the plan he had
first proposed to Salvemini in America. It was one that would not
demand the cooperation of associates, who might be forced to
suffer. He would return to Rome, in a way that would renew the
honour of his family and make the purity of his intentions clear
to the world.

17 THE FLYING CONCIERGE

In joining the *fuorusciti*, the community of exiles from Mussolini's Italy, Lauro de Bosis entered a maddening limbo.

In Rome, he had worked side-by-side with the Fascist *gerarchi*, whom he considered at best second-rate intellects, at worst thugs, their March on Rome a massive bluff enabled by a weak and indecisive king. Through his work alongside Thomas Lamont at the Italy America Society, he knew that the Italian economic miracle was in fact a transitory mirage, one that had been enabled, temporarily, by American loans. And he knew it was only Mussolini's control of Italian media, and his successful manipulation of foreign reporters, that prevented the world from learning what life was really like under the dictatorship.

Lauro also knew that thousands of Italy's bravest and brightest citizens had been tortured, jailed, and sent into internal exile, and believed that Il Duce was leading the nation, and the world, towards another war.

As 1931 began, the rest of the world saw a very different Italy. At a time when economies were reeling into depression after the collapse of the American stock market, Fascist Italy appeared confident, progress-oriented, triumphant. The year would see the launch of the luxurious passenger steamer *ss Rex*, known as "the Riviera afloat," which would break records by crossing the Atlantic in just four days, at an average speed of 29 knots. Guglielmo Marconi's ongoing innovations in radio and telegraphy were eclipsing Thomas Edison's inventions. The six-foot-six boxer Primo Carnera helped erase the image of Italians as diminutive, ill-nourished emigrants every time he flattened another challenger. "The Ambling Alp," as he was known, would beat out the American Jack Sharkey for the title of world heavyweight champion in 1933. The following year, Italy's team would win the world soccer championship, and the Fascist playwright Luigi Pirandello would receive the world's top honour for literature, the Nobel Prize.

Nowhere was Italy's achievement more impressive than in that most up-to-date of fields, aviation. From the early days of manned flight, the derring-do of fliers had mesmerized the nation. Six weeks after his solo crossing of the English Channel, the French aviator Louis Blériot brought his flying machine to the 1909 Brescia air show. Present in the crowd was Gabriele d'Annunzio, who talked his way into the passenger seat, and gave a press conference in which he read a poem dedicated to Icarus. (Mussolini, still a Socialist, wrote that Blériot's flight was a "triumph of Latin genius," and hailed early aviators as the "first champions of a future race of Supermen," for translating the "dream of Icarus into reality.") In 1911, the first Italian-made aircraft, built by d'Annunzio's friend, the engineer Gianni Caproni, was rolled out of a factory in Milan. In the same year, an Italian pilot tossed four grenades from his monoplane on Turkish troops in Libya, becoming the first person in history to drop bombs from a heavier-than-air machine. By 1919, the Italian aviation industry employed a hundred thousand people and was producing 6,500 planes a year.

The Fascists, like the Futurists, were obsessed with flight. During the First World War, command of the skies had brought freedom from the sordid mire of trench warfare, and the figure of the dashing pilot, aloft in a streamlined flier, meshed with the national cult of stylish, devil-may-care bravado. Mussolini was an enthusiastic aviator; while still a member of parliament, he completed eighteen flights, emerging from a 1921 crash with only scratches and a twisted knee. When Charles Lindbergh touched down in Paris after his solo trans-Atlantic flight six years later, Il Duce rushed a congratulatory telegram to the American ambassador: "A Superhuman will has taken space by assault and has subjugated it. Matter once more has yielded to spirit and the prodigy is one that will live forever in the memory of men."

Italian factories were already producing aircraft that could beat the Americans on their own turf. In 1926, sleek Italian seaplanes with liquid-cooled Fiat engines captured the Schneider Trophy in Virginia, setting a world record for speed. (In the thirties, the Macchi M.C.72 seaplane, which hit 709 kilometres an hour, held the title of world's fastest plane of *any* type for five years.) In 1928, the world watched in awe as the Airship *Italia* flew from Milan to the Arctic, circumnavigated the North Pole, and dropped the Italian flag on the ice, an exploit diminished only when the dirigible crashed on the return journey. If the British maintained their command of the seas, and the Germans would soon throw their efforts into army-building, Italy devoted its efforts to mastery of the skies. Aviation was turned into a tool of Fascist propaganda, and no one marshalled it with more panache than the Minister of the Air Force, Italo Balbo.

Lauro was well acquainted with Balbo; he'd been forced to welcome him to the Casa Italiana when the *ras* of Ferrara had visited New York. Balbo's position in the Fascist hierarchy was assured by his role in organizing the March on Rome. "He's a violent young man of great courage," Lauro wrote in an unpublished article, "but a political non-entity. Moreover, he has on his conscience the assassination of a priest." In 1923, Balbo had ordered the murder of Giovanni Minzoni, a left-wing Catholic from Ferrara. Lauro related the story of an event given in Balbo's honour by the Lord Mayor of London, in which a forged telegram sent by anti-Fascists was read aloud:

"'Impossible to attend banquet but am present in spirit. Signed Don Minzoni.' Balbo and his followers became as pale as Macbeth when he saw Banquo's ghost."

By 1931, Balbo had turned the Aeronautica into one of Italy's most modern and disciplined ministries. At spartan new headquarters near Rome's Termini Station, fitted out with glass walls, black marble tables, chromium-trimmed desks, and a pneumatic mail service, twelve hundred employees followed an American-style work schedule, which allowed just forty minutes for lunch. Balbo's first coup was a "cruise," in which he led a squadron of 61 seaplanes, flying in arrowhead formation, to the western ports of the Mediterranean. Having conquered *Mare Nostrum*, Balbo then set his sights on the Atlantic. As Lauro waited for news of his mother's trial, the goateed Balbo, dressed in a tight-fitting white uniform over his black shirt, took off from Orbetello, a peninsula north of Rome. At the head of a squadron of a dozen flying boats, he skirted the west coast of Africa before making an eighteen-hour crossing of the Atlantic. As the planes circled the harbour of Rio de Janeiro, filmed by the world's leading news agencies, the eight support boats that had followed them offered a forty-eight-gun salute. Ashore, Balbo made a radio broadcast announcing that his next exploit would be a "cruise" to the United States.*

The Fascist regime's penchant for turning aerial stunts into successful propaganda was particularly galling to Lauro. His play *Icaro* had equated flying with liberty and the triumph of science and reason over tyranny. Yet now a tyrant and his henchmen were laying claim to the sky, as they'd laid claim to the land by turning Rome's archaeological treasures into expressions of the glory of *Romanità*. While Balbo was straddling continents, Lauro's total air time amounted to a few short hops over the English Channel and an excursion to Athens and Istanbul.

It was obvious to Lauro that the skies that Mussolini claimed to have mastered were also his weak point. Before the invention of radar, it was all too easy to penetrate Italian airspace, a fact illustrated by the exploit of a lone aviator the previous summer. Just after noon on July 11, 1930, a small plane, piloted by Giovanni Bassanesi, a young left-leaning Catholic, appeared in the sky above Milan, and circled the city centre, dropping leaflets that urged non-payment of taxes and active resistance to the regime. Workers, emerging from the factories for lunch, jeered at the police as they scrambled to scoop up the sheets. Only one in ten of the 150,000 leaflets were recovered; the rest were pocketed, to be read and re-read and then passed from city to city. By the time fighter planes were scrambled, the pilot had already crossed the border into Switzerland. From Rome, Bocchini, the Fascist chief of police, shot off furious telegrams dismissing the officials who

---

* Balbo would succeed in crossing the Atlantic in 1933 with twenty-five seaplanes, which touched down in Lake Erie after making stops in Shediac, New Brunswick, and Montreal in time for the Century of Progress World's Fair in Chicago. The city welcomed him by declaring an "Italo Balbo Day," erecting a Roman column donated by Mussolini in Burnham Park in his honour, and renaming a three-block stretch of Seventh Street "Balbo Drive," which controversially still bears his name. On the return voyage, Balbo was greeted in New York with a tickertape parade down Broadway.

had let the culprit slip through their hands. Mussolini called for the maximum penalty for "violators of the inviolable sky."

A front-page article in the *Corriere della Sera* lamented that the airplane, "which we celebrate for its beauty, for its audacity, for its power, as an expression of a new life" had been turned into a "hateful device" in the hand of the regime's enemies. Alluding to Gabriele d'Annunzio's First World War raid, the editorialist concluded that "we prefer to celebrate another flight with entirely different manifestos: the flight over Vienna."

As a boy, Lauro had thrilled to d'Annunzio's feat, in which he had urged the residents of the Austro-Hungarian capital to surrender in a shower of red-white-and-green pamphlets. Now the perpetrator of the raid on Milan, working with the left-wing resistance group *Giustizia e Libertà*, had turned the tables, flying into Italy to protest a homegrown tyrant. Though he suffered from severe airsickness, Bassanesi, who had been stirred to action by the murder of Matteotti, had succeeded in spite of the fact that he had only thirty hours of flight time to his credit. Arrested after his plane crashed in a field over the Italian border, Bassanesi was released by the Swiss authorities after a trial that allowed prominent witnesses to make spirited denunciations of the regime. Bassanesi returned to Paris a hero, cheered by Italian exiles at train stations along the way.

Lauro was impressed, and more than a little jealous. In Paris, he'd learned of the feat from Gioacchino Dolci, a young Roman who had accompanied Bassanesi on his flight and helped him toss pamphlets out of the cockpit. Bassanesi, who had conceived his plan after seeing the furor caused after he tossed anti-Fascist pamphlets from a theatre balcony, was four years Lauro's junior. In Paris, Lauro found his mind returning to the question he had first asked Gaetano Salvemini in New York, a year before Bassanesi's flight. What would be the effect of a message exhorting the people to rise up against their servitude—this time in the name not of Socialism, but of liberty and democracy—if it were delivered by a pilot who dared to bombard an Italian city?

Not Milan this time, but the capital, Rome. A city whose airspace, Mussolini was fond of boasting, had never been violated by enemy planes. The city, not incidentally, that Lauro most longed to see again.

"Hélène," Lauro shouted up the staircase of the Hôtel Victor-Emmanuel III, "prepare the bath for number 28!"

Since early in February, 1931, he had been working at a bourgeois hotel—"clean, yes," he wrote to Ruth, "but a little bit shabby"—on the Rue de Ponthieu, just off the Champs-Elysées. In return for his duties as concierge, telephone operator, desk clerk, and bookkeeper, he was given room and board, and paid 800 francs ($32) a month. After his years frequenting New York's high society, his pride was stung when well-heeled travellers patronized him with their tips. It helped that he was able to send most of his first month's pay back to Italy to help the families of his imprisoned National Alliance lieutenants, Rendi and Vinciguerra.

The irony of working in a hotel named for Italy's king appealed to him, as did his anonymity. During the day he worked on the preface to an anthology of Italian poetry he'd been asked to write for Oxford University, though guests' demands interrupted his literary endeavours.

"Don't believe that I chose this hotel for its name," he wrote his friend from Harvard, Giorgio La Piana, on the hotel's stationery. "I'm not a guest, but a porter. The owner is very interesting, but he keeps me busy from nine in the morning until eight at night with bells that ring, guests that shout, or come to share their confidences with me."

Lauro kept aloof from other members of the Italian expatriate community, who congregated in the cheap hotels and smoke-filled cafés around the Rue de la Tour-d'Auvergne, on the north side of the Grand Boulevards. Of the million Italians who had fled the country since the March on Rome, the largest group, an estimated 150,000, had settled in and around Paris. (The French, predictably, dubbed them *les macaronis*.) Most were Socialists or Communists, far to the left of Lauro politically. The Concentrazione Antifascista, founded in 1927, had claimed to speak for the exiles—all except the Communists, who looked after their own—until the formation of *Giustizia e Libertà*. Among its founding members were Vincenzo Nitti, son of the former prime minister, and Carlo Rosselli, who had collaborated with Lauro's friend, the historian Gaetano Salvemini, on the Florentine anti-Fascist newspaper, *Non Mollare*. Rosselli had been arrested after helping the former head of the Italian Socialist party, Filippo Turati, flee by boat to Corsica. Sentenced to *confino*, or internal exile, Rosselli had humiliated his captors by pulling off a daring motorboat escape with Nitti and another political prisoner from the southern island of Lipari. Gioacchino Dolci, who had accompanied Bassanesi on his flight over Milan, had escaped on the same boat.

Now, from Paris, the *giellisti*, as the members of *Giustizia e Libertà* were known, claimed to represent the vanguard of the fight against Mussolini. Their symbol—devised by Dolci—was a flaming sword, and they promised to organize "noisy, vast and violent" acts of resistance. "We Italians, and no one else," the *giellisti* declared, "will defeat Fascism." A botched attempt by *giellisti* to set off phosphorous bombs in several Italian cities on the eighth anniversary of the March on Rome happened to coincide with the National Alliance arrests. Unlike Lauro, Rosselli endorsed violence, praising a failed assassination attempt against Crown Prince Umberto, heir to King Victor Emmanuel II's throne, as justifiable tyranicide. He refused, however, to approve a plan by Bassanesi to drop real bombs on Mussolini's offices in the Palazzo Venezia.

Lauro wasn't surprised when, after his mother's arrest, the Italian exile community in Paris had sneered at his attempts to rouse the Italian people through chain letters. The National Alliance's endorsement of Liberalism, as well as its tolerance of the king, discredited it in the eyes of most left-wingers. The poor showing Vinciguerra, Rendi, and his mother made at their trial sharply contrasted with the moving speech Rosselli made at his.

"I had a house," he told the judge, "they destroyed it. I had a magazine: they suppressed it. I had a university chair: I was forced to give it up. I had, as I have today, ideas, dignity, an ideal: for these I have been sent to prison. I had teachers, friends— Amendola, Matteotti, Gobetti—they killed them."

While Rosselli had escaped to France after enduring imprisonment in Mussolini's jails and hunger and privation in exile on remote islands, Lauro had avoided punishment while enjoying almost complete freedom of movement. To other anti-Fascists, the only real suffering Lauro had endured was injured pride.

"I have not met among the exiled," Lauro wrote to the *Guardian's* Cecil Sprigge in London, "any capable of discussing things serenely and objectively. They are all too hurt and out of touch with Italy to have a really realistic vision of things there."

Salvemini, then splitting his time between France and England, observed that his young friend was spending his days in Paris in "silent sadness." In letters to Ruth, Lauro confessed to occasionally succumbing to a "tiny blue mood." But his belief in the justice of his cause roused him from depression. "I have had *not one instant* of doubt that I did the right thing and the simple duty. All the rest is irrelevant." Grateful for Ruth's support, he wrote to her that she was his "protective halo," and "an armour of strength."

The shabby hotel provided cover for his real work. While answering requests for butter from demanding guests, he continued the mission of the National Alliance. He had collected and translated the Alliance's newsletters into English, which would be published in an edition of five hundred copies. (H.G. Wells, who believed Lauro to be a staunch monarchist, declined to write the preface.) He continued to nurture his international network of supporters, including former Popular Party leader Don Sturzo in London, Salvemini in Paris, and Luigi Ferrari, the ex-secretary of the Popular Party, in Brussels. He'd solicited $500 from Giorgio La Piana, and poured the gifts that Ruth had sent him into the Alliance's war chest. The funds were wired to "Tristram Shandy," Lauro's "war name" at the Paris office of the Morgan Bank. Bestowed as a parting gift by Thomas Lamont's right-hand man, the box was intended to allow him to dispatch funds to his mother before her trial. Now it was proving useful for the organization of another venture.

"Word of honour, nothing violent," he wrote to La Piana. "I can only guarantee that you'll approve it. (Burn this letter.)"

After his mother's arrest, Lauro had started to correspond with Eric Wilbur Wood, a pilot he'd met while teaching summer courses at Harvard. Wood, the vice-president of a New York aviation firm, was an experienced flier known for establishing a world record for completing the most loop-the-loops in a single flight.

"I don't know whether you read about in the papers," Lauro wrote Wood, "but a young Italian called Bassanesi learned to fly and after only 10 hours of flight, flew from Switzerland over Milan throwing down innumerable antifascist manifestos... unfortunately the manifestos were not good, because he was a socialist, but anyhow they made a tremendous hit in Italy and his gesture became a great spur, and symbol. Now I must absolutely do the same thing!" Lauro peppered Wood with questions. Should he consider buying a seaplane? Did Wood know any qualified pilots in Europe? Would a night flight help him avoid anti-aircraft guns? He concluded: "It would be glorious!"

Wood at first discouraged the plan, pointing out to Lauro in an eight-page letter that he was too valuable to Italy to risk his life. A pilot who undertook such a flight would have to be among the best in Europe, with between six and eight hundred hours of flight time under his belt, and considerable experience in navigating over unfamiliar ground at night. If his destination was Rome, he advised leaving from Corsica, a route that would call for overflying just nineteen kilometres of Italian territory. He enclosed photos of a Lockheed Vega, a Boeing airmail plane, and other types of aircraft he thought suited to the job.

"I think your best chance for success," Wood concluded, "would be to fly with a very fast plane on pontoons in cloudy weather, and to arrive at your destination just as the sun goes down, approaching from at least 12,000 to 15,000 feet [3,600 to 4,600 metres]."

Lauro welcomed Wood's letter, and others that would follow, while ignoring the pilot's main piece of advice. He had no intention of letting anyone else fly the plane.

"The whole object," he wrote back to Wood, "is to acquire the right to speak to the Roman People and to the King through some daring and gallant enterprise." Lauro hoped that Wood would consider accompanying him, "if the glory or the fun of the enterprise appeals to you at all." Once he'd solicited enough money from supporters, he would add them to his earnings from the hotel and immediately begin flying lessons.

Behind a desk covered with maps and half-finished letters, the concierge at the Hôtel Victor-Emmanuel III silently exulted as he drafted an open letter to the king of Italy on the back of an old room bill. In the margins, he sketched images of Icarus and Pegasus, wings lifted in flight.

Ruth's mid-April arrival in Paris was as long-awaited as it was ill-timed. The couple had been apart since Lauro left New York at the end of the previous November. Since then, the arrest and trial of Lauro's mother and the National Alliance members had riven their world. After a five-month separation, Ruth longed for a few tranquil weeks with her lover before her season in London began that June.

"Lauro met me at the station here," she wrote a friend from her sitting room in the Hôtel Lancaster, a more elegant address a five-minute walk away from Lauro's hotel. "We love each other more than ever, I think. He looks well, seems older, steadier, but no less charming. He is no longer managing the hotel; he is writing and full of ideas but it's better to say nothing and be perfectly ignorant. I count each hour of happiness—that's all I can say."

By then, Lauro had revealed his plans to her. He'd quit his job at the hotel, and, on the day of her arrival, passed the necessary medical exams. His flight training was to begin in three days. Ruth was shocked to learn what he had in mind, but supportive.

"I'm deeply troubled by all it involves," she wrote her friend, "and it's hard to cast off the shadows, and the ominous element in the future." But she knew that there was nothing she could say to deter him. "One can hardly advise or criticise or suggest—where such a nature is involved—and such ideals at stake. I feel so far off from the vision he sees—so unequal—so unworthy."

After a few idyllic days with Ruth visiting Chartres and Fontainebleau, Lauro pedalled off on a bicycle, singing all the way, to a private airstrip six kilometres beyond Versailles. Introducing himself to the instructor as "Louis Russell"—another of his many aliases—he began to learn the rudiments of flying. Lauro proved a natural: within a month of his first lesson, he was confident enough to undertake a solo flight.

He was cheered by his new sense of focus, as well as news from Rome that National Alliance newsletters continued to circulate. What's more, members of the anti-Fascist exile community who had initially denounced the Alliance were now actively seeking to contact him. Nitti, one of the founding members of *Giustizia e Libertà*, had offered his support, as had the wealthy editor of a liberal newspaper in Belgium. Donations from sympathizers were beginning to fill the box of "Tristram Shandy" at the Morgan Bank when Lauro learned that Fascist spies had got wind of his plans. He quickly packed his bags, and, after telling his coworkers at the hotel he was sailing for America, followed Ruth to England. (A memo on Lauro in Bocchini's files suggests his stratagem worked, at least temporarily: "The individual is moving to America, where he is having his mail delivered to 745 Fifth Ave New York.")

In Heston, a western suburb of London, he found what looked like a suitable plane for the job. Sylvia Sprigge, who by then had been recalled from her role as the *Guardian*'s Rome correspondent because of concerns over censorship, related a chance meeting with her old friend from Italy.

"On a London tube platform, I suddenly saw Lauro de Bosis," she later recalled. "He was like a man with a single mission in life, and in great haste." At a teashop, he told her how "he minded desperately" that his comrades were in jail, and explained that it was Ruth who had discouraged him from returning to Rome. "So he had devised another course. He would fly to Rome and shower new *Alleanza* leaflets on the capital."

A few days later, Sprigge drove him to Heston, stopping at a printer along the way to pick up his leaflets, a half million of them, printed on diaphanous onion-skin paper. At the airfield, Lauro solemnly introduced Sprigge to the plane he intended to buy. It was a De Haviland 60 Cirrus Moth, a two-seater biplane newly painted silvery grey with blue trim, which he thought he could buy for 50,000 francs ($1,950). The name he'd chosen for the aircraft was, of course, *Pegasus*. Sprigge, an experienced flier, thought it looked like an old-fashioned army scout plane, and doubted it would serve for a long-distance flight. Nonetheless, she agreed to act as a mule and carry a suitcase packed with some of the leaflets across the Channel.

The prospect of returning to Rome in triumph made Lauro rejoice.

"Does Mussolini really believe that he can prevent me from returning to Italy?" he wrote in an unfinished letter addressed to his mother. "What do his three hundred thousand bayonets, his fifty thousand spies count against Pegasus? Pegasus is my beautiful winged horse which I finished taming just three days ago and which now carries me far into the skies with a grace all his own. He is all silver with blue harness and has the power of eighty mortal horses. He takes no food, but drinks a sweet and transparent nectar—at the rate of five gallons per hour! His speed is but eighty miles an hour, so that when compared with the Fascist chimeras who can do two hundred, he looks like a little pigeon or a lamb. This does not matter; thus he can fly over Rome as silently as a shadow."

Lauro continued to take lessons, funded by Ruth, switching instructors almost weekly until he settled on the London-born Owen Cathcart-Jones, a Royal Canadian Air Force veteran known for a record-breaking flight from England to Australia.

"De Bosis was one of the bravest and most charming men I had ever met. He was full of the finest ideals," Cathcart-Jones would recall in his memoirs. The young man was also in a hurry to learn. "In order to get as thorough a flying training as possible in the extremely short time—he only allowed me ten days—he was with me constantly all day from sunrise to sunset; flying, taking-off and landing."

But Cathcart-Jones, deciding Lauro's temperament was "too excitable for a really reliable pilot," refused to let him fly alone, in spite of his assurances that he'd already soloed in France. Lauro told him he wanted to take a few days off. A week later, he reported back to the airfield at Hanworth, a broad smile on his face. He'd visited a flying school in Croydon, and talked the management into letting him go up alone. Cathcart-Jones, though put off by this breach of etiquette, agreed to help his impatient student by piloting Cirrus Moth across the Channel. He would rendezvous with Lauro in Cannes.

On the afternoon of July 12, an idyllic summer day, Cathcart-Jones touched down next to the aerodrome on the edge of the Côte d'Azur. Lauro arrived by car, and proceeded to upend a suitcase full of leaflets London into the cockpit. The tissue-thin papers began blowing around, forcing Cathcart-Jones to scamper around the field retrieving them. He stuffed them back into the cockpit, and, full of misgivings, wished his student luck.

"I watched him disappear in the distance over the blue Mediterranean in the direction of Corsica," Cathcart-Jones recalled. "Finally I lost sight of him in the haze." The Cirrus Moth could manage 130 kilometres an hour. The distance from Cannes to Lauro's destination in Corsica was 260 kilometres, a two-hour flight. From there to the Italian coast, Lauro had calculated a distance of just over five hundred kilometres. If Lauro's refuelling stop in Corsica went smoothly, he would be in Rome well before sunset.

Cathcart-Jones made an overnight return journey on the Blue Train, the luxurious express that ran from the Riviera to Calais, interpreting every lingering gaze as evidence he was being shadowed by Fascist agents. At home in London, he found a detective from Scotland Yard's Special Branch waiting for him.

"He told me that a British light aeroplane had been found crashed and abandoned in Corsica—with my name in its logbook."

Cathcart-Jones would only learn the whole story later. At six in the afternoon, residents of Ghisonaccia, midway up the east coast of Corsica, saw a small plane circling the town square. The Cirrus Moth then descended towards an unplowed field to the south. But the landing was rough, and a wing and the engine were damaged on touchdown. Panicked that he was being followed,

Lauro ran to the car where an associate was waiting for him with fuel for the next leg of the flight, while leaflets that had escaped the cockpit wafted into the air. The support vehicle became a getaway car, and Lauro and his helper sped northwards along backroads to L'Île-Rousse, on the island's north coast.

On the ferry back to the mainland of France, Lauro cursed his luck. He'd lost his *Pegasus*. As it turned out, he needn't have fled from his crash site so quickly: it was a Sunday, and the police were off-duty. Yet the plane would be found, as would the leaflets, every one of which bore the signature of the "National Alliance." It was a name that was amply documented in the files of Bocchini's secret police. Every Fascist agent in France, Lauro now believed, would be hot on his trail. From that moment on, there could be no security, and every day that passed reduced his mission's chances of success.

Lauro was a man on the run.

18 MERRILL & MORRIS

France, an ideal launching point for Lauro's raid on Rome, had suddenly become a very dangerous place for him to be.

Pegasus, with crucial information in its logbooks and National Alliance leaflets littering its hastily abandoned cockpit, had been examined by the French Sûreté, a Scotland Yard inspector dispatched to the crash site. The details weren't shared with the Italian authorities, but the Fascist espionage network in France was robust, and Lauro was convinced spies were already on his trail.

Since 1926, when OVRA was founded, Arturo Bocchini's agents, identified with such code names as "Ulisse," "Apollo," "Socrates," and other figures from Classical antiquity, had been hard at work infiltrating the Italian exile community in France. Each spy reported to a consulate—Mussolini was committed to making his diplomatic corps "exquisitely Fascist"—and the Consul-General in Marseilles, Commendatore Sillitti, was known to be a particularly zealous scourge of anti-Fascists. Undercover agents used private homes and hotels as drops for their reports, which were then sent to Rome's main post office, to be collected, transcribed and summarized by a team of four hundred shorthand typists, and placed on Bocchini's desk every afternoon. The most important dispatches would then be brought to Mussolini's attention. Lauro had already been forced to flee France once, after—as he wrote to Ruth—that "scoundrel of a Bino [sic] had given the secret away to no less than two fascists." (Lauro was almost certainly referring to Livio Bini, who claimed to be a Florentine Socialist in exile, but was actually one of OVRA's most successful agents in Paris.) Now Lauro feared the French authorities, under pressure from Italy, would issue an expulsion order, ending all hope of making a raid on Rome from the Mediterranean coast.

Until the crack-up in the field in Corsica, Lauro was convinced that his extraordinary precautions had allowed him to outwit Bocchini's spies.

"On behalf of my dream," he wrote in an unsent letter to his mother, "I have crossed the sea seven times; three times I went to London, twice to Corsica. I have gone under ten different names; have had to surmount incredible difficulties and find a solution for ten thousand minor problems."

Now he was convinced that both his identity and his intentions had been revealed. The logical move would have been to return to the United States, where he could enjoy freedom and a privileged life, safe in Ruth's Upper East Side apartment. "Happiness," as he often told his lover, "is also an act of the will." His conscience, however, wouldn't allow him to choose happiness. His actions had led his National Alliance comrades in Italy to be tortured, his mother jailed, his brothers and sisters humiliated.

"It required superhuman willpower to begin again," an admiring Gaetano Salvemini would write later. "Lauro began again."

A new airplane would have to be located, new leaflets printed, and a new departure point chosen, as the airfield in Cannes was sure to be under surveillance. (In reality, the name of the pilot who crashed in Corsica with a payload of anti-Fascist propaganda wouldn't appear in Bocchini's files for another three weeks.)

From that point on, Lauro was determined to stay one step ahead of any pursuers, and believed every day was counted.

FRIDAY, JULY 17, 1931

Lauro is staying at the Hôtel de l'Europe on Rue Robert-Céard, a modest inn four blocks from Geneva's lakefront. He has checked in as "William Morris," in homage to the nineteenth-century Socialist designer and poet. Ruth, who identifies herself as "Mademoiselle Merrill," joins him after driving over the border from Paris. Geneva is home to Lauro's trusted friend, the *New York Times* correspondent Carlo Emanuele A Prato, a baron from the Trentino region in northern Italy. A former collaborator of Salvemini's in Florence, A Prato also gained flying experience as a pilot in the First World War. Lauro explains his predicament: his last plane, the British Cirrus Moth, was too light to handle a landing on rough terrain, and couldn't carry enough gas to reach Rome from the southern coast of France without touching down to refuel. A Prato suggests a German aircraft, like the Klemm, a light monoplane ideal for longer-range flights. The current weakness of the Deutschmark means he might be able to find a bargain at a German flying club. Lauro dashes off a letter to Luigi Ferrari in Brussels, the former Popular Party secretary who helped fund the purchase of the first plane, disguising the planned flight as "a concert." He envisions working with Bassanesi, who he has learned has plans to cross the Alps again for another aerial raid on Milan.

"I have thought that one could take advantage of the German crisis to find a second-hand violin in Germany, much better than the English or French ones." Lauro sets a tentative date, either in mid-August or the first two weeks of September, on a night with no moon. "Could one not play a duet, he with the alpine horn and I with the sea trumpet?" He hopes that Ferrari will offer to work as his assistant before the flight.

The spectacle of planes bombarding Italy's two most important cities, Lauro knows, would simultaneously madden and humiliate Mussolini.

SUNDAY, AUGUST 2

Ruth is sitting at the desk of a room of the Palazzo Josty, a hotel in the village of Madulein, working on a letter. After driving across Switzerland from west to east, Lauro and Ruth have opted for a secluded hotel near the Austrian and Italian borders, registering as American tourists. There are only three other guests at the hotel, all Swiss.

"It's a beautiful old manor house," Ruth writes to her closest friend. "Cows go by the front door, and sweet peasants. Stables and the post office and one store are all crowded to-gether, near a rushing river, and a great sweeping valley of hay fields. So I've been out working, and L. and I also played tennis, and walked, and sat in the forests, and read and slept and it's been too lovely."

But Ruth has been warned by Salvemini that her fame will point an arrow directly at Lauro. He's correct: in Bocchini's files, Ruth is clearly identified as Lauro's lover. She agrees that they should be seen in public as little as possible—particularly not in big cities, where people are sure to recognize her. Lauro ends their Swiss idyll by announcing that he is leaving that day for Germany, where he has a lead on a new airplane.

SATURDAY, AUGUST 8

At Munich's light airplane flying club, Lauro stares fondly at a handsome two-seater monoplane with cream-white wings, its upper fuselage, nose, and tail-wing detailed in crimson. With a top speed of 135 kilometres an hour, the wood-framed Messerschmitt

M.23b, fitted with an 83-horsepower engine, is significantly faster than the Cirrus Moth. It also has a longer flying range. Though it is small, the M.23b, which has won several races for planes of its class, is fleet and solid. Nowhere near as fast as the high-powered fighter planes of Italo Balbo's Aeronautica, but enough, Lauro believes, to get the job done.

He has found his new *Pegasus*.

After introducing himself as "Adolf Morris," Lauro signs a contract for the two-year-old plane with Hans Böhning, the jovial director of the flying club. (Böhning, a memo in Bocchini's files will note, "is a member of Hitler's National Socialist party," and the flying club is known for its "conservative and right-wing orientation.") "Mr. Morris" tells Böhning that he has been hired to distribute publicity fliers over Barcelona, and will need somebody from the club to fly the plane to the south of France. The price is set at eight thousand marks ($1,888): a better plane, for less than he paid for the Cirrus Moth. There will be enough left over for Lauro to pay for two crucial modifications: a front-mounted leaflet-release mechanism, and two additional gas tanks in the wings, which will extend the flying range by three hours, to nine hours and 36 minutes.

"Fortunately, I have now found a magnificent German machine, capable of ten hours of flight, so I will no longer have refuelling problems," he writes to his friend Giorgio La Piana at Harvard. Rome is within his reach. "For me, no joke, it's a thousand times better, in every sense, to break one's neck succeeding, then save it by giving up. From now on [Rome] has become for me like Cape Horn for the Flying Dutchman."

Ruth, unable to refuse her lover, provides the money to buy the plane.

FRIDAY, SEPTEMBER 4

Ruth is ensconced in yet another small hotel. This one is in Starnberg, a town in the Bavarian lakes district, thirty kilometres southwest of Munich. She has had a few good weeks with Lauro this summer, entire days when she has been able to forget about his plan. During the day they would go on long bicycle rides in the Black Forest; in their room at night, they would take turns reading aloud, Lauro from a biography of the Risorgimento statesman Count Cavour—a hero for his role in unifying Italy— she from a collection of P.G. Wodehouse's short stories. But now, her lover's obsession is pushing her to the breaking point. He's planned his flight for the following Monday, when the moon will be waning, but a problem with the release mechanism has forced him to put it off. Now he is often absent, splitting his time between Munich, Starnberg, and other small towns, hoping that constant movement will throw off any Fascist pursuers.

"I've gotten so superstitious," she writes to her friend. "The delays and things that happen are fantastic and fate seems to mock us— illness of friends who promised to help—miscarriage of letters—fears of detection—bad weather—all added to my increasing fear and nearly exhausted patience. He is so wonderful—I bow before his spirit and nerve—and I cannot leave him. I can't speak of the awful thoughts that nearly overwhelm me—I don't see why he isn't unnerved by the lack of faith and optimism and courage in me—so I fail in hiding it—but I still feel my presence helps—so I stay."

On the rare nights they are together at Starnberg, Lauro continues to perfect the wording of the National Alliance leaflets, and writes to his friend in Brussels for advice on which airfield he should use in the south of France. (Ferrari replies with a coded telegram, cabling "Louis" to indicate Marignane, twenty kilometres north of Marseilles.)

Lauro also adds the final touches to an article he first started in June. It's one he plans to mail to the world's leading newspapers on the eve of his flight.

The title, which he hasn't shared with Ruth, is "The Story of My Death."

MONDAY, SEPTEMBER 21

Lauro's frustration continues to grow. The take-off has once again been delayed. The previous Thursday, Böhning and another pilot from the flying club, Max Rainer, successfully landed *Pegasus* at the airfield at Marignane. There, Lauro decided to have magnesium flares installed on the wingtips, which would provide the illumination necessary for a night landing. Without Lauro's permission, the German pilots decided to test the flares, lighting up the airfield over Cannes, the very place from which the first *Pegasus* had left on its ill-fated flight to Corsica. Then a problem developed with the plane's electrical-ignition system, forcing the pilots to fly back to Germany for repairs. Lauro returns to Munich, where he checks into a hotel near the central train station.

In Munich, at least, there is one piece of good news. The new run of his leaflets is complete. In August, Lauro approached a local publisher to ask Georg Hirth, AG, a fine-art typographer established by a founder of Germany's Art Nouveau movement, to do a small print job for him. There are four separate texts. One is addressed to his "Majesty," the King of Italy, entreating him to declare once and for all whether he is on the side of liberty, or of the oppressors who have made the Italian people into "servile sheep." Another is addressed to members of the militia and the *balilla*, the Fascist youth movement, and urges the mothers of Italy: "Do not allow your sons to be torn from you at the age of eight years in order to be made into cannon fodder." Two other leaflets enjoin Italians to imitate the Spanish, who have recently thrown off their oppressors by declaring a Republic, and to follow a ten-point program of resistance to the regime. The leaflets are six-by-eleven-centimetre rectangles, printed on translucent stock as thin as the paper used to roll cigarettes.

Neither the publisher nor the printer can speak Italian, but they are happy to accept money from this well-dressed Englishman, who, as the publisher later reports, "speaks German very badly." After hastily reviewing the texts, Lauro packs 400,000 leaflets into a large suitcase. Back at the Fränkischer-Hof Hotel, he phones the German pilots, arranging to meet them at the Marignane airfield Friday of the following week.

FRIDAY, OCTOBER 2

At four in the afternoon, Lauro puts Ruth on a train to Cannes at the Gare Saint-Charles, Marseilles' main train station. They have spent ten days together in Geneva and the French Alps, waiting for good weather and a dark night best suited for the flight. From Cannes, Ruth will travel to Paris to await news in a friend's apartment.

Lauro walks down the stairs that cascade from the train station towards Marseilles' old port, and checks into the Hôtel Terminus with his suitcase full of leaflets. At seven in the evening, he receives a call from Böhning, who has arrived with Rainer in Cannes after an uneventful flight. It is too late, he tells the Germans, for the take-off to happen that day. Lauro urges Rainer to arrive at Marignane the following morning: "Make sure the machine is here about ten o'clock!"

In his room that night, Lauro writes two letters to Ruth. The first he dispatches to Paris as soon as the ink is dry: "I have still on my lips the perfume of yours, and if I close my eyes I feel you so close as if I might hold you in my arms. I think I could live 100 years on the sweetness accumulated these days. What a bewitcher you are! If only Flaubert had known you!... I burn to go and be through with this thing. I feel absolutely sure of this success, and am not even excited about it. It has become almost a matter of 'routine.'"

The second letter, though, he sends in care of Ferrari. His friend in Brussels is instructed to mail it only in case Lauro fails to return.

"You wanted me to play a role in the life of my country," he writes to Ruth, "I can assure you that not even in 50 years of successful work I could have attained such a role. Wait and see! Not right away but I will become a symbol and achieve 100 times more this way than if I were alive... Be happy and continue your glorious life not as if something had been taken away from it, but as if something had been added... be happy. '*Sta allegra*'... and please love somebody else. I will consider it indirectly as love to me."

Late into the night, he works on the final draft of "The Story of My Death," which will be mailed to Ferrari the following morning. Like the youthful Icarus on the eve of his escape from Crete, he exults in the glory of the coming deed:

"Pegasus—my airplane's name—has a red body and white wings; although it is as strong as eighty horses, it is as slim as a swallow. Drunk with fuel, it can leap in the sky like its ancient brother, but if it wants, at night, it knows how to glide through the air like a ghost... its former master is going to bring it to me on the coast of the Tyrrhenian Sea, truly believing that it will serve the leisure hours of a young Englishman. My bad accent has not awakened his suspicions: may he forgive my ruse!"

As Icarus scorned the tyrant Minos, he condemns Mussolini and his regime:

"One cannot both admire Fascism and deplore its excesses. It can only exist because of its excesses. Its excesses are its logic. For Fascism, the logic of its existence is to exalt violence... they say that the murder of Matteotti was a mistake; from the Fascist point of view, it was a stroke of genius. They say that Fascism is wrong to use torture to extort confessions from its prisoners; but if it wants to live it cannot do otherwise. The foreign press must understand this. One cannot expect Fascism to become peaceful and human without desiring its complete annihilation."

And, again like Icarus, who has been forewarned by his father Daedalus not to fly too close to the sun, Lauro is aware of the risks he's taking:

"Though I have only done seven-and-a-half hours of solo flying, if I fall it will not be from lack of experience. My plane does only 150 kilometres an hour [sic], whereas those of Mussolini do 300. He has nine hundred of them, and they have all received the order to bring down at any cost, with machine-gun fire, any suspicious airplane. However little I may be known, they must know that after my first try, I have not given up. If my friend Balbo has done his duty, they are now there waiting for me. So much the better: I will be worth more dead than alive."

He addresses the envelope to Ferrari, with instructions that, in case of his death, it is to be published in *Le Soir* in Brussels.

SATURDAY, OCTOBER 3

It is a good day for flying, the German pilots agree, as they walk back to the Marignane airfield after a hearty lunch. A band of high pressure has passed, visibility is excellent, and the skies are brightening over the western Mediterranean. There is even a slight tailwind, which is good news for "Mr. Morris," who leaps from a taxi at the airfield to greet them with a smile on his face. In the hangar, Lauro seems nervous as he empties several small bags of printed material into the front cockpit. Rainer, who goes off to look for a can of oil, attributes his agitation to the fact that it's been three weeks since his last flight. He advises him to make at least one trial flight before setting off for Barcelona.

"I have no time!" Lauro tells him. "It will be all right."

Böhning, meanwhile, inspects *Pegasus*. He estimates that, with the reserve tanks on the wings, the plane has an eight- to nine-hour range, plenty of time to circle Barcelona and fly back to Nice, which Lauro has told them is his final destination. He gives the Germans one thousand francs, about $40, enough for food and train tickets. He will meet them in Nice that evening, and they will enjoy a nice meal together.

"Don't forget pumping the gasoline from the wing tank to the main tank in time," Rainer urges Lauro. "Otherwise the engine will stop."

Lauro seems calm as he straps on his silk parachute and lowers himself into the cockpit. He is wearing a rumpled business suit with a carefully buttoned vest, a neat bow tie, and goggles, and carries a glass bottle full of coffee. Rainer hands him a flashlight, a last-minute gift, and Lauro chuckles when the punctilious German advises him once again to pump the wing tanks.

Böhning and Rainer push *Pegasus* out of the hangar with the help of the taxi driver. Rainer turns the propeller by hand. When the engine catches, he shouts to Lauro: "Good bye, good luck and *auf Wiedersehn* at Nice tonight!"

Their client's take-off, the Germans agree, is most excellent: rapid and smooth. They watch *Pegasus* rise, until it turns into a dot in the blue Mediterranean sky, and then set about packing their belongings into the taxi. They are not particularly worried about the airfield officials, who have been told their client is merely out for a pleasure spin. It is just after three o'clock. If all goes well, in a few hours they will be toasting his success with a late-night bottle of champagne.

PART IV

"I know of no other bomb than a book."
—Stéphane Mallarmé

PART IV

19 BOMBARDING THE BOSS

The weather in Rome on the evening of October 3, 1931 was gorgeous, indeed miraculously so. The sky, according to the *bolletino meteorologico* in the evening papers, was cloudless and *"sereno,"* with the mercury that afternoon rising to twenty-six degrees centigrade. It was warm enough that many were calling it an *"estate di San Martino"*—a St. Martin's Summer—after Martin of Tours, a Roman soldier in Gaul who was said to have made the heavens clear, and the summer heat return, after giving his cloak to a shivering beggar. Though life was now hard for many—a million out of work across the country, the price of bread at an unheard of 2.25 lire a kilogram, twice what the unemployed received in benefits per day—the people of Rome were still able to enjoy the timeless pleasure of the *passeggiata*. Families were out on their evening strolls, inspecting the windows of the elegant shops on the Corso, or staring at the live she-wolf, the symbol of Rome, that paced in a cage midway up the stairs leading to Michelangelo's piazza atop the Capitoline.

Even for an unseasonably warm Saturday, the streets were unusually busy. Since the previous afternoon, columns of black-shirted teenage boys—the so-called "rapid divisions" of the Fascist Youth—had been pouring in from the six regions of central Italy through the city gates, after crossing the *campagna* on motorcycles, horseback, and racing bicycles. They would assemble over the next few days at the "Campo Mussolini," a tent city set up on the vacant land between the Vatican and the new Fascist sports complex rising on the right bank of the Tiber. The climax of the event was to come the following Thursday, when Il Duce himself would address forty thousand members of the *Fasci giovanili* on the first anniversary of the movement's founding. While they waited, the boisterous youths thronged the bars and cafés, and made the *piazze* echo with choruses of *"Giovinezza."*

Outside the Palazzo Venezia, the piazza beneath Il Duce's balcony resounded with the fall of the pick-axes of labourers, busy reducing another nineteenth-century tenement to rubble. The work continued the "isolation" of the Vittoriano monument, part of the newly announced Master Plan of 1931, which set out to erase "the stain of material and moral misery" by creating new neighbourhood-clearing boulevards to serve a city with a projected population of two million, double its current size. The demolitions—which could continue on weekends now that unions had been outlawed—were done without the benefit of dredges or steam shovels, all part of Mussolini's aim to boost employment by favouring hand-labour over costly mechanization.

On Via Nazionale, the broad avenue leading from the Piazza Venezia to Termini Station, crowds were lining up outside Palazzo delle Esposizioni, where two days earlier, the first *Mostra d'arte coloniale* had been inaugurated. For the occasion, the neoclassical palace had been transformed into a showcase for the art of Tripolitania, Cyrenaica, Italian Somaliland, and Italy's other colonial possessions in Africa. Beneath the arches of the portico, the *zaptié*—native gendarmes dressed in hooded red burnoose—stood at attention with unsheathed sabres raised. Within, the palazzo's rotunda had been turned into a replica of a Bedouin tent, and visitors wandered through a simulation of an African souk, where dark-skinned natives squatted around hookahs and fez-wearing weavers laboured over looms. Mussolini and the king had been given a lengthy tour, pausing before paintings of bare-breasted maidens and lingering in the Futurist room, which featured African-inspired works by Marinetti's wife, Benedetta Cappa. The exhibition made Fascist Italy's vision of North Africa as a colonial dependency of the Third Rome abundantly clear.

Also present at the inauguration was Lauro's old friend Italo Balbo, recently returned from his successful seaplane raid on Rio de Janeiro. As Under-Secretary for Air, he had welcomed "the natural marriage between chemical weapons and the sky" in Africa. Within two years, he would be named Governor General of Libya, where he would go on to oversee the aerial deployment of poison gas over the holy city of Kufra. Fascism, having consolidated its hold over the Italian peninsula and chased out or banished its Communist and Socialist enemies, was ready to renew the most shameful project of nineteenth-century Liberalism: the subjugation of the people of Africa for material gain.

For most Romans, though, it was just another Saturday, a day of leisure to wander the streets or escape their cares for an hour or two in one of Rome's sixty movie theatres. Most of the movies were German or Italian productions, preceded by mandatory newsreels from the state film institute Luce extolling the latest Fascist triumphs in aviation, city-building, and engineering. Exceptions were made for a few of Hollywood's lighter diversions. At the Modernissimo in the Corso Umberto I, people were humming along to the talkie *The Big Pond*—retitled "*La Conquista dell'America*" for Italian audiences—featuring Maurice Chevalier as a Venetian tour guide who sings his way into the affections of an American heiress and ends up working in her father's chewing-gum factory. At the Cinema Vittoria in Testaccio, women admired Rudolph Valentino as he glowered beneath a fur cap as a lieu-tenant in the Russian Imperial Guard in *The Eagle*. And at the Excelsior in Via Cavour, Mussolini's favourite comic duo, Laurel and Hardy, were mugging and simpering their way through a pair of two-reelers.

On the Janiculum Hill, a few fellows from the American Acad-emy had joined couples and families who had wandered up from the streets of Trastevere to watch the sun set over the Alban Hills. The Depression was taking its toll on enrolment at the Academy, which had fallen from a high of 66 fellows and students in 1929 to its present low of a few dozen. Those that had chosen to cross the Atlantic were unnerved by growing evidence of xenophobia in the streets; excursions into the city were made less appealing by the challenging stares of swaggering Fascist youth and the conspicuous eavesdropping of waiters. Some chose to remain in their studios, or, as on this pleasant evening, confine their walks to the serpentine streets around the Academy.

Those who had adventured out looked with interest at the dot that appeared in the western sky. Aircraft had lately become a rare sight in the skies over Rome, as Balbo had temporarily sus-pended night patrols to spare the air ministry's budget after the previous month's intensive manoeuvres.

Yet, there was no mistaking it: an airplane had made an incur-sion in Italy's apparently inviolable airspace, and was now rapidly losing altitude. To those on the Janiculum that evening, the little plane seemed to be headed for the city's historical centre on the other side of the Tiber.

Inside the Palazzo Chigi, preparations were being made for that night's meeting of the Grand Council of Fascism, where Mus-solini planned to discuss strategy with foreign affairs minister

Dino Grandi, justice minister Alfredo Rocco, and other leading party *ras* until the early hours of the morning.

The little plane was plunging, like a dagger from above, directed straight at the heart of Fascist power.

It was one year, to the day, since Lauro had bid farewell to his childhood friend Giorgio de Santillana as he boarded a Naples-bound train. A year since he had last seen Rome. And he had never experienced the Eternal City like this, laid out beneath the wings of *Pegasus*, whose silent glide allowed him to hear the barking of dogs and the screech of trams rounding the street corners of Trastevere.

Though his heart was racing, his spirits were high, for the flight had gone according to plan. Before taking off, he had sketched out his route in pencil on the back of the draft of a National Alliance leaflet. From the take-off at Marignane to the base of Corsica's northern peninsula—that finger of French territory raised up towards the crook of the Italian Riviera—would take two hours and ten minutes. Another thirty-three minutes to reach Pianosa, one of the penal islands to which enemies of the regime were banished. More island-hopping, flying by sight from Montecristo to Giglio: three quarters of an hour. Then, after ten more minutes over the Tyrrhenian Sea, he would climb to four thousand metres as he approached the Italian mainland to avoid being sighted. Following the coast southwards, *Pegasus* would overfly the ancient Roman port of Civitavecchia, then turn inland at Palidoro, and begin its downwards glide twenty kilometres outside of Rome, when the dome of St. Peter's was in sight.

He had estimated a total flight time of 303 minutes, but a tailwind pushed the Messerschmitt beyond its maximum speed of 135 kilometres an hour. The German pilots had clocked his take-off at 3:15 in the afternoon; now, at eight o'clock, eighteen minutes ahead of schedule, he was bearing down on the unmistakable bend in the Tiber River that marked the heart of Rome. In theory, he had fuel for four and a half more hours of flight—not enough to reach Nice, but surely enough to reach the east coast of Corsica, where the magnesium flares on his wingtips could help him find a landing field.

The city he now saw below him was no longer the endearing backwater he had grown up in. Approaching the Janiculum, he saw how Rome had spread beyond the old Aurelian Walls, modern apartment blocks and worksites bleeding into the old pasture land beyond the city gates. A broad boulevard thrust through the Ghetto towards the left bank of the Tiber, and a new road had been driven from the Piazza Venezia to the Coliseum, cleaving the Forum. Taxis and the black sedans of government officials—there were now thirty thousand automobiles on the streets of Rome—jostled for space in the *piazze* where once only the hoofs of cabmen's horses had clattered on the cobblestones.

It was a comfort, as he came in low over the Tiber north of the Ponte Cavour, to see that the streets of the historic centre, near his family's apartment, seemed untouched by Mussolini's hand. The vegetation-covered mound that was Augustus's mausoleum was directly below him, the Pantheon's oculus-pierced dome on his right. Drawing a bead on the triangle of the Piazza di Spagna, he opened the throttle, and the plane's engine roared as the whirring propeller drew him upwards towards the church of Trinità dei Monti. From below, it must have looked like *Pegasus* was galloping up the Spanish Steps. At the last second, he pulled the lever to release a load of leaflets from the underbelly. Circling the piazza where he'd asked his friend Giorgio de Santillana to loan him the money to buy the machine to print the first National Alliance chain letters, he saw he'd scored a direct hit. The leaflets dropped in clumps, and then, separating in the light breeze, fluttered earthwards. Some were plucked out of the air by leaping children. Others papered the tiles of roof of the house where Keats had died, or drooped over the wales of Bernini's boat-shaped fountain.

Picking out the rooftop terrace of the family's palazzo, he loosed another load. In a letter to his mother, he had imagined her being informed of his triumphant return to Rome by a snow-fall of leaflets, and pictured her joy should he alight on their rooftop terrazzo beneath a silk parachute. She might be there even now, as it was her custom to have an evening coffee while enjoying the sunset. Circling back towards the Villa Borghese park, where he'd first courted Ruth Draper, he papered the wind-ing paths and ornamental temples with his little tracts. Next came the Quirinal Palace, the royal residence. He bombarded its gar-dens with leaflets addressed to the king, imploring him, in the name of the forty million Italians who looked to him for guidance, to choose liberty over oppression.

Over the Palazzo Chigi, where the "Boss" was sure to be work-ing, he came in low. Another direct hit. For good measure he hurled copies of a book from the cockpit: *Fascism in Italy*, a blis-tering dissection of the weaknesses of the regime by a British author, which he'd had translated and printed in a lightweight edition. The street lamps turned the paper that drifted past Il Duce's balcony into glowing rectangles, like sheets torn from a medieval gilder's book.

For thirty minutes, perhaps forty, Lauro circled, dove, and loosed payloads of his little bombshells. They fell on the terraces of cafés in Trastevere, on a crowd gathered at an outdoor cinema, on the luxurious hotels in the Piazza Barberini, on the curving arms of Bernini's colonnades that embraced St. Peter's Square. No searchlights pivoted to follow his progress. No airplanes of Balbo's Aeronautica dropped from above to bring him down.

As Icarus had dared to defy the tyrant Minos, Lauro had outfoxed and shamed the dictator Mussolini.

But, unlike the ingenious Athenian, there was no need for him to fall. He had perhaps lingered too long over the city, but there was fuel in the auxiliary tanks, surely enough to take him beyond the borders of Italy. As a final taunt before leaving the sky over Rome, he came in low over the military airfield at Ciampino, as if he were going to land. Instead, pulling up *Pegasus's* nose at the last second, he released more leaflets, these illuminated green, white, and red—the colours of the Italian flag—by the navigation lights on his wings.

All that remained was the return, to freedom and Ruth, perhaps to glory. He flew towards the darkness of the *campagna*, following the ancient roads of Empire northwards, turning back only for one last glimpse of the lights of Rome, her domes glowing silver as a half-moon rose over the horizon.

The spectacle of the lone plane, flying free, low, and unpursued over the "inviolable" sky of Rome astonished all who witnessed it. Police and militia rushed to gather up the leaflets, ordering those who had stooped to retrieve them to surrender their prizes. Outside the luxurious Hotel Bristol, guards shouted and trained flashlights on the facade, convinced agitators were dropping manifestos from an upper-floor balcony.

Many who plucked the papers from the air, or grabbed them from the cobblestones, glanced quickly at the words—*lies, boycott, resist, accept nothing*—and tucked them in coat pockets or purses.

In their homes, they marvelled at what was written, in language clear and direct, on those papers. Words that, in a nation where every publication was subject to state censorship, had been unsayable for years.

On one of the four leaflets, they read that Mussolini was a "Hapsburg in a black shirt" who treated the liberty for which so many had given their lives in the First World War as a "putrefied corpse." His regime was "not only the most tyrannical and corrupt but also the most bankrupt of all governments." The world, they were told, "looks with horror at a regime" which "exalts the brutality of its henchmen" in order "to reduce you to slavery." They were informed that the National Alliance had "launched its program of a union of all forces against Fascism." The severity of the sentences against its leaders was proof "how much its program frightens the regime."

Another leaflet set forth an action plan for non-violent resistance to Mussolini.

THE NATIONAL ALLIANCE

Rome.   *Year VIII after the murder of Matteotti*

Whoever you are, you are sure to be a severe critic of Fascism, and you must feel the servile shame. But even you are responsible for your inaction. Do not seek to justify yourself with the illusion that there is nothing to be done. That is not true. Every person of courage and honour is quietly working for a free Italy. Even if you do not want to join us, there are still TEN THINGS which you can do. You can, and therefore you must.

1. Do not attend any Fascist celebration.
2. Never buy a Fascist newspaper. They are all lies.
3. Do not smoke. (The tobacco monopoly provides Fascism with three billion lire a year, enough to pay for its worst extravagances...)
4. Do no action and speak no word in praise of the regime.
5. Boycott all the servants of the regime in your personal and business relations. They are your exploiters.

6. Boycott or hamper every Fascist initiative by a policy of obstructionism. Even the best initiatives only serve to add another chain to your burden...

7. Accept nothing of Fascism. Whatever it offers you is the price of your slavery.

8. Circulate the leaflets of the National Alliance. Spread every piece of truthful news you may get hold of. The truth is always anti-Fascist.

9. Make a chain of trusted friends on whom you may rely whatever happens.

10. Believe in Italy and in Freedom. The defeatism of the Italian people is the real foundation of the Fascist regime. Tell others of your belief and fervor. We are in the fullness of the Risorgimento. The new oppressors are fiercer and more corrupt than the old, but they will also fail. They are only united by a conspiracy, and we are bound by the will to be free. The Spanish people have freed their country. Do not despair of yours.

THE DIRECTORATE

When Mussolini learned of the appearance of an unidentified plane over the Palazzo Chigi, he was enraged. First Bassanesi had mocked the regime by bombarding Milan with propaganda. Now an unknown pilot had penetrated the sacred skies of Rome, and dared to dive-bomb his own palace. Had the books and manifestos been explosives, he and the leading members of Fascism's Grand Council could well have been blown to bits.

What was worse, the pilot seemed to have made a clean getaway. His air minister Balbo had been caught flat-footed; all of the air force's machine guns and swift pursuit planes were useless against the intruder. At two airfields, Ciampino and Centocelle, pilots had leapt into their cockpits, but by the time their fighters were airborne, the little plane had disappeared into the darkness.

It was essential that the people of Rome be seen as rejecting the invader. At a quarter to midnight, blackshirted youth converged on the Corso Umberto, and marched northwards. Their route took them directly beneath the de Bosis family's apartment on Via dei Due Macelli. By the time the columns reached the Piazza del Popolo, they were estimated to be twenty thousand strong. The papers the following day would call it a "spontaneous demonstration." But Mussolini himself had ordered the march, which was then hastily organized by his federal secretary Nino d'Aroma, who used the presence of thousands of idle Fascist Youth in the city to make it appear like citizens were professing their unshaken faith in the regime. Entering the Piazza Venezia, the teenagers mechanically chanted d'Annunzio's doggerel refrain, *"Eia, Eia, Eia, Alalà!"* D'Aroma derided the "miserable attempt" of the aviator as a "useless gesture," and assured the crowd that, at Il Duce's signal, "Roman Fascism is ready for any eventuality." By 2:30 in the morning, the boys, happy for the outing, wandered back across the bridges of the Tiber to their camp beds in the tents of the Campo Mussolini.

The people of Rome were not fooled. Only a few thousand of the hundreds of thousands of leaflets that snowed down that night would ever be handed over to the police. Street sweepers around Termini Station stashed them in their rubbish carts, waiters on the Via Veneto tucked them in their aprons, nuns in the Vatican slipped them into the sleeves of their habits. These messages of hope from the outside world were taken to homes, to be hidden beneath flowerpots, between the pages of books, and under floorboards, to be read and re-read in the dark years to come.

Each of them was a little ember, snatched from a fire that had only begun to spread.

20 "DOV'È DE BOSIS?"

After leaving Marseilles, Ruth went by train to Paris to wait for news of Lauro with her friend Léa Dessay, who had an apartment on Avenue de Wagram, one of the boulevards that radiates from the Arc de Triomphe. She spent the night of October 3 pacing the floor, torn between hope and anxiety, waiting for the phone to ring.

"Can you imagine?" she asked Dessay. "Even now, he's flying!"

But the phone didn't ring, and no telegram came, not that night, nor the following morning, which was a Sunday. It wasn't until Tuesday that the Parisian newspaper *La Volonté* reported the flight of a lone aviator over Rome. The author—who Ruth suspected was Lauro's childhood friend, Jean Loyson, writing under a pseudonym—seemed both well-informed and sympathetic. The Fascists may have conquered Italy's soil, the writer exulted, but this daring feat proved the skies were still free: "At five hundred metres over the Palazzo Chigi, there is no dictatorship." The same day the article appeared, Ruth received

Lauro's letter, forwarded by his friend Ferrari in Brussels, imploring her to *sta allegra*, "be happy," for his sake.

"You have made my life a real paradise for over three years," she read. "Don't [do me] the injustice of rendering me a cause of sadness."

After the article appeared, Ruth was brought in for questioning to the local police headquarters. Moved by her story, the *préfet* rose from his desk and kissed her on both cheeks, declaring: "*C'est un amour extraordinaire!*"

Meanwhile, Ferrari, following Lauro's instructions, mailed "The Story of My Death" to a friend, the editor of Brussels' *Le Soir*, on October 13. The following day, it was picked up by *The Times of London* and the *Guardian*. The Manchester paper, edited by Lauro's friend Cecil Sprigge, commented admiringly: "His feat in flying over Rome distributing the literature of liberty in the Duce's own garden and in the thronged streets at their most crowded hour is of the kind Italians regard with adoration." (In homage, Cecil and Sylvia Sprigge would name their newborn son Timothy Lauro.) *The New York Times*, whose news from Italy was still filtered through pro-Fascist journalists based in Rome, published the document in full, but without comment.

Around the world, readers were now presented with Lauro's version of his story: the clandestine network that spread the National Alliance chain letters; the arrest and trial of Vinciguerra, Rendi, and Lillian de Bosis; the months spent plotting his flight while working at a small hotel in Paris. For many, it was the first time they'd heard criticism—or rather, a blistering denunciation, from a patriotic Italian—of a regime that had built an image as a benign and effective dictatorship.

"It takes the children from all families," Lauro informed the world, "at the age of eight, imposing on them the uniform of executioners and giving them a barbarous and warlike education.

'Love the rifle, worship the machine-gun, and do not forget the dagger,' wrote Mussolini in an article for children."

The newsletter of *Giustizia e Libertà*, the left-wing group that had dismissed Lauro as a monarchist and a dilettante, now proclaimed him a "Hero of Liberty," pointing out that had he been carrying bombs rather than books and leaflets, the Fascist capital would be filled with rubble. "From now on," the newsletter declared, anticipating the end of Fascism, "a Republican Italy will be able to consider him one of its precursors." ·

Though Lauro appeared to have announced his own death to the world, Ruth believed he was still alive. The day after the flight, she'd wired 45,000 francs ($1,800) via the Morgan Bank to Cannes. It was only on Monday afternoon, more than two days after the flight, that a seaplane was launched from Antibes to scour the east coast of Corsica. The pilot returned at sunset, reporting he'd seen no signs of a wreck. Meanwhile, the German pilots, in spite of protesting their genuine ignorance of "Mr. Morris's" intentions, were arrested and expelled from France.

Ruth's young nephew, Bill Carter, who happened to be on his way to start work at an institute in Geneva, read about Lauro's flight in the London *Times* as he was eating a croissant in a café in Paris. He rushed to Dessay's apartment, where he found his aunt being consoled by Salvemini. Ruth was desperate to get news to Lauro's family in Rome. Carter agreed to pose as a tourist and find out what he could about Lauro's whereabouts. Salvemini wrote out a list of the names and addresses of potential informants in Rome, which he gave to Carter rolled up and tucked into a silver pencil case.

Carter, feeling rather "cloak-and-daggerish," arrived in Rome a week after Lauro had flown away into the night, and checked into a hotel at the top of the Spanish Steps. He met a Miss Cohen, an employee at the American Library, at an outdoor café in the nearby Villa Borghese gardens, where she was giving English lessons to a student. Though Cohen was nervous about being overheard by government spies—she was hard of hearing, which made public subterfuge a challenge—she agreed to pass on a letter from Carter's aunt to Lillian de Bosis. Lauro's family, in fact, hadn't been at their apartment on the night of the flight; his mother and his sister Charis were staying in the family's seaside tower in Ancona, where they'd learned from the radio that Rome had been bombarded with National Alliance leaflets. On hearing the news, they'd immediately guessed that Lauro was the pilot.

When Cohen's student told him that her husband had ventured out into the streets when the leaflets rained down, Carter arranged a private meeting at his apartment.

"He was especially struck," Carter reported to Ruth, "by the attitude of the crowd. He seemed to sense something different in the atmosphere. None dared really read the paper 'out loud,' though the police did not stop them. Rather they would shove it into a pocket and take it home to read in peace and quiet. He said that coming into the square was like coming into a new world; something he had not felt for years."

Working down Salvemini's list of contacts, Carter arranged to meet Umberto Zanotti Bianco, an archaeologist who had agreed to help Lauro distribute National Alliance chain letters, at his palazzo. Zanotti Bianco's research focussed on sites in Magna Grecia, the parts of southern Italy that had been colonized in Classical times by Greek settlers, providing proof of Hellenistic influence that did not endear him to a regime devoted to glorifying Augustan Rome. Liberal in politics, and a signatory of Benedetto Croce's Manifesto of Anti-Fascist Intellectuals, his every move was monitored by OVRA agents. Fearing that even his servants might be eavesdropping, Zanotti Bianco invited Carter to carry on their conversation in French.

"He told me," reported Carter, "of the furtive proprietor of the café who had slipped a paper under his beer, of the gardener who had come in next morning with one from a flower bed... many, he said, were especially impressed with the sense, and educated simplicity of the manifestos—not the usual Fascist panache and rhetoric... he then affirmed Mussolini's personal anger at the complete surprise of the exploit." Zanotti Bianco also passed on a rumour from a typist in the aviation ministry: she'd overheard a report that Lauro had first headed for Corsica, but after encountering Balbo's fighters, had headed towards the Adriatic Sea.

After only forty hours in Italy, Carter returned to Paris, where he had a chance to debrief Salvemini. Searchlight defences, he reported to the historian, had been reinforced in Rome, as had aerial night patrols over the city, suggesting the Fascists feared another incursion. After reporting for work in Geneva, Carter sent another letter to his aunt, describing a meeting with Carlo A Prato. Lauro's sponsor, Carter wrote, "thinks it quite conceivable that Lauro might have landed in the trees and is in hiding until he can get away." A Prato told Carter he'd advised Lauro to ditch his plane in the treetops if he couldn't find a landing field. "The anti-Fascist feeling is such [in Sardinia] that he would have a reasonable chance of safety; especially as it is very wild and mountainous."

Ruth, who had taken refuge at a chateau near Fontainebleau, was suddenly filled with hope.

"My whole state of mind has changed now about the possibilities that Lauro is safe," she wrote a friend. "These are the hypotheses: 1—that he flew East, was picked up by fishermen in the Adriatic and is being hidden, or got to Jugo Slavia. 2—that he was picked up in the Mediterranean and is on a vessel bound for a far-off port, and can't communicate with anybody. 3—that he got to Algiers and that the French police are hiding him until Italy is less angry and stops pressing the government for some accounting of his activity and the origin of the whole affair. The police have strongly hinted that he is alive—but have told me *not to tell*, save to my close and *trusted friends*. They won't say where—

how—or how they know. At first I thought it was a trick—but now I'm told they wouldn't say so unless it were true." She was now able to exult over the exposure "The Story of My Death" was receiving in the international press. "The publicity given it will make Mussolini boil; it's terribly important for the 'Cause,' and a newspaper correspondent of Rome told me the British papers have never given such prominence to a thing before."

If Lauro had not only succeeded in dive-bombing Rome, but also survived to tell the tale, he would at once humiliate the Fascists in Italy who had let him escape and provide an inspiration to Italians in exile. Once he emerged from hiding, he would immediately become a living symbol—and perhaps a leader—of the anti-Fascist resistance.

Which is exactly what Mussolini, fuming in his offices in the Palazzo Venezia, was afraid of.

Nancy Cox McCormack had a bone to pick with Mussolini.

The formidable sculptor had returned to Italy, after an eight-year absence, five weeks after Lauro's flight. In Rapallo, she was met by a gaunt Ezra Pound, who hailed her, his tweeds dripping, from beneath an umbrella on the station platform. Pound had been in Rome at the time of the flight. As much as the poet admired feats of aviation, he dismissed Lauro's act as "sheer romanticism." To Pound, Cox McCormack complained about how she'd been treated on the Rome Express. An officious porter had the temerity to *demand* a tip of twenty lire—one dollar—before making off with her travel documents. It was only after enlisting the aid of an aristocrat in an adjoining compartment that she could get her passport returned before alighting at Rapallo; the brute had tossed it out the window as the train was pulling out of the station. Such things would have never happened to a well-heeled foreign lady in the days before the March on Rome.

"If this was Fascist Italy," she railed, "I wanted none of it!"

Arriving in Rome, Cox McCormack checked into the Hotel d'Inghilterra, two blocks west of the Spanish Steps, where she was greeted by Lidia Rismondo, the widow who'd arranged her sittings with Il Duce eight years earlier. She was disappointed to note the change in the hotel's gay atmosphere. The Depression meant Americans were travelling less, and many of the foreign-run shops and hotels in the *ghetto degli inglesi* centred around the Piazza di Spagna had closed; of Rome's million inhabitants, only five thousand were now foreigners. The hotel's dining room, once filled with the lively conversation of English-speaking guests, was now occupied by a few dour Germans. But Angelo, the old coachman who used to wait for her in the piazza, was still waiting for clients beside his horse-drawn Victoria. Greeting the Signora with tears, he told her that things had gotten so bad in Italy under the new regime that he barely had enough money to feed his horse. After making a pilgrimage to the grave of Giacomo Boni on the Palatine, where Lauro had first introduced her to Italy's most prestigious archaeologist, she instructed Angelo to drive her to the Palazzo Venezia.

In the Renaissance palace, she walked up a broad staircase and was ushered through iron grills into the Sala di Mappamondo, the immense room named for the world map that had adorned its walls until the seventeenth century. (The lights here were always kept burning—even when Mussolini retired early to his home in the Palazzo Torlonia or rode his motorcycle to his beach house—to convey the impression that Il Duce worked tirelessly for the nation.) Beneath a coffered ceiling, candelabras illuminated walls decorated with *trompe-l'oeil* frescoes. As her eyes adjusted to the gloom, Cox McCormack saw that Mussolini was standing next to a desk, atop which he kept a photo of his beloved Angora cat, watching her from the far end of the room.

Il Duce was eyeing her, she thought, "like a human spider conscious of its own dramatic psychological advantages." The room was eighteen metres long, which forced visitors to walk for long seconds along a formal strip of red carpet laid down over a new mosaic floor, flanked by a pair of fasces, depicting the Rape of Europa by Jupiter. Aware of the dark eyes inspecting her from head-to-foot, Cox McCormack broke the tension by hailing her former subject in a hearty voice:

"Now *Eccellenza*, don't try to frighten me!"

With mock gravity, Mussolini asked her if she happened to know a sculptress with her name whom he had last seen eight years and four months earlier. When she replied that she had never heard of such a person, Mussolini laughed, and the stern look dropped from his face.

They spoke of common friends, and Mussolini expressed his delight at the warm reception his foreign minister Dino Grandi had recently received on his visit to her homeland. When she complained about her treatment at the hand of the rude porter, she was shown documents about a similar complaint from a group of Rotarians who had been delayed at the border by an overzealous official; the culprit, she was assured, would be forced to resign. When she wondered aloud that *il Capo del Governo* found the time to devote his attention to such minor affairs, Mussolini turned playful.

"Look, Nancy!" he said. Rolling up a sleeve to flex a bicep, he invited her to give it a squeeze. "I'm as strong as a lion!"

When Nancy brought up Lauro's recent flight, his levity vanished.

"The boy was lost at sea." That's all he would consent to say. The interview soon came to an end.

Cox McCormack rode in her carriage back to the Hotel d'Inghilterra, where the wife of the hotel's owner had something to show her.

She handed her a little white rectangle of printed paper, weather-worn but still legible, that had been found in the fireplace of Cox McCormack's room the day before her arrival. It was one of Lauro's leaflets, which must have been blown into the chimney.

"Fascism," she read, "encamped among you like a foreign garrison, besides corrupting your very souls, destroys your substance: it paralyzes the economic life of the country, it wastes billions to prepare for war and to hold you oppressed."

Cox McCormack, the first foreigner to glorify Mussolini's image in bronze, had been an early and very public supporter of Fascism. But on this short visit, she had seen signs of fear and poverty among the citizens of Italy, and the exercise of arbitrary power by petty officials. The words Lauro had put down on paper rang true.

And the regime's treatment of her young friend's family after the flight would make her see Fascism as something to be shunned, not celebrated. It would take some time, but the rest of the world would soon come to a similar conclusion.

Mussolini told Cox McCormack that Lauro had been "lost at sea." The truth was, both he and the Fascist police feared he was very much alive, and might resurface in triumph at any time to humiliate the regime.

Lauro's Political Police dossier, which is now filed away in the State Archives, includes his birthdate, but there is no indication of a time or date of death. The folders of many other dossiers are stamped with the word "MORTO" in purple ink, indicating that an enemy of the state had died and no longer constituted a threat. The contents of the Political Police files show that Bocchini and the agents of OVRA had no idea what had happened to Lauro, and indeed were obsessed with determining his current whereabouts.

On the night of the flight, coded telegrams were sent by provincial prefects responding to the Ministry of the Interior's demands for information about an aerial incursion over Italian territory. Dozens reported no activity, but a few, from towns northwest of Rome, confirmed the presence of an unidentified civilian aircraft on the night of October 3. In the days that followed, hundreds of Lauro's leaflets were discovered littering fields and forests of the towns of Monterosi, Sutri, Capranica, and Ronciglione. The last sighting, of a plane flying low and releasing leaflets, occurred in the town of Tuscania, twenty-four kilometres from the coast of the Tyrrhenian Sea. From there, the trail went cold. The office of the Merchant Marine reported that the commanders of the ports of Genoa, Viareggio, Naples, and other coastal cities had heard nothing from local fishermen about any plane going down in Italian waters.

Then the rumours began, each to be duly noted and entered into the files. From an "unverifiable source": de Bosis was rescued four nautical miles from Civitavecchia, and taken to safety in Philippeville (the Algerian coastal city now known as Skikda). From an anonymous informant in Rome: after his flight, de Bosis destroyed his aircraft and was picked up by a motor launch, which took him to Corsica; he is now hiding on French territory, where he is plotting to launch "another enterprise of a similar kind." From the Air Union offices of Marseilles: a seaplane pilot has reported seeing an aircraft being towed by a steamer off the coast of Sardinia. From a German newspaper: the remains of de Bosis's aircraft, with the marks of machine-gun bullets, were found off the Italian coast and secretly transported to Rome. From an OVRA informant in Marseille: an anarchist who frequents the Maison du Café says that de Bosis is alive and being supported by funds from the ex-Liberal Party of Italy. From an agent in Barcelona: a young man speaking fluent Italian, wearing his moustache clipped "in the American style," is passing himself off as Portuguese, but in fact is suspected to be the notorious Lauro de Bosis.

In Italy, the regime had almost completely blacked out news of Lauro's feat in the press. Four days after the flight, a newspaper called *Il Tevere*—later to become a venue for vile invective against Italian Jews—published one of the few accounts of the flight in the Italian press, identifying Lauro as the possible perpetrator. It was titled *"Una Carogna,"* a term of abuse to describe the putrefying corpse of an animal. The undersecretary of state supplied foreign correspondents in Rome with anecdotes that seemed to minimize the impact of Lauro's flight. The Republican *New York Herald Tribune,* for which Walter Lippmann was now a columnist, played along, dismissing the flight as an ineffective stunt. Under the headline "Romans Smile at Anti-Fascist Leaflets Showered on Rome," readers were informed that the leaflets were thrown away or handed over, with laughter, to the police.

It is also clear from the evidence in the State Archives that Lauro's family in Italy were made to suffer for his actions. The files are filled with letters that had been intercepted—to be duly reproduced and translated—before being sent on to his mother. His siblings were followed, harassed, their requests for passports and other documents questioned and often denied. Some of them came to understand what their brother had done. Three months after his flight, his sister Elena wrote: "We are left without our pride and our love and our youth and everything that made our family bright—what can ever console us?" (In 1938, Elena would flee Italy for England with her husband Leone Vivante, who was Jewish.) Lauro's eldest sister Virginia, who had always considered him spoiled, found it impossible to forgive him. And Charis would write: "Much as I loved Italy, I loved my mother more."

For her part, Lillian was filled with regret, particularly for the way she'd written to Mussolini to beg for clemency for her and her family.

"I never failed Adolfo," Lillian told Cox McCormack, "but I did fail my dearest Son. I could not do otherwise: but I knew when I made the choice, as coldly as I could under those circumstances, that I should repent it every day of my remaining life, and I am."

Lillian kept an album of images from the life of her youngest son. There was a photo of Lauro at the Villa Diana, in short pants and a sailor's suit, leaning affectionately into his father's shoulder. Another of Lauro, aged fifteen, smiling widely as he teeters on a bicycle. Lauro as a young man, his moustache full, dressed in one of his recently deceased father's suits, chin reposing on his hand in a portrait taken on the eve of his American lecture tour. Then, towards the end, Lauro in the rear cockpit of the Messerschmitt, turning towards the camera, grim-faced and determined in his aviator's cap.

But the final photo in Lillian's album is of Lauro as a toddler with blond curls, dressed in a white blouse, standing in front of a haystack. Between chubby knees, the boy who dreamt of winged horses, and would go on to tame his own *Pegasus*, clenches a pole that ends in the bridled head of a white hobby-horse.

21 | THE NEW AUGUSTUS

Lauro de Bosis was right to think that by penetrating Italian airspace and blanketing the streets and squares of the capital with anti-Fascist propaganda, he would be delivering a symbolic blow to the regime. Mussolini's rage, and the secret police's obsession with determining his whereabouts, showed that *"il volo su Roma,"* as the flight became known, had wounded Il Duce where it hurt most, in his pride. But Italian Fascism's hold on the Italian people, at this stage in its development, was nowhere near as fragile as Lauro had imagined. Eventually, the regime's claims to have mastered the economy, gained universal approval from the Italian people, and built a powerful war machine would be revealed as grossly—and tragically—over-inflated. But in the early thirties, Fascist Italy was still able to maintain the bluff that it was a force to be reckoned with on the world stage.

The nation had entered what historians now refer to as the "years of consensus," a seven-year period, starting in 1929, during which the people of Italy offered almost no resistance to the dictatorship. The Fascists were able to claim that they had resolve two historic failures of the Liberal state. After moving its black-shirted officials into the south, and staging show trials of hundreds of alleged gangsters at a time, the regime declared the Mafia defeated, and banned any mention of its existence in the press.* In Rome, peace had been made with the Vatican, which for decades had reproached Liberal Italy for seizing church property after the country's unification. With the signing of the 1929 Lateran Accords, seventy years of dissension between Church and state came to an end. Close to two billion lire were paid out to the church in cash and bonds, the Vatican City was recognized as a fully independent state-within-a-state, and crucifixes were restored to classrooms.

Making good on the concept of totalitarianism, the state continued to invade every aspect of daily life. University professors were forced to take an oath of allegiance, and elementary teachers had to wear Fascist uniforms at official functions. First-grade students were given primers that taught them to spell "Benito," "Duce," and "*fascismo*," and a new youth organization, the *figli della lupa* (the "sons of the she-wolf") was established for boys aged six-to-eight years. Girls were taught to march in formation carrying dolls, as their mothers cradled infants. Mussolini launched a "Battle for Births," rewarding mothers who gave birth to more than ten children with gold prizes. In spite of such inducements, the birth rate continued to drop, barely hitting replacement levels in north and central Italy by mid-decade. Fortunately for the regime, restrictions on emigration staunched the outflow of population, which dropped from a high of a million a year early in the century to just 70,000 in 1934.

---

* The Mafia had merely been driven underground. In Sicily, where years of bad harvests had led to near-starvation conditions, leading Mafiosi were released from jail to quietly resume their time-honoured old roles as enforcers using a tradition of culturally sanctioned private violence to further their economic ends.

Though the Italian stock market lost a third of its value in the three years following the Wall Street collapse, the nation's largely agricultural economy spared it some of the worst effects of the global depression. The regime increasingly felt empowered to turn its back on the world. Achille Starace, the party's dim-witted but zealous secretary, banned the handshake as an effete Anglo-Saxon import, and insisted all meetings begin with a *Saluto al Duce*. (Mussolini exempted himself from the convention, and continued to greet foreign visitors with an outstretched palm.) Foreign words like "croissant" and "sandwich" were replaced by the Italianate neologisms *bombolino* and *tramezzino*; a "cocktail" became a *coda di gallo*. In the *dopolavoro*, the state's after-work recreation clubs, workers were encouraged to play a high-speed cross of rugby, soccer, and basketball with eight players to a side, whose Fascist promoters claimed had existed since Roman times. (*Volata* was never able to usurp the national cult of soccer, particularly after Italy defeated Czechoslovakia by one goal in overtime at the 1934 World Cup in Rome.)

As the Depression killed off foreign demand for olives, wine, nuts, and other traditional export products, Italy gradually embraced "autarky," a policy of building self-sufficiency through a strictly national economy. By the end of the decade, state ownership of the industrial sector in Italy would be surpassed in Europe only by the Soviet Union. Instead of uniting industry and labour in a harmonious national economy, the much-vaunted "Corporative State" succeeded only in providing work for a bloated class of Fascist bureaucrats. (In practice, it transformed every boss and foreman into a miniature Duce, allowing employers to exploit their employees at will.) The policy of self-sufficiency would also prove a failure: only a fifth of the nation's needs was ever met by domestic production, and Romans would eventually be forced to subsist on a ration of "autarkic" bread made of mashed chickpeas, mulberry leaves, and an extract of elm bark.

The *Decennale*, the tenth anniversary of the March on Rome (marking the midpoint of the *Ventennio*, as the twenty-year period of Mussolini's rule became known) provided an opportunity for the Fascists to swagger about their perceived successes. Its centrepiece, the *Mostra della Rivoluzione Fascista*, opened on October 28, 1932. The beaux-arts Palazzo delle Esposizioni, which a year before had hosted the Exhibition of Colonial Art, was redecorated in an angular Rationalist style, with eight-storey-tall fasces of oxidized copper towering over the entrance staircase. Twenty-three rooms, one for each year since the beginning of the First World War, presented artifacts from Fascist history, including d'Annunzio's original constitution for the city-state of Fiume. The exhibit culminated in a darkened altar to Fascist martyrs, where a seven-metre-tall crucifix on a blood-red pedestal was illuminated by a thousand electric lights while *"Giovinezza"* played softly in the background. Four million visitors came to the exhibition during its two-year run, though many of them were taking advantage of the specially discounted train fares to enjoy a cheap Roman holiday. The Mostra's guests of honour included future prime minister Anthony Eden, the King of Siam, the British Fascist leader Sir Oswald Mosley, and Joseph Goebbels.

In the final week of the exhibition, Mussolini announced another state spectacle: the celebration of the two-thousandth anniversary of the birth of Augustus, the Emperor who replaced ancient Rome's constitutional government with dictatorship. Preparations began with the now-familiar ritual of Il Duce wielding a pick-axe, raining down blows on a condemned building next to the Mausoleum of Augustus.

If any tourist had doubts that Il Duce saw himself as inheritor of Augustus's mantle, they would be dispelled by a taxi ride down the twenty-metre-wide Via dell'Impero. The regime boasted the new parade route through the Forum, now lined with statues of Julius Caesar, Augustus, and Trajan, had carried

6.2 million automobiles in its first year of use. On April 21, 1934, traditional anniversary of the city's founding, four enormous maps of gold, bronze, and marble were unveiled along the Via dell'Impero on the brick wall at the base of the Basilica of Constantine. From its earliest days as a dot on the west coast of the Italian peninsula to its greatest extent in the second century, Rome and its empire were depicted in grey-white stone—with the barbarous outlying regions of Germania, Arabia, and Caledonia shown in pitch-black Apuan marble.

Two and a half years later, a fifth map would go up on the cathedral's wall. This one, the largest of all at 24 square metres, would be titled *"L'Impero dell'Italia Fascista,"* and showed Italy's possessions in Africa, including *Libia, Somalia*, and a newly conquered territory labelled *L'Impero Etiopico*. The conquests of the new Augustus, who had taken Italy from post-war humiliation to imperial glory, were rendered in stone for all to marvel at.

Lauro had gambled that a single, poetic act of heroism would be enough to expose Fascism's bluff before the eyes of the world. He was right: the regime's mastery of the economy and the Italian people, like its twentieth-century imperium, was a sham. But Lauro had played his hand too early. Mussolini still controlled the deck. For the time being, the Fascists still had plenty of cards hidden up their sleeves.

The Bagnanis watched the ongoing transformation of Rome with uneasiness. In "Ten Years of Fascism," an article written for, but never published in, a Toronto newspaper, Stewart recorded her thoughts about the Via del Mare, one of the roads inaugurated by Mussolini on the anniversary of the March on Rome.

"[The road was driven] unmercifully through a network of old narrow streets whose houses seem to have collapsed like card houses, so quickly have they disappeared. The treatment is a little drastic. When I first came to Rome I wandered through many dark little streets, some quite mediaeval, where one walked with the feeling that adventure might await around every corner. They are no more; but on their way these roads have been careful not to touch one ancient monument and instead, those ancient buildings lying on their route have been excavated, restored and cleared of surrounding debris till they stand out in unimagined splendour."

Despite these misgivings, Stewart believed Fascism had been good for Italy. She found the spectacle of black-shirted children and teenagers marching in the streets during the *Decenalle* celebrations invigorating. "The streets are thronged with youths from all over Italy in their picturesque uniform, with a brightly coloured scarf knotted about their necks and a black cap with a large tassel—a cap worn by the storm troopers in the war." She noted with approval the new neighbourhoods rising in small towns, the introduction of modern farming methods, and the planting of trees on once-barren hillsides.

"But besides all these material achievements Mussolini has been able to accomplish the far more difficult task of altering the psychology of a nation. He rose to power when the morals of his countrymen were at a low ebb, disillusioned by post-war conditions, headed by an impotent government, threatened by Communism." For Stewart, Il Duce had succeeded in moulding "a people of widely different characteristics, of separate loyalties and distinct ideas, into a patriotic nation and a great world power."

Such glowing assessments were common in the early nineteen-thirties. As a resident foreigner, Stewart might have felt the need to make a public show of support for the regime. But such a stance only served to bolster Mussolini's prestige abroad, and reinforce his power at home. Stewart, in short, looked at Fascism through the lens of the wealthy aesthete. Like so many of her class, she approved the superficial manifestations of progress while choosing to ignore abundant evidence of violence, the muzzling of the press, and the loss of individual and intellectual freedom.

Gilbert was too much the sophisticate to indulge in such naive outpourings. While in Italy, he confined his political observations to his correspondence. When he learned that the mother of his old friend Lauro de Bosis "had been arrested as being implicated in a conspiracy against the government," he sent his mother a newspaper clipping about the trial. "The de Bosis as you see did not make a *bella figura*. I feel very sorry for Bobby [her son-in-law], I am sure no one will give him a job for ages." (Gilbert was not in Rome on the day Lauro made his flight, and there is no record of his reaction to it in his letters.)

The de Bosis trial must have been a reminder, too, that Gilbert's own chances of making a career in Fascist Italy were limited. If he wished to maintain a residence in Rome, securing an academic or administrative post was crucial. As long as the regime insisted on using archaeology to glorify *Romanità*, Gilbert's unorthodox views made it unlikely he'd find a position in an Italian university. But when his friend Carlo Anti proposed that he run the Graeco-Roman Museum at Alexandria, his candidacy was rejected. The director wrote that Gilbert was a "snob who affected to speak English, married to a Canadian, presumptuous and antifascist."

In the nineteen-twenties, Gilbert's wealth had allowed him free rein to pursue his interests in ancient Rome. But the Stock Market crash of 1929 had taken a bite out of his savings, and Rome's countryside, now riddled with construction sites, was fast losing its charm. He was also disturbed by the death of his collaborator on the topographical dictionary to the *campagna*, the former director of the British School. In 1931, Thomas Ashby's body was discovered next to the railway tracks fifteen kilometres south of Waterloo Station. The archaeologist had been on a train bound for Oxford, where he was to start a research position at his old college, Christ Church. The post-mortem disclosed a brain tumour, which might have caused him pain and giddiness; friends speculated he'd opened the carriage door by accident, mistaking it for the toilet. The coroner recorded an open verdict. Ashby was fifty-six when he died, a year older than his father had been when he'd committed suicide.

Gilbert contributed a heartfelt tribute to Ashby, written with an Italian colleague, to *The Times of London.* "To us he was more a fellow-Roman than the director of a foreign school. He was respected for his unrivalled knowledge of the past history of our city; he was loved for his understanding of our modern life... As master, colleague, and friend, *quel caro Ashby* will be no less mourned in Italy than in his native land."

By then, Gilbert, reconciled to working outside of his own native land, had already started his excavations in Egypt. What he found in Tebtunis was thrilling. His Fascist colleague Anti had been at work with an architect clearing the streets around the houses to establish the layout of the town, in an effort to show evidence of Roman city planning in Egypt. In 1931, Gilbert, focussing his attention on the contents of the houses and temples, discovered an enormous sanctuary dedicated to the crocodile god, with priests' houses and workshops intact, its vestibule lined with a spectacular sculpted frieze. Buried in the sand, he found the temple's archives, which would prove to be the second-largest cache of papyri to ever come out of Egypt.

It was the find of a lifetime. Gilbert, often with Stewart as his assistant, spent much of the next five years sleeping in tents, weathering sandstorms, and painstakingly unrolling fragile papyri and translating their hieroglyphics. His work did nothing to endear him to his Fascist overseers. They had spent enormous sums on the Egyptian mission not to dig up crumbling scrolls, but to convince the world that Rome, since the days of Antony and

Cleopatra, had been the true master of Egypt, and deserved to rule it again.

Gilbert's discoveries in Tebtunis were making a mockery of Fascism's overblown claims of *Romanità*. For that, he and his Canadian wife could expect to pay a price.

On October 3, 1935, exactly four years after Lauro's flight, Italian troops crossed the border into the ancient east African kingdom of Ethiopia. The forces of emperor Haile Selassi amounted to 300,000 men, 371 bombs, and eleven slow aircraft, three of which couldn't take off. Mussolini would dispatch 650,000 troops to east Africa, two million tons of supplies, and 450 aircraft, two hundred of them bombers. In a war of machine guns against bolt-action rifles, and modern airpower against tribesmen on horseback, Italian victory was inevitable.

Bombs rained down on the market town of Aduwa, where Liberal Italy had experienced a humiliating defeat in 1896. Mussolini's son Vittorio led some of the most brutal dive-bombing raids—including one on a British Red Cross unit—and came back with hideously aesthetic descriptions of the impact of bombs on native huts and horsemen. Chemical weapons were massively deployed, often in the form of arsine and mustard gas sprayed as a vapour from airplanes. (Italy denied such atrocities, claiming that photos of chemical burns on villagers' bodies merely showed the symptoms of leprosy.) When the League of Nations condemned the invasion and imposed sanctions, defiance grew among the people of Italy. Women lined up to contribute their wedding rings for the war effort on the *Giornata della Fede* (the "Day of Faith")—the American archaeologist Esther Van Deman among them—and the playwright Luigi Pirandello contributed his gold Nobel Prize for Literature to be melted down for the cause. By the time Addis Ababa fell, at the beginning of the following May, as many as

275,000 Ethiopians had been killed. Italy, by contrast, lost only 4,500 troops.

"Our peninsula is too small," Mussolini had told Parliament a decade earlier, "too rocky, too mountainous to be able to feed its forty million inhabitants." Just as Nazi Germany would cry for *Lebensraum*, Fascist Italy needed *spazio vitale*, room to live. The Vatican endorsed the project of colonization, and the new imperialists imagined half a million relocated peasants happily cultivating oases and fertile palm groves. To make room for prospective settlers in Libya, one hundred thousand nomads, most of them women, children, and old men, would be marched up to a thousand kilometres across the desert, where 40,000 died of hunger and typhus in concentration camps.

After Ethiopia was conquered, Mussolini announced "the reappearance, after fifteen centuries, of empire on the fated hills of Rome." On hearing the news, the King, who had been bestowed with the title "Emperor of Abyssinia," reportedly wept with joy. The aged d'Annunzio sent a telegram from his castle on Lake Garda saluting Mussolini for "his incomparable and courageous gesture," adding: "you have nothing more to fear." *Africa Orientale Italiana* was to prove a fleeting, threadbare imperium. Only 3,200 Italian peasants ever "colonized" Ethiopia, and Italy's African possessions cost far more to maintain than they ever contributed to the national economy. In the effort to add new white spaces to the map of empire, an extraordinary deployment of arms and men proved such a drain that Italy was unable to keep up with other powers in arming for the bigger war to come. While Germany ramped up arms production, Italy coasted on bombast with a navy completely lacking aircraft carriers, and an army—in spite of the "eight million bayonets" supposedly at Mussolini's command—that boasted only the lightest of tanks.

And while Mussolini's empire-building had gained him approval at home, it was dealing a fatal blow to the credit he'd built up in the western democracies. In 1934, Cole Porter had written the line "You're the top—you're Musso—li—ni!" for the stage musical *Anything Goes*. (The reference would be edited out for the movie version.) A year later Ernest Hemingway, who went to Ethiopia as a correspondent, was deriding Il Duce in the pages of *Esquire* for trying to make Africa "fit for Fiats" and condemning Fascism as a form of "mechanized doom." The world's sympathy had fallen on the side of the outgunned Ethiopians, and Liberals and Conservatives on both sides of the Atlantic denounced the egregious flouting of international law.

As a short-term strategy, Mussolini's bluff had succeeded. Though Italy remained poor and its economy underdeveloped, swamps had been drained, roads built, the monuments of a Third Rome erected—enough at least to convey the impression of progress. With its new colonial adventures, it had exported the bluff, erecting triumphal arches and sphinxes in the sands of Africa— enough to at least temporarily satisfy a disappointed nation's hunger for lost glory.

The long-term costs, though, would soon become apparent. Defying the League of Nations had pushed Italy away from its former allies, France and Britain, and would from now on draw Mussolini into an ever-closer relationship with Nazi Germany and its increasingly bellicose chancellor.

And Il Duce, who had always prided himself on being the most informed of dictators, would start believing in the biggest bluff of all: the myth of his own infallibility.

Adolf Hitler, chancellor of Germany since January 30, 1933, was an early admirer of Mussolini.

"The March on Rome, in 1922, was one of the turning points in history," he would concede during the Second World War.

"The brown shirt probably would not have existed without the black shirt."

Though Nazi racial theorists would consign Italians to the "Mediterranean" race, the third and worst of European blood groups, Hitler made an exception for the founder of Fascism, and was known to keep a life-sized bust of Il Duce in the party's Munich headquarters. Mussolini, by contrast, was wary—and occasionally contemptuous—of Hitler and the Germans.

"Thirty centuries of history," he told his fellow Italians in a 1934 speech, "allow us to look with utter disdain on certain doctrines from the other side of the Alps which are espoused by the descendants of people who were illiterate at a time when Rome had Caesar, Virgil, and Augustus." At his first meeting with Hitler, arranged by the industrialists Henry Ford and Giuseppe Volpi at a golf club in Venice in June of that year, Mussolini was bored by the Führer's incessant ranting, particularly his diatribes against the "degenerate" modernist art Italy had permitted to be shown at the Biennale.

Nor did Mussolini share Hitler's deep-seated hatred for Jews. Italy's Jewish population was small—numbering just 50,000, compared to half a million in Germany—and well-integrated. Italian Jews had played a prominent role in the founding of the Fascist party in Ferrara; more than two hundred Jewish Fascists had participated in the March on Rome; and Mussolini's long-time mistress, Margherita Sarfatti, was born to a family of wealthy Venetian Jews. In the early days of Nazi persecution, Italy allowed three thousand German Jews to seek refuge in Italy. But the nation's increasing involvement with Germany encouraged the racism of the more zealous party *ras*, and Mussolini himself began to signal that he was willing to follow Hitler's lead. The fact that the leading anti-Fascist-in-exile, *Giustizia e Libertà's* Carlo Rosselli, was a Florentine Jew, as well as Mussolini's belief that the main authors of the international media backlash against the Ethiopian invasion were Jewish, probably helped drive Italy's belated embrace of anti-Semitism.

And the benefits of cooperating with Hitler seemed to outweigh the potential drawbacks. In 1936, Italy's young foreign minister, Count Galeazzo Ciano—who also happened to be Mussolini's son-in-law—returned from a visit with Hitler energized about the prospect of Germany expanding east into the Baltics, while Italy would be left free to rule the Mediterranean. Mussolini, relishing the vision of a Europe divided between Rome and Berlin, came up with a new term, describing the partnership as an "Axis around which all the European states motivated by a desire for cooperation and peace can collaborate." The following year, he would be welcomed in Berlin, where, in execrable German, he told a crowd of nearly a million how "an imposing and ever-increasing mass of 115 million spirits"—the new Axis—would unite against the forces opposing them in "one unshakeable will."

The Axis's first battleground would be Spain, where Republican forces were waging a desperate war against a right-wing coalition of Nationalists, monarchists, and Catholics led by General Francisco Franco. The Spanish Civil War would prove an excellent training ground for the Nazi war machine, and a sinkhole for Italian Fascists. While Britain and France declined to support the Republicans, left-wing volunteers from around the world poured in to prevent the triumph of Fascism in Spain. The cause was a rallying point for Italians in exile, including Rosselli, who led a company of forty riflemen and rallied the volunteers with broadcasts from Barcelona under the slogan "Today in Spain, tomorrow in Italy." While Italy tried to maintain a facade of non-intervention, it unofficially dispatched regular troops and Fascist militia to the conflict. When three Fascist divisions marched on Madrid in 1937, confident they would easily take the capital, they were routed by anti-Fascist countrymen at the Battle of Guadalajara.

The humiliating defeat made it clear to the world that Italy had no compunction about projecting its power into sovereign states, as it had in Ethiopia. Determined to be avenged, Mussolini would eventually pour 50,000 men into Spain, and billions' worth of lire of armoured vehicles, aircraft, and artillery. Very little of the materiél would return to Italy. Already hard hit by the League of Nations sanctions, Italy was forced to leave the gold standard and devalue its currency.

Whatever spurious glory Italy had gained in Africa was spent on the Iberian Peninsula, and the new Augustus's growing belief in his own omnipotence would allow him to be gulled by the promises of his commanders, who assured him Italy was amply armed for the war to come. On the eve of the conflict, Italian industry had produced bombers whose engines routinely failed, submarines that were deadly to their crews, and tanks with armour so thin that they were nicknamed "sardine cans." Mussolini claimed to have 150 divisions at the ready; at most, he had ten, all of them under-equipped and below strength. By the time his son-in-law Ciano signed the 1939 "Pact of Steel" with Germany, even he was writing in his journals that Fascist military power was a "tragic bluff."

Lauro had been one of the first to call attention to that bluff. The battle that first led Italy to squander its military resources in Spain was fought by the Italian volunteers of the Garibaldi battalion, in honour of the nineteenth-century mercenary general who fought to unify the Italian nation. The battalion was organized into five companies, each named after a leading anti-Fascist.

The fourth, which helped turned the tide against the Fascists at the Battle of Guadalajara, was named the "Lauro de Bosis company."

22 THE DESPOT'S RAGE

In the weeks and months that followed the flight, Ruth Draper continued to hope that her lover was alive. Lauro's silence might be explained if he were crossing the Atlantic on a freighter, or stranded on a Mediterranean island, or merely waiting for an opportune moment to come out of hiding and announce his triumph to the world.

"Who knows," she wrote to a friend from a château in Fontaine-bleau, "if Lauro should call me up perhaps from Spain, or South America, or Egypt—It's so hard to know what to do, where to go, but my instinct is just to stay here and wait and be ready for anything!"

Her optimism was nourished by the French authorities, who continued to transmit reports of possible sightings.

"I've lived in alternate despair and hope—for five days was sure he was alive—told by the Ministry of the Interior who based the announcement on unfounded rumors that he'd been picked up by Algerian fishermen! It was Machiavellian in its cruelty."

She hoped that the standing offer of a $40,000 reward through the Paris office of the Morgan Bank would lead to information on his whereabouts.

In Rome, Bocchini's Political Police would never close their files on the "notorious" Lauro de Bosis. When, in the early months of 1932, a young English governess in the employ of Lauro's sister Elena travelled from her villa in Siena to Naples, and greeted a dark-haired young man of Italian appearance who'd disembarked from a ship newly arrived from South America, both were arrested. They were only released, after several days of interrogation, when it was pointed out that the suspect's eyes were blue, while Lauro's were clearly recorded in the files as being brown. OVRA agents intercepted letters to Lillian de Bosis claiming to be from her son; all were revealed to be hoaxes. Fully six years after the flight, an anonymous informant in the United States reported:

"I've learned that Lauro de Bosis is still alive. Recognizing his handwriting, I read a letter... in which de Bosis covertly confesses to being disillusioned and nostalgic. After having spent a long period of time in Russia, he can now be found forty-eight hours from New York. I haven't managed to determine his precise place of residence."

Paying attention to such rumours, Ruth realized early on, would only madden her. In the weeks after the flight, she was consoled by the company and kind words of Salvemini and Amey Aldrich, the sister of Chester Aldrich, the former president of the Italy America Society and the man responsible for inviting Lauro to lecture in America. Amey, who was heading to Rome, where she and her brother would take over the management of the American Academy, promised to carry Ruth's letters to Lillian. Irene di Robilant, the Society's former manager, wrote to send her sympathies. Di Robilant, who had conceived the plan to set up the news service funnelling pro-Fascist bulletins to America, seemed to have changed her mind about Mussolini. On a Mediterranean voyage di Robilant later took with Ruth, in which they made a pilgrimage to the airfield Lauro had taken off from outside Marseilles, she would echo his disparaging term for Il Duce.

"The 'boss' has never had greater prestige and power," she lamented to Ruth. "How strangely things work out—and how rare really great men are."

For Ruth, the remedy for despair was to throw herself back into her work. She set out on a series of a dozen one-week engagements through Britain, opening in Brighton on January 11, 1932. At first she found returning to the grind of touring difficult—the shabby dressing rooms in old theatres, living out of suitcases in endless hotel rooms—but the auditoriums were packed, and the pleasure she brought to audiences, conveyed by their laughter and applause, gratified her. It also kept her mind off her greatest regret: the fact that she and Lauro never wed. (In a letter addressed, but never sent, to Lauro's friend Giorgio La Piana, she wrote: "Lauro and I would have been married had he returned.")

After a restorative autumn at her property in Maine, where she · recalled idyllic days sailing with Lauro in the bay of Dark Harbor, Ruth embarked on a lengthy and gruelling world tour. As the months and years wore on, she began to focus on curating Lauro's legacy. Between appearances in Capetown and Khartoum, she found the time to work on a translation of *Icaro*, which was published by Oxford University Press. In 1932, the same press had released Lauro's *The Golden Book of Italian Poetry*, with a preface by Gilbert Murray, a renowned scholar of classical Greece. The cover of the anthology, which featured a poem about Icarus by the sixteenth-century poet Jacopo Sannazaro, bore the golden imprint of a winged horse.

With the help of La Piana, Ruth founded a chair in Italian civilization at Harvard, eventually endowing it with $50,000. In 1934, Salvemini became the first appointee to the Lauro de Bosis Lectureship in Italian Civilization, a position he would occupy until after the Second World War. While Salvemini regretted abandoning the anti-Fascist struggle in Europe, it was the only way he could see to make a living. "As for America," he told his friend Carlo Rosselli, "I am going there as to prison." Perhaps it was for the best that Salvemini left when he did, for OVRA had embarked on a ruthless and efficient campaign of extra-territorial assassinations.

After his experience fighting the Fascists in Spain, Rosselli was willing to embrace the violence that Lauro had rejected in the cause of overthrowing the dictatorship. By 1937, he was telling friends: "As for Italy, there is one absolutely necessary thing that we must do first: and that is *to kill Mussolini*." The Fascists had come to a similar conclusion about the troublesome Rosselli and his brother Nello. In June of that year, the Rosselli brothers were vacationing at a spa town in the north of France, when they stopped their Peugeot on the side of a deserted road to help a group of men changing a tire. It was an ambush, arranged by the French Fascist group *La Cagoule*, named for the Ku Klux Klan-style hoods worn by its members. Nello was stabbed to death, and Carlo shot down when he tried to come to his brother's aid. Salvemini accused Il Duce's son-in-law, Ciano, of ordering the French *cagoulards* to carry out the hit, almost certainly with Mussolini's knowledge. The murder, so reminiscent of the roadside butchering of Matteotti in 1924, sent a chilling message to the surviving anti-Fascists of *Giustizia e Libertà*: nobody was safe from the long tentacles of Bocchini's OVRA.

At the Political Police headquarters in Rome, the Rossellis' dossiers were stamped in purple ink with the word "MORTO."

With Ruth's oversight, awareness of and esteem for Lauro's flight continued to grow. A French edition of *Icaro* was published, with a lyrical preface by the poet Romain Rolland. A beautiful edition of *The Story of My Death* was published in London, translated by Ruth herself, with the complete texts of the leaflets he'd dropped on Rome. Rebecca West, reviewing the book in *The Daily Telegraph*, praised Lauro's bravery, and recognized him as "a superbly gifted writer of polemics." The pacifist Unitarian minister John Haynes Holmes delivered a sermon at the Community Church of New York, subsequently published as "The Single Greatest Deed of Heroism in Our Time," comparing Lauro to George Mallory, who died trying to scale Everest, and Charles Lindbergh.

"Lauro de Bosis's attack on Rome was a voluntary action," pointed out Haynes. "He was not ordered, or conscripted to make this flight... this Italian poet moves into the ranks of the supreme heroes because, among other things, he was absolutely a free agent in what he did."

Owen Cathcart-Jones, the British aviator who gave Lauro some of his first flying lessons, concurred, writing in his memoirs: "Only pilots can realize the courage and determination of this very gallant gentleman who, with only a few hours' instruction in flying, took off and flew across two hundred miles of water on a pitch black night, without blind-flying apparatus, and successfully reached his objective." Don Sturzo, the former Popular Party who had encouraged Lauro with advice and funds from his London exile, wrote: "the memory of the young poet and hero is always present to my mind and heart, and the future Italy will never forget him."

Ruth had long agonized about the fate of Lauro's National Alliance co-conspirators. After six years' imprisonment, they were freed, probably in response to pressure from abroad. (Aldous Huxley and the poet Paul Valéry were among those who wrote to Mussolini demanding their release.)

"Renzo Rendi and Mario Vinciguerra have been released on parole," Ruth wrote to the novelist Stark Young. "Though closely watched and unable to get work, they are out of prison—which I suppose means heaven to them and their families. I feel a great weight off my heart." For years, Ruth had been sending money to Rendi's wife and twin sons, and supporting the widowed Vinciguerra's daughter Claudia, who kept a photo of Lauro over her bed. Solitary confinement had severely incapacitated Rendi, who would die fifteen years to the day after the National Alliance trial. An undaunted Vinciguerra continued active resistance, and was briefly jailed with his daughter during the Second World War for distributing anti-Fascist literature.

Ruth herself became the subject of OVRA surveillance. A 1935 letter she'd addressed to *Mia carissima cara madre* ("My dearest dear mother," Lauro's affectionate term for Lillian) was intercepted by Bocchini's police, who concluded that, since all the remaining de Bosis children were accounted for, it must have come from Lauro himself. Agents were dispatched to Ruth's performances while she was touring America; a telegram from Cleveland claimed she was "continuing her program, anti-Fascist in character, of holding our race up to ridicule." Though Ruth's performances had always been devoid of political content, a Ministry of the Interior bulletin alerted all consulates and embassies to "promptly signal her movements, and hinder, or at least limit, any initiatives of an anti-Fascist character." Most of all, by tailing Ruth, OVRA hoped to determine whether Lauro was still alive and still represented a threat to the regime.

Doubts about Lauro's fate hampered Ruth's ability to mourn. She learned to repress the thrill that arose when she heard the engine of a small airplane passing overhead. And gradually, she resigned herself to acting like his widow. The sixty-nine letters and telegrams Lauro sent to her—the passionate tributes to his "archangel" after their first meeting in Rome, the yearning messages dashed off from the desk of the hotel in Paris, the final imprecation to "be happy" and love again sent from Marseilles—were carefully collected into a green leather letter-case, to be kept as a record of the three-and-a-half years they had spent together.

Among Ruth's papers, only a single scrap of a letter addressed to her lover survives. "You have shown me such beauty," she wrote to Lauro, "as I did not know was possible. Such exalted, blazing purity and beauty and tenderness. You saved me and quickened my spirit to a new life...

"To me you have from the first been utterly perfect."

As he piloted *Pegasus* into the darkness north of Rome, Lauro must have known that if he was going to make it to the coast of the French territory of Corsica and so to freedom, fortune would have to be on his side. The Messerschmitt had burnt seven hours' worth of fuel, leaving just enough for one-and-a-half hours—two at the most—of flight time.

At take-off the plane, laden with National Alliance manifestos, was thirty per cent past its recommended load. By showering the little towns in the Roman *campagna* with the last of his leaflets, Lauro reduced the plane's weight, buying himself precious minutes in the air. But when he finally cleared the Italian mainland, he met a headwind, eighteen-kilometres-an-hour at ground level and probably more at altitude, which increased his fuel consumption. He'd set his compass mark on a west-northwest route, towards the east coast of Corsica. *Pegasus* had neither radar nor radio, and scattered clouds obscured both the stars that could serve as guides and the rare lighthouses and navigation beacons on the small islands below.

Should he reach the French coast, the magnesium flares installed on his wingtips would allow him to turn night into day, and scout out a farmer's field or a stretch of earth level enough to touch down on. Failing that, he would take his friend Carlo A Prato's advice and aim for the treetops. But first he had to clear the dark expanse of the Tyrrhenian Sea. He carried no life raft, and should he use the parachute strapped to his back, he might be tangled in the silk when he hit the water, as his brother Valente had been tangled in the struts of his seaplane when he'd drowned off of Sicily. It would be just as well to ditch the plane, clamber out of the cockpit, and try to swim for land.

Somewhere east of the Corsican coastline, *Pegasus* drank the last of her fuel. The German pilots had neglected to replace the 23 litres of gas that had been consumed when they'd flown the plane from Cannes to the airfield outside Marseilles. Filling the tanks to capacity might have bought the Messerschmitt an additional hour's flying time, certainly enough for Lauro to reach land and safety. At some point, the engine stalled, and the plane went into a glide, slowly losing altitude until it splashed down on the softly swelling sea.

Pegasus, like the hobby horse Lauro clutched between his knees as a child, was made of wood. It was a calm night, so, for a few minutes at least, the plane would have floated on the surface, rocked by small waves. Lauro would have had time to shed his parachute and goggles, and crawl out on one of the cream-coloured wings.

Looking up into the "solid darkness black," and towards the "dim low line before / Of a dark and distant shore," Lauro surely would have recalled that before him, the vessel of another young poet had foundered in these very waters. And, before the weight of the plane's engine dragged it to the bottom, he might have whispered to himself words from Shelley's "Lines Written Among the Euganean Hills":

Men must reap the things they sow,
Force from force must ever flow,
Or worse; but 'tis a bitter woe
That love or reason cannot change
The despot's rage, the slave's revenge.

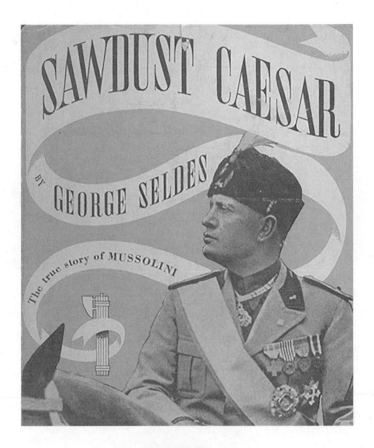

PART V

"A nationalist will say that 'it can't happen here,'
which is the first step towards disaster. A patriot says
that it could happen here, but that we will stop it."
–Timothy Snyder, *On Tyranny*.

23 THE HELL IT CAN'T

By 1935, much of the world was finally seeing what had become clear to Lauro de Bosis a decade earlier. The brutal invasion of Ethiopia had provoked international revulsion, and Mussolini's embrace of Hitler was starting to raise eyebrows. Since the March on Rome, foreign correspondents, Liberals, and people of conscience had been sounding the alarm about the violence and repression that was the essence of Italian Fascism. Yet it was only after over a decade of dictatorship that some of them were being heeded. The blank cheque handed to the regime, which had been credited with bringing American-style progress to the perennially undisciplined Italians, was about to be cancelled.

Mussolini, it turned out, wasn't the regular guy—the "right dictator"—that Will Rogers had praised in his syndicated column. One of the first signs that public opinion was turning came in a 1931 speech delivered by General Smedley Butler of the Marine Corps at a private luncheon in Philadelphia. Butler told the story of a friend who was invited to accompany Mussolini on a driving tour of the Italian countryside. Travelling at 110 kilometres an hour, Il Duce's car struck a child, "grinding it to death under the wheels." Butler's friend reported that Mussolini ordered his driver to keep going, shouting, "What is one life in the affairs of a State?"

Mussolini's travel companion, who was later revealed to be newspaper publisher Cornelius Vanderbilt IV, corroborated the story, adding that when he'd turned to "see a shapeless little form lying on the road behind us," he was told: "Never look back, my friend. Always forward." When the Italian government denied the story, President Hoover took the extraordinary step of ordering the first court-martial of a general since 1862. But the damage to Mussolini's reputation had been done. The graphic account of the slaughter of an innocent child, as Butler's biographer noted, "cast a shadow over the dictator's heretofore almost immaculate image."

Mussolini's reputation in the United States was about to receive another blow—in fact, a powerful one-two punch—from a pair of early eyewitnesses to the rise of Fascism. Ever since being chased out of Rome in 1925 for reporting on Mussolini's involvement in the murder of the Socialist deputy Giacomo Matteotti, the muckraking correspondent George Seldes had been plotting his revenge. Holed up in a Revolutionary-era house near South Woodstock, Vermont, Seldes spent years gathering testimony and documents that laid bare Mussolini's overinflated war record and his shift from Socialism to Fascism. When the manuscript was completed in 1932, it was rejected by editors in New York and London as being inflammatory and potentially libelous. Publication was only deemed propitious after the invasion of Ethiopia. The brilliantly titled *Sawdust Caesar*, one of the great hatchet-jobs of political biography, was finally published in 1936. The first major exposé of Mussolini by an American journalist, it portrayed him successively as a lonely, beaten child, a thief, a draft dodger, an intellectual poseur, and a political opportunist addicted to violence.

"Reactionary dictators are men of no philosophy," wrote Seldes, "no burning humanitarian ideal, nor even an economic programme of any value."

The book began with a prescient warning. "Fascism not only exists in America," claimed Seldes, "but it has become formidable and needs only a Duce, a Fuerher, an organizer, and a loosening of the purse strings of those who gain materially by its victory, to become the most powerful force threatening the Republic."

Seldes's words were given extra weight by the revelation of an alleged conspiracy to install a Fascist dictatorship in the United States. In 1934, the same General Butler who had dared to insult Mussolini astonished America by revealing that he had been approached by a representative of leading corporations— among them the same House of Morgan responsible for bankrolling Italian Fascism—to lead half a million First World War veterans on Washington to overthrow then-President Roosevelt. The new regime, Smedley reported, was to be led by Hugh S. Johnson. As head of the National Recovery Agency, the hard-drinking businessman distributed copies of a book on Italy's corporative state by a leading Fascist economist and invoked the "shining name" of Mussolini in speeches. The "Business Plot," as the press labelled it, was strenuously denied by its alleged perpetrators—among them Morgan's Thomas Lamont—who dismissed it as "perfect moonshine." The congressional committee charged with investigating the plot, by contrast, concluded there was "definite proof" that an American-bred Fascist putsch was "actually contemplated."

As he was writing *Sawdust Caesar*, Seldes traded stories with his friend Sinclair Lewis, who had loaned him the money to buy his house in Vermont, and owned a property in nearby Barnard. Travelling in Italy 1921, Lewis had been delayed by a strike in Florence, where he'd watched Fascist thugs beating up workers in the street. "The so-called Communisti are workmen," Lewis wrote to his father at the time, "union men, very few of whom are really Socialists at all; and the Fascisti are a kind of American Legion, but much more violent." In Rome, where he'd been introduced to *fettuccine al burro* at Alfredo's restaurant by Lilian and Edgar Mowrer, Lewis was regaled with first-hand reports from the Chicago *Daily News* correspondent about the Fascists' punitive raids on Socialists in the countryside.

Soon after, when the Mowrers were transferred to Germany, they shared an apartment with Lewis's wife Dorothy Thompson, then a reporter for Philadelphia's *Public Ledger*. The globe-trotting Thompson was a spirited critic of dictators, and her analysis of Europe's embrace of strongmen echoed, in plain-spoken prose, the philosopher Gaetano Salvemini's scholarly definition of Fascism as the voluntary abandonment of free institutions.

"In country after country," Thompson warned her readers, "under one slogan or another, the people are retreating from freedom, and voluntarily relinquishing liberty to force and authority, with instructions to bring order into men's affairs." For daring to belittle Hitler and draw attention to the persecution of Jews, Thompson became the first foreign journalist to be run out of Nazi Germany—an expulsion that made her famous and cemented her reputation as the nineteen-thirties' "First Lady of Journalism."

Mowrer would also incur the ire of the Nazis. While many North American newspapers—particularly the 28 owned by William Randolph Hearst, who was a guest at the 1934 Nazi party rally at Nuremberg—lavished praise on Hitler for bringing progress and defeating the Communists, Mowrer published the best-selling book *Germany Sets the Clock Back*. He also infuriated Hitler by reporting graphic accounts of anti-Semitic violence, gathered at covert appointments with his doctor, who happened to be the son of the grand rabbi of Berlin. After Storm Troopers gathered outside Mowrer's office, threatening violence, he bowed to encouragement from the American embassy to accept a posting in Japan. The Nazi official who accompanied him to Zoo Station to make sure he got on his train asked: "And when are you coming back to Germany, Herr Mowrer?"

Mowrer turned and said, before fellow correspondents who had come to witness his expulsion: "Why, when I can come back with about two million of my countrymen."

Familiarized with Fascist tactics through the Mowrers and Thompson, as well as his own experiences in Italy, Lewis spent long evenings in Vermont with Seldes, who shared all that he'd seen as a correspondent and learned in the research of *Sawdust Caesar*. "I had to relate every meeting with Mussolini," Seldes would later recall, "every glimpse of him, every day I could remember of the year and more [I lived] in Rome under Fascism. He pumped day and night, lunch and dinner, cocktail hour and auto trips." In the summer of 1935, Lewis sequestered himself at Twin Farms and set to work on a novel, completing the manuscript in two months of twelve-hour days.

The result was *It Can't Happen Here*, the second major literary assault on Fascism's reputation in America. Told through the eyes of Doremus Jessup, the Liberal editor of the *Daily Informer* in the fictional town of Fort Beulah, Vermont, the novel begins in a recognizable America, where Roosevelt is president and 28 million people are out of work. Jessup watches with concern as Senator Buzz Windrip, a plain-speaking populist who resembles Huey "Kingfish" Long, the recently assassinated governor of Louisiana, beats out Roosevelt for the Democratic nomination by promising a minimum income of $5,000 a year while railing against unions, Jewish bankers, and the Liberal press.

Jessup is at first perplexed that "there could be a dictator seemingly so different from the fervent Hitlers and gesticulating Fascists and the Caesars with laurels round bald domes; a dictator with something of the earthy American sense of humor of a Mark Twain, a George Ade, a Will Rogers." He is then chilled as local layabouts and thugs don the white shirts of Windrip's version of Italy's Fascist militia, the Minute Men, and take over his town. Windrip, who professes to admire both the Founding Fathers and Mussolini, is endorsed on the radio by Reverend Prang, modelled on the Hamilton, Ontario-born Father Coughlin, who in his popular broadcasts from Detroit denounced bankers and Jews and celebrated Nazis and Fascists. Backed by Prang's "League of Forgotten Men," unemployed veterans who resemble the demobilized *squadristi* of Fascist Italy, Windrip easily wins the presidency. He sets up a "Corpo State," modelled on Mussolini's corporative state, in which unions are banned and the unemployed are rounded up and put to work in $1-a-day labour camps.

Jessup joins the New Underground, led by Republican Senator Trowbridge, and—like Lauro—turns his talent to writing anti-regime newsletters, which he slips into copies of *Reader's Digest* in drugstores. When Trowbridge escapes by plane to the Fort Garry Hotel in Winnipeg, Jessup drives to Montreal, headquarters of the resistance, whose squabbling exiles recalls the anti-Fascist community in Paris. ("It is commonly asserted," Jessup muses, "that without complete political independence the United States would not have developed its own peculiar virtues. Yet it was not apparent to him that America was any more individual than Canada or Australia; that Pittsburgh and Kansas City were to be preferred before Montreal and Melbourne, Sydney and Vancouver.") As the book ends—with Windrip deposed by one of his lieutenants, who is in turn ousted by rebellious generals—Jessup returns to the United States, where, pursued by posses of white-shirted Minute Men, he works to rid the last pockets of the Corpo-occupied Midwest of the dictatorship.

As satire, the hastily written *It Can't Happen Here* was heavy-handed, but its vision of the form a right-wing dictatorship could take in the United States—particularly in the wake of General Butler's revelation of the "Business Plot"—hit the mark. Early in the book, one of Jessup's friends scoffs at the idea that a Fascist dictatorship could take root on native soil. "'That couldn't happen here in America, not possibly! We're a country of freemen.'" Jessup responds: "The answer to that... is 'the hell it can't!'"

It Can't Happen Here was published on October 21, 1935, just as front pages around the world filled with headlines about Italy's aerial bombing of Ethiopian villagers. Lewis's reputation—he had become the first American to win the Nobel Prize for Literature five years earlier—ensured it was widely reviewed. In the *New Yorker*, Clifton Fadiman called it "one of the most important books ever produced in this country," and declared that reading it was "a public duty." It would eventually become Lewis's best-selling book, with 320,000 copies sold. A movie version, with Lionel Barrymore playing the role of Jessup, was planned but never filmed. (Lewis would claim the Hays Office, newly formed to enforce a moral production code on the movie industry, had banned the film to avoid offending Hitler and Mussolini.) The Federal Theater Project's stage version of the book, which included Yiddish and Spanish versions, was attended by over a hundred thousand people in eighteen cities.

When Lewis learned that Nazis had started burning the book in Berlin, he instructed his German publisher to address him as "Sinclair Levy."

By 1935, the Bagnanis were forced to face the obvious: they had no future in Mussolini's Italy.

For five years, Gilbert's strategy of pursuing his archaeological career outside of Italy seemed to work. The excavation of the town of Tebtunis had proved wildly successful. Stewart arrived in 1932, and a "dig house" made of mud bricks was erected so the couple could live in relative comfort. Gilbert oversaw a team of up to 160 workers—among them a resourceful native boy known as "Mohammed the Cat"—and an industrial railway was built to remove the sand from the site. A processional way was uncovered, revealing two colossal limestone lions, still on their pedestals. An entire church, frescoed with Coptic inscriptions, was also unearthed. Gilbert, who feared that clandestine diggers had already plundered the site, was overjoyed when the sand was removed from the cellar of a building that served as a public records office. The floor was a solid mass of papyri, which collectively provided a priceless record of life in second-century Tebtunis. After celebrating the find with a bottle of Champagne, they set to work unrolling the documents, some of which were three-metres long, and preserving them by attaching them to gummed transparent paper.

"At this work," wrote Gilbert, "which requires infinite patience, very delicate fingers and excellent eyesight, my wife far outshone... myself and to her is due of the merit of preserving these magnificent documents."

Some of the most important papyri were discovered in a vast cemetery of elaborately mummified crocodiles. Tebtunis had served as the sanctuary of the crocodile god Souchos. A live crocodile was kept in the temple, which the priests fed with grain, scraps of meat, and wine. Pilgrims were encouraged to make an offering by buying live crocodiles, which were slain and buried in family groups. The priests used discarded documents in the mummification process, and the Bagnanis spent long hours unwrapping the mummies to recover the papyri.

"Not to put too fine a point on it," wrote Gilbert, "they stank to high heaven. We started to do the job in the courtyard, but after a few days of it my wife struck and insisted the examination and disembowelling of crocodiles should take place on the dig, a mile or so away. Even then, with a high wind..."

But even in the Egyptian desert, the Bagnanis couldn't escape Italian politics. In 1933, they learned that Victor Emmanuel III and his wife had expressed a desire to visit the site. The king was keen on archaeology, and had often personally contributed funds to support digs. A new road had to be built to welcome the royal visitors and their entourage. On the way to the dig, disaster struck: a driver in the caravan, after accelerating to one hundred kilometres per hour so one of his royal passengers could shoot a gazelle from the window, flipped his truck, killing a soldier. Though Gilbert fretted about the crash, the king seemed to take it in stride, and after a lunch was treated to a demonstration of the unwrapping of one of the pungent sacred crocodiles.

But papyri, Coptic churches, and mummified reptiles were not what the Fascists had in mind when they made money available for the dig in Tebtunis. They wanted evidence of Roman influence, not of the vigour of Egyptian civilization. At best, Oriental relics were fit to be plundered. After the invasion of Ethiopia, the Fascists looted the Obelisk of Axum and the Lion of Judah, transporting them to Rome for display. Gilbert was annoyed when Fascist bureaucrats ordered him to stop his work, and immediately drive to Dandarah, five hundred kilometres to the south, where he was instructed to make a cast of one of the walls of the Temple of Hathor. A replica of the enormous relief sculpture depicting Cleopatra and her first son, fathered by Julius Caesar, would be shown at the Mostra Augustea in Rome as proof of the Roman Empire's influence in Egypt.

Because of his lack of Fascist credentials, it was easy for ambitious colleagues to sideline Gilbert and his work. After working alongside Gilbert on his dig, a well-connected papyrologist from Milan, Achille Vogliano, published a paper on Tebtunis, claiming the discovery of the most significant cache of documents unearthed in Egypt in a generation as his own. Gilbert, officially only the "acting director" of the site, was powerless to object. It was becoming obvious that, if he hoped to gain recognition for the work he'd done in Tebtunis, he would have to take the oath of loyalty to the Fascists.

At the beginning of 1935, when he was on the verge of obtaining his *tessera*—the card that would prove his membership in the Fascist party—Gilbert learned of his mother's sudden death in Rome. That summer, the Bagnanis left Egypt and sailed for Canada to settle her estate. Shortly after they arrived, Stewart's mother also died after suffering a heart attack in Toronto.

Gilbert would return to Tebtunis the following year, but only for a month. Not only politics, but also economics, were conspiring to make his dreamt-of return to Rome impossible. The previous year, the Fascists had passed a decree that would allow them to seize the assets of wealthy expatriates. If the Bagnanis didn't move their residence from Italy, Gilbert would be forced to declare all his Canadian securities, and convert them to Italian lire on demand.

Making a life in Canada, which the Bagnanis had viewed as a last resort, now became their only option. For Stewart, it would mean a return to the land of her ancestors. For Gilbert—with his doubts about the extent to which civilization had penetrated into the "Wild and Woolly West" of Ontario—it meant expatriation and exile.

The Bagnanis' return to the American continent in 1936 coincided with a major shift in public attitude towards Fascist Italy. Together, Seldes's excoriating takedown of Mussolini and Lewis's chilling vision of a dystopic near future provoked a major shift in popular opinion, and made the familiar clichés about Fascism—how it made the trains run on time, and put a nation to work—ring hollow.

But for many British and American Conservatives, European Fascism continued to be a palatable alternative to the perceived dangers of Socialism. Two of the most influential sympathizers were also two of the most famous people on the planet, Anne and Charles Lindbergh. When Lindbergh made the first solo aerial crossing of the Atlantic in 1927, Lauro de Bosis had joined the crowd of one hundred thousand who gathered to greet him at Le Bourget airfield; the sight of *The Spirit of St. Louis* successfully touching down, after thirty-three hours in the air, almost certainly offered inspiration for his own solo flight over the Mediterranean. Since then, the couple's high-flying reputation had been darkened by the kidnapping and murder of their twenty-month-old son. Invited by Hermann Göring to inspect military air installations in 1936, the aviator found himself deeply impressed by the new Germany. To Lindbergh, the Third Reich's industrious workers were lovers of nature, good music, and hearty food, and seemed to be building a new society based on the racist principles he endorsed—especially the creation of a purer "Nordic" race through eugenics. Germany and Italy, Charles wrote to a friend, were "the two most virile nations in Europe."

The couple's flights around the world seemed to drive Lindbergh—already a staunch Nativist—deeper into his support of the isolationist America First movement. Their travels also convinced Anne Spencer Morrow of the merits of dictatorship. They had met through her father, Dwight Morrow, who was Lindbergh's financial adviser. (The pint-sized senator was a lover of Italian culture; at the House of Morgan, where he'd been a partner with his friend Thomas Lamont, Morrow helped underwrite both the American Academy and the Italian dictatorship). In *The Wave of the Future: A Confession of Faith*, Anne Lindbergh would argue that democracies that had failed to solve unemployment and poverty should make way for the new order promised by Nazism and Italian Fascism. In the same decade hundreds of thousands were reading *Sawdust Caesar* and *It Can't Happen Here*, Lindbergh's polemic shot to the top of the bestseller lists, and became a Book-of-the-Month Club selection.

The Lindberghs had old friends in Rome. In 1935, Lauro's colleague Chester Aldrich, the former president of the Italy

America Society in New York, was appointed the new director of the American Academy in Rome. As a bachelor in Paris in the twenties, Chester had given a twenty-year-old Anne Morrow, on her first European tour, a taste of Continental nightlife. Chester was also the architect who designed Highfields, the New Jersey home—since abandoned—from which the Lindberghs' son had been abducted. Amey Aldrich followed her brother Chester to Rome in the role of the Academy's official hostess, and unofficial assistant to the director. A long-time friend of the Morrow family, Amey was a gifted writer who maintained a spirited correspondence with Lindbergh's wife.

On August 28, 1936, Amey invited Anne to stay at the Villa Aurelia on the Janiculum Hill. "You, who have braved Nazi Germany, can no longer be reluctant about Fascist Italy!" she wrote on the back of a postcard. "You've evidently no scunner [strong dislike] for dictatorships—so no such excuse... no one is educated really who hasn't seen Rome."

The Aldriches got the good news after Christmas. The Lindberghs would be flying over the Alps in the new year, and were expected for tea at the American Academy in the first week of February.

24 BACK TO THE ACADEMY

There were times, in the early thirties, when things had looked bleak for the American Academy in Rome.

As the Depression bit deeper, study and travel stipends for fellows were drastically lowered, and many artists and sculptors opted to stay in the United States to find employment in federal works projects. The few that took up residence were aware that the Academy's perch on the Janiculum had become precarious. In 1933, Mussolini, dressed in top hat and spats, had strolled through the studios on a visit to mark Washington's Birthday, pausing to lavish praise on a sculpture by Robert J. McNight titled "Fascist Allegory." Though some fellows obligingly greeted him with stiff-armed Roman salutes, others suspected Il Duce resented the foreign academy's presence in his Third Rome, and might be sizing up the premises for later use by the regime. (The King, who made a near-annual trek to the Academy from the Quirinal Palace, would later observe: "I wish I could live up here. My place is so damp.") The Villa Aurelia had to be completely shuttered in 1934, and the entire Academy shut down for the summer session, the first time its doors had been closed since the First World War.

The arrival of a new director the following autumn brought new hope and energy to the institution. Chester Aldrich, a member of the Academy's board since 1924, was fluent in Italian, a music-lover, and a close friend of Bernard Berenson, the art-collector whose villa I Tatti was a kind of unofficial outpost of American culture in the hills outside Florence. With the firm Delano and Aldrich, Chester had designed residences for Rockefellers and Vanderbilts, and his familiarity with the Wall Street elite helped attract an influx of gifts and new grants to the cash-strapped Academy. Chester's directorship also conferred another significant advantage: the presence of his charming and spirited sister Amey, who, between her duties as official hostess, found the time to research works on the ancient Roman history of the Academy properties.

Liberal in outlook, the Aldriches were dismayed by the disappearance of Lauro de Bosis. When they arrived in Rome in October, 1935 to reopen the Academy—just as Italian troops were invading Ethiopia—Amey carried with her a package for Lauro's mother given to her by Ruth Draper. Lillian was driven to the Academy, where a framed portrait of Lauro, wrapped in a red-white-and-green ribbon, had been hung on a wall. Back at the family palazzo on the Via dei Due Macelli, Lillian opened the package and was for the first time able to read the letters that Lauro had been unable to send before his flight for fear they would be seized by Fascist censors. Since the trial, she'd fretted that her son believed she'd betrayed him for writing to Mussolini to beg clemency for the de Bosis family.

"I have just finished reading all the letters, after midnight, with silence—and no danger of interruption—all around me," Lillian wrote to Ruth. "They are the confirmation of all that my heart desires... now and for some time past I have left sorrow behind me and live in the presence of such unspeakable beauty and greatness... I feel that you too have come to the same triumph of life over death."

Her son's words heartened her. "I will alight at the mouth of the Rhone and renew my gasoline supply," Lauro had written, describing his planned flight path should he successfully reach Corsica after leaving Rome. "Then to Geneva where my angel is waiting for me. Oh why can't I find you also there to welcome me?... with the prestige of the flight over Rome I will return to America in triumph and will go on a lecture tour which you will hear about!" Her beloved "Fofo," in other words, had no intention of throwing his life away. Lauro's unsent letters also made it clear that he had—deeply and unreservedly—forgiven her.

For her part, Amey was anticipating another aviator's arrival in Rome. Her letters urging her childhood friend Anne Spencer Morrow to visit the American Academy had borne fruit. On the morning of February 2, 1937, a streamlined monoplane with orange wings, striped with black, landed in the Littorio airfield north of Rome. The M.12 Mohawk had been custom-built by the British engineer George Miles for Charles Lindbergh, who had asked for a twin-seater capable of making long flights. If Lauro's little Messerschmitt was a Volkswagen, the Mohawk was a Cadillac, with a 200-horsepower engine, almost three times as powerful as *Pegasus*'s, that gave the plane a top speed of 220 kilometres an hour. After taking delivery of the Mohawk at the Woodley Aerodrome in Berkshire on the first of February, the Lindberghs had crossed the English Channel and soared over France. Touching down the following evening in Rome, the Lindberghs were greeted by the crowd at the airfield with flowers and applause. Charles told reporters how they'd encountered a violent storm over the Alps, which had forced them to change course to avoid the thunderheads, before making a refuelling stop in Pisa. He professed his delight at being in this "marvellous country, whose ancient and modern history represents the height of civilization."

Then they were whisked away in a taxi to a hotel. Amey convinced them to stay with her at the Villa Aurelia. The hilltop haven provided a respite from the crowds that gathered wherever the famous couple stayed, and the week the Lindberghs enjoyed atop the Janiculum was idyllic. Spring-like weather allowed them to take their meals with the Aldriches on the villa's terrace while they looked out over the city's spires and domes. The couple visited St. Peter's and newly excavated ruins in the Forum, but Charles also pursued his own eccentric touring agenda. For several years, he'd been following the research of Dr. Alexis Carrel, a Rockefeller University surgeon who was notorious for his belief in telepathy and his preference for operating on patients while dressed in a monk-like black cowl. (Carrel also admired Mussolini, listing him with Caesar and Napoleon as one of "great leaders of nations grown beyond human stature.") Charles was intrigued by the surgeon's work on keeping human organs alive outside the body, and in Rome paid a long visit to the *Istituto di biotipologia umana*, where similar work was being carried out by one of Carrel's Italian colleagues. The regime's progress in "'human reclamation,'" noted the *Corriere della sera*, "was highly admired by foreigners."

Charles had worked with Carrel to develop the Lindbergh Perfusion Pump, a "mechanical heart" to keep organs alive outside the body. Though he had dropped out of college and had no formal training as a biologist, Charles longed to be considered more than just a showman famous for aeronautical exploits. Yet it was his political escapades that increasingly made headlines.

On February 8, the Lindberghs climbed into the cockpit of the Mohawk to continue their voyage. Amey, who watched with regret as the plane turned into a "speck in the sky," would write to Anne that "your visit was the nicest we've had or will have here." In the coming days and weeks, the *Corriere della sera* would publish front-page reports of the Lindberghs' landings in Tripoli, Cairo, and Bombay.

Later, though, Amey followed with alarm the controversy that followed the Lindberghs' public statements in support of European strongmen. Invited to witness displays of Nazi air power in Germany, Charles would accept the Order of the German Eagle from Hermann Göring. While Hitler and Mussolini annexed and invaded neighbouring territories, Charles would condemn Britain and France for their "stupidity" in resisting what he saw as the inevitable, and salutary, rise of Fascism.

Amey continued to send letters to her friend, hoping she'd once again be her guest in Rome. "We still hope you may come," she wrote a year after their visit, as the violence against Jews in Germany intensified. "But not full of Nazi praises—we couldn't bear that. Wonderful air force, if you like—but oh!—"

The Lindberghs never returned to the Academy. The couple's defiant embrace of order, discipline, and racial purity was already starting to look like a holdover from the twenties, when their glamour and fame were at their peak and Fascism still seemed a shiny novelty. As the world chose sides in the looming conflict, those Americans who supported isolationism in the face of dictatorship would themselves become isolated.

Amey knew which side she was on. She had chosen it by honouring a more selfless aviator than Lindbergh, and ensuring that—for a time, at least—the portrait of Lauro de Bosis occupied pride of place on the walls of the American Academy.

There was another American who never lost faith in Italian Fascism. Like Lindbergh, Ezra Pound made no apology for glorifying strongmen. For years, the poet had sought an audience with Mussolini, assiduously pursuing Nancy Cox McCormack and others for an introduction. His wish had finally been granted in 1933, when he was granted an audience in the Palazzo Venezia. After brushing aside the eighteen-point summary of abstruse economic theories Pound had brought with him, Mussolini pleasantly thanked his visitor for sending him a copy of his epic poem, *The Cantos*. He'd found it *divertente*—entertaining.

On the basis of this brief visit, Pound would claim to have gained mystic insight into Il Duce's mind. He had long argued Mussolini was the greatest leader in the modern world—the one sure bulwark against the demon of "Anglo-Jewish" capitalism— but now he ranked him with Thomas Jefferson and Confucius as a man of culture and discernment. Not only was Mussolini a born leader of men, he was also a creative genius.

"I don't believe any estimate of Mussolini will be valid unless it starts from his passion for construction," the awestruck Pound said after the meeting. "Treat him as *artifex* [a skilled workman] and all the details fall into place. Take him as anything save the artist and you will get muddled with the contradictions."

Mussolini, proud of building new towns on what had once been malarial swamps, would have concurred with Pound's assessment. "Architecture," he said, in one of his in-depth conversations with the Swiss journalist Emil Ludwig, "is the greatest of all the arts, for it is the epitome of all the others." When Ludwig observed his attitude was "extremely Roman," Mussolini—a son of provincial Predappio—replied: "I, likewise, am Roman above all."

From this perspective, Mussolini's most ambitious work of art was Rome itself. The culmination of his remodelling of Rome came with the anniversary of Caesar Augustus's birth in 1937. Yet the bimillenary's prestige project, the excavation of the emperor's tomb—where Mussolini himself hoped to be buried in glory one day—proved a disappointment. The mausoleum on the left bank of the Tiber turned out to be little more than a shallow cone, forty-four metres in diameter, which even reinforcing brickwork couldn't elevate into an awe-inspiring monument. (It resembled, in fact, a *dente cariato*, a rotten tooth, which is what Romans call it to this day.) Next to the mausoleum, Augustus's Altar of Peace, the *Ara*

Pacis, with its relief sculptures of Aeneas and the imperial family, had to be pieced together with reproductions of fragments held by museums in Florence and Paris. The final result was housed in a sterile edifice that looked more like a clinic than a shrine.

At least the bimillenary's official opening, in the same Palazzo delle Esposizioni where the Exhibition of Colonial Art was held during Lauro's flight over Rome, offered an opportunity for the kind of pomp the regime favoured. For the occasion, the building was clad in white marble topped with "DUX"—the Latin term at the origin of the title "Il Duce"—reiterated eightfold in huge letters. Its facade was carved with such inspirational slogans as "May the glories of the past be surpassed by the glories of the future!" Within, 21,000 plaster casts, models, and artifacts led visitors through the history of Rome, from legends of its founding by Aeneas, through the problematic Republican period, and finally to the glorious era of the Emperor Augustus, whose reign was portrayed as "one of the decisive turning-points for all of humanity." At the September 23 opening, as ranks of Fascist youth dressed in knee-pants sang hymns to the regime, Mussolini was presented with a live eagle, a symbol of the continuity between the ancient and modern empires.

The *Mostra Augustea della Romanità,* as it was officially called, leaned heavily on the research of foreign archaeologists who—whatever their original intentions had been—were now called upon to glorify Imperial Rome. The pioneering topographical work of Esther Van Deman of the American Academy and the late Thomas Ashby of the British School in the *campagna* was consulted for the painstaking reconstructions of the ancient aqueducts. The centrepiece of the exhibition was a vast 250:1 scale model of Rome in the fourth century, which featured a Coliseum the size of a bathtub. One of the most enthusiastic participants was Eugénie Sellers Strong, the British School's former assistant director, who in her scholarship had obligingly championed the merits of the painting of ancient Rome over the art of classical Greece. The regime's most powerful archaeologist, Boni's old protege Giulio Giglioli, invited Strong to introduce Mussolini at the inauguration of Augustus's Altar of Peace.

Turning to Il Duce, the doughty septuagenarian praised the Ara Pacis—and by implication the man responsible for its restoration—as "the outstanding monument that the emperor Augustus—that great pacifier who always preferred to celebrate a restored peace than the related victory—built as the perpetual reminder of a wise policy reawakened in our day under your auspices." For her collaboration, Strong was presented with the Gold Medal of the City of Rome.

By the time the Augustan Exhibition closed in November 1938, it had drawn a million viewers. Though judged a success by its organizers—the following year, select artifacts would be displayed at the Metropolitan Museum of Art in New York—attendance was in reality a quarter that of the earlier exhibition of the Fascist revolution in the same location.

Italians didn't need to visit an exhibition to realize the Augustan scale of Mussolini's ambitions. They were inscribed in the streets of Rome itself. New neighbourhoods—Parioli, Garbatella, Magliana, Ardeatina—had risen on what had until recently been fields. The Tiber River was now traversed by ten bridges, two more than in Classical times. Entirely new "cities" had been built within the city: the sprawling Foro Mussolini sports complex; the rationalist buildings of the Città Universitaria, now the main campus of Rome's Sapienza University; the new neighbourhood of EUR rising to the south of the city; and the sound stages and studios of Cinecittà, the Fascist version of Hollywood, on the old Via Torlonia. Most of the elegant Baroque parks and villas that had interspersed their greenery through the city, providing much of its charm, were gone. Sharp-edged post offices and pretentious ministry buildings, surrounded by barren concrete *piazze*, dotted the city.

Under Mussolini, Rome would spread southwards towards the sea, its population eventually reaching 1.4 million. Even the sewer grates, which bore the images of eagles and she-wolves, showed the imprint of Fascism. When American loans dried up, Mussolini continued to fund the rebuilding of Rome by raiding the health care and pension funds purported to be a cornerstone of his corporative state.

Two thousand years earlier, Augustus Caesar boasted of finding Rome a city of brick, and leaving it a city of marble. Mussolini would succeed in leaving Rome a city of "isolated" ruins and roads—roads that would end up choked with cars whose exhaust would blacken and degrade the monuments of antiquity.

They were the same roads that, as Italian Fascism engaged in its final, fatal embrace with Nazism, would prove so admirably engineered to speed the arrival of the city's next rulers.

It was still possible, in the final years of Fascism, to look down from the Janiculum and reflect that Rome, in spite of all the changes, remained the Eternal City. It was, of course, an illusion. The hill, which had once marked the western limits of the city, had merely been leapfrogged by urban development. Just out of sight of the Fontana dell'Acqua Paola, a grim complex of eight-storey *case popolari*, or housing estates, was being built to house three hundred working-class families, many of them relocated from the area razed to build the Via dell'Impero.

Nor would the serene Academy on the hill be spared from the next phase in Rome's history: war and occupation.

Amey, a keen observer of everyday life in Rome, recorded the changes in her letters, noting the increasing presence of Nazis with unease. "This week 500 Hitler boys were here," she wrote to her brother Richard, "hand picked blondes, all large and fine of physique who marched solemnly about with swastika flags... they were reviewed by the Duce, and [I] thought them remarkably fine looking, but I could not bring myself to salute the swastika."

Soon Amey would watch as the city was put into service to welcome Hitler on his second visit to Italy, and his first to Rome. On the evening of May 3, 1938, the Führer of Germany and Austria—the sovereign nation annexed by the Nazis two months earlier—arrived in Ostiense station on a train that had brought him through the Brenner Pass and down the spine of Italy. The station, built for the occasion, was elaborately decorated with eagles and swastikas. Hitler was welcomed with a military salute and a handshake by King Victor Emmanuel III, who, as the head of state, was required by protocol to greet foreign dignitaries before Mussolini, who was officially merely *il Capo del Governo*. The Führer's motorcade proceeded down the new Viale Adolfo Hitler, following a five-kilometre route to the king's palace. Waving to the crowds from the back of an open limousine, Hitler passed gilded fasces, huge pylons spouting flames, and the floodlit ruins of the Circus Maximus, the Coliseum, and the Forum. On the Via dell'Impero, the car slowed to allow closer inspection of the five maps showing the Roman empire from ancient to modern times. In the *piazze*, Fascist soldiers executed the newly introduced *passo romano*—which to foreign observers looked identical to the Nazi goose-step, but which Mussolini would always insist was a venerable march invented in Piemonte.

Hitler, a champion of classical art over "decadent" modernism, was impressed by what he saw. He visited the Pantheon and was taken to the ruins of the Forum by the rising young archaeologist Ranuccio Bianchi Bandinelli, whose German ancestry made him an ideal guide. At the Augustan Exhibition, he peered at scale models of aqueducts and amphitheatres, before being driven to the Foro Mussolini, where, before a crowd of 35,000, well-drilled marchers arranged themselves into a giant "M" and a swastika for his approval. Il Duce seemed to have turned Italy's glorious past into present power, betokening a fruitful collaboration between the two nations.

The people of Rome, whose instinctive antipathy to all things German dated to the days of the barbarian invasions, were less impressed. On the eve of the visit, Amey wrote to Anne Lindbergh: "Rome is all topsy-turvy (and in a blue funk) for the Führer's visit— such a Hollywood scenario as they have made of the streets with standards and fountains and swastikas. The poor man won't see our lovely old yellow Rome at all. It is being scrambled beyond recognition. We are all of one mind about the visit."

Eyewitnesses reported that the applause for Germany's chancellor at public appearances was short-lived and unenthusiastic. Many were disgusted by the money spent to erect a Potemkin Village for the leader of what, under the ancient empire, had been a race of Goths and Vandals. A new *pasquinato*—the age-old verse form that epitomized popular Roman disdain for authority—was on the lips of the residents of Trastevere:

Roma di travertine
Rifatta di cartone
Saluta l'imbianchino
La sua prossima padrone.

"Rome of travertine marble / Redone in cardboard / Salutes the house-painter / Its next boss."

With their habitual fatalism, the people of Rome anticipated the dire times to come. Two months after the Führer's visit, the regime published its "Manifesto of Racial Scientists," declaring that "the people of Italy are of Aryan origin," and "the Jews do not belong to the Italian race." Mussolini, who had until then looked askance at Hitler's anti-Semitic ranting, now assured an anthropologist that his family was, in fact, "Nordic." Nuremberg-style legislation introduced in November 1938 excluded Jews from the military, banking, education, and the party bureaucracy, and marriages with non-Jews were prohibited. Mussolini's long-time Jewish mistress Margherita Sarfatti was quietly spirited off to Portugal, and from there to exile in the United States.

After that, events moved quickly for Italy, with a logic of their own. When the Pact of Steel with Germany was signed with Germany in May, 1939, Mussolini warned that he'd need three years to prepare the country for war. But Hitler was working on a faster time frame. While Italians were building scale-models and model villages, Germans had been industriously preparing for total war. Italy remained on the sidelines as a "non-belligerent" when Germany invaded Poland, but when the invasion of Francé began in May 1940, Mussolini decided that the time was right to add his ill-prepared forces to the irresistible Blitzkrieg.

On June 10, the sixteenth anniversary of the murder of Matteotti, Mussolini appeared on the balcony of the Palazzo Venezia to declare war on France and England. True to form, he predicted that victory was preordained by Italy's history: "We will win because twenty years of Fascism has prepared us magnificently in spirit and in arms, because of our past glories and greatness, from Rome to the Risorgimento." (The applause greeting the speech was so muted that cheering from recent Olympic trials had to be dubbed into the Luce newsreels.) The next day, Allied aircraft bombed the northern cities of Genoa and Turin, emphasizing what Lauro de Bosis and Giovanni Bassanesi had already made manifest: Italy's capacity to defend its cities from aerial attack was virtually non-existent.

The nation's inability to prosecute a modern war soon became equally evident. Only the intervention of Germany prevented Italian forces from being driven into the Adriatic Sea after a botched invasion of Greece. When an advance into Egypt was repelled by a smaller British army, General Rommel's Afrika Korps had to be rushed to the battlefield. Italian troops joined the invasion of

Russia, where they served listlessly and sometimes mutinously on the front lines. When General Goebbels remarked that "we have the worst allies that could possibly be imagined," even Hitler had to agree that Italy had become a "laughing stock."

Those expatriates who remained in Rome began to plot their escape. "It is strange to be living here," Amey wrote to Anne Lindbergh, "and to face the uncertainty of the how and when of getting back... I suppose something of the cynicism of Romans gets into one here—after all, so much has happened and so many Romes have been swept away, and the sight of all that has been is so present still, that it doesn't seem to make so much more difference here who is elected as president next week."

Rome, which for so long had rung with the fall of pick-axes, suddenly fell silent. The demolitions of nineteenth-century apartment buildings ceased, as did work on the new suburban city of EUR, which would never host E42, the 1942 world's fair planned to coincide with the twentieth anniversary of the March on Rome. German tourists in ill-fitting suits and shoes of ersatz calf swarmed shops looking for silk stockings and dresses, but the pickings were slim. Customers still came to the famous *trattoria* where Sinclair Lewis had discovered fettuccine Alfredo, but the atmosphere wasn't the same. Instead of butter-slathered egg noodles, they were served a few hundred grams of grey spaghetti, and then only on presentation of a ration card. Alongside the signed photos of Gary Cooper and Mary Pickford, owner Alfredo had hung a portrait of the gluttonous Hermann Göring in a tight-fitting white uniform.

On the day after Christmas, 1940, Chester Aldrich died in a Roman hospital after an operation. Amey was forced to take over the directorship of the Academy, and began to prepare to close it down. Portuguese visas were found for the remaining fellows who would return via neutral Lisbon to the United States. The *New York Times* reported that William Tongue, an Academy student stranded in Italy without funds, was forced to don a white steward's uniform and serve tea to passengers on the *uss President Monroe* to earn his passage home.

"The monuments are sandbagged," reported Amey in a typewritten letter to Anne, "the guns are mounted on our gates, all foreigners, except from points north, have gone." In a pencilled postscript, she excused herself for not writing more: "the censor blacks out all political comments so this is an innocuous letter. One I just received had a whole page solid black so it looked as if the whole family had died." In June 1941, after putting the Academy buildings under the protection of the Swiss embassy, Amey finally left Italy on a New York-bound ship.

Four days after Pearl Harbor was attacked, Mussolini once again emerged onto his balcony, this time to join Germany in declaring war on the United States in support of their Axis partner, Japan. Il Duce, increasingly wracked by stomach pains, insomnia, and anxiety, and more than ever aware of the discrepancy between the bluster of his ambitions and the reality of Italy's inadequate armed forces, seemed to lack his usual vigour. The few Americans left in Rome reported that it was one of the shortest speeches of his career.

The Bagnanis tried to make the best of their departure from Italy, viewing it as a new start in a young country. They bought a century-old farmhouse on eighty hectares of land not far from Port Hope, where Gilbert's mother had been raised. They named it "Vogrie," after the Dewar family's ancestral estate in Scotland, and enlarged the Neoclassical brick building by adding a two-storey wing with a soaring ceiling, filling its shelves with Gilbert's library of rare volumes, which included a fifteenth-century copy of the *Nuremberg Chronicle*, one of the first books ever printed. Stewart slept in a sleigh bed that had once been owned by her ancestor, Bishop Strachan. Vogrie became a Baroque enclave in backwoods Ontario, a place where visitors were served vintage wine from immense Georgian decanters, and could enjoy a collection of paintings that ranged from the Rococo to Abstract Expressionism.

"It was a typical Canadian farmhouse," remarked a visitor England, "with Piranesi hanging up the stairs."

But even in Canada, the Bagnanis were not immunized from politics. With the coming of the Second World War, Gilbert's Italian nationality meant he was considered an "enemy alien," and he was barred from employment for the duration of the conflict.* Forbidden to travel without government permission, Gilbert turned Vogrie into a working dairy farm, raising a large herd of Hereford cattle and keeping graceful, long-haired Saluki dogs, the first of their breed in Canada.

Gilbert was finally given the academic position that had eluded him in Italy when he was invited by a colleague to teach in the classics department of the University of Toronto in 1945. Stewart became an administrator of the Art Gallery of Ontario, and taught art to prisoners at Kingston Penitentiary. Gilbert electrified generations of students with his erudite lectures, delivered in a charming lisp, on the "Gleeks and the Romans." For his work on Petronius, the author of the *Satyricon*, he was inducted into the Royal Society of Canada.

Though the Bagnanis would be able to return to Rome after the war, they never lived in Italy again. Nor would Gilbert to return to his Egyptological studies. It will likely take generations

---

* Lauro de Bosis's nephew, Arturo Vivante, suffered a similar fate. At the age of sixteen, he was interned near Liverpool and shipped to Canada along with two thousand prisoners of war. Ruth Draper secured his release after writing to Prime Minister Mackenzie King on his behalf. Vivante went on to study medicine at McGill University, before moving to the United States, where he became a noted author who contributed vivid stories to the *New Yorker* about his uncle Lauro and his grandmother, Lillian de Bosis.

for the papyri he discovered in Tebtunis, now scattered in collections around the world, to be translated and fully analyzed.

The Bagnanis never had children. After Stewart's death in 1996—Gilbert had died eleven years earlier, after helping set up the classics department at Trent University in Peterborough—Vogrie was sold, later to be demolished, and its contents put up for auction. Much of the extraordinary collection of books and art Gilbert had acquired in his travels was donated to the Art Gallery of Ontario.

Among the thousands of photos, diary entries, and letters in the Bagnani Archives at Trent University is an undated one-page poem, written by Gilbert while he was at Vogrie. He observes a neighbour working on his roof, notes the fall of his hammer, and gestures which seem like an act of defiance against a chill wind, borne over the waters of Lake Ontario, that portends the coming of the Canadian winter.

> Now is the worst: the wind barbed, the pigeons
> Nodding sagely to each other of what's to come,
> The western sky in fantastic ruins, the actor
> Dried in his speech, his gestures frozen in air.

Gilbert called the poem "Against the Cold." The words, with their hints of impotence and nostalgia, could have been written by a Stoical nobleman who, after failing to court favour with some despot in ancient Rome, was forced to endure exile far from the beloved city of his birth, on a distant and barbarian shore.

One mild and sunny day in December, 1945, three years after Italy's declaration of war on the United States, a bespectacled American officer, well into middle age, stepped out of the back seat of the open command car that pulled up outside a luxurious hotel near the upper end of the Via Veneto. Lieutenant-Colonel T.N. Wilder, staff officer at the Mediterranean Allied Armed Forces headquarters in Caserta, near Naples, would be billeted at the Albergo Maestoso, one of the luxurious hotels commandeered for high-ranking officers of the U.S. Air Force.

He recognized the address from his youthful explorations of Rome. It was the old Hotel Majestic, whose English name had been Italianized by the Fascists as part of their attempt to purge the nation of foreign influences. The last time he had arrived in Rome, two decades earlier, it had been on a slow, under-heated train from Naples. Already, in the short time it had taken to drive across Rome, he could see the city had changed. The arches of ancient aqueducts still paralleled the road they'd driven along through the *campagna*, but now modern apartment blocks rose from fields where he had once enjoyed long moonlit rambles. Within the city walls, the Coliseum and the Forum, shorn of the atmospheric mazes of alleyways that had made their discovery such a delight, stood starkly exposed. His driver followed new roads, as broad as Midwestern main streets, which, apart from American Jeeps and staff cars, were virtually empty of traffic. Wartime rationing and fuel shortages kept streetcars, buses, and private cars out of circulation. Rome, that paradise for walkers, had—temporarily at least—been restored to its former status as a city of pedestrians.

Thornton Wilder had a week's leave from his duties to renew his acquaintance with the city. It was time sorely needed. For the previous two years, his military service had kept him at work seven days a week, for up to twelve hours a day, and he was nearing exhaustion. He had been 45 when he sought, and gained, assignment to U.S. army. Other prominent figures had been refused—among them William Faulkner and Charles Lindbergh, whose air corps commission was revoked by President Roosevelt—so he was surprised when he was sworn into the Army Air

Corps as a captain in 1942. After weeks of training in Florida, Pennsylvania, and California, he had flown out of Maine for a posting at the Air Force headquarters in Constantine, Algeria.

The two-time Pulitzer Prize-winning author, whose works had been staged on Broadway and filmed by Hollywood, turned out to have a knack for strategic planning. Under the command of General Eisenhower in Algiers, he'd helped orchestrate the first act in the reconquest of Axis-occupied Europe. North Africa, wrested from Italian and German control, would become the launching point for Operation Avalanche, the combined British and American invasion of Sicily and mainland Italy. Wilder had been charged with helping to formulate the air plans for the Allied landings at Salerno and Taranto.

Following the progress of the war in Italy, he'd agonized about what would happen to Rome. A week after the Allies landed in Sicily, the first British and American planes had appeared in the skies over Rome, taunting the Fascists with leaflets that read: "Today we choose to drop pamphlets even though tomorrow we can choose to drop bombs." On July 19, 1943, waves of B-26 bombers, five hundred in all, targeted the marshalling yards southeast of the city. Flying in perfect formation at ten thousand feet, beyond the range of Italian aircraft-guns, they dropped one thousand tons of high explosives, all but destroying the fourth-century church of San Lorenzo, one of the city's seven sacred basilicas. The thickly populated district around the church was hit particularly hard, and other outlying districts would be targeted in the weeks that followed. In the Protestant Cemetery, the graves of Keats and Shelley were torn open by the bombs. In all, seven thousand Romans would die in the Allied bombings.

The virtually unopposed raid on San Lorenzo had made it clear to the world that Mussolini and his regime were finished. King Victor Emmanuel III, at whose pleasure Il Duce governed, had finally had enough. When Pope Pius XII visited San Lorenzo to distribute money to the survivors of the bombing, he was met with cheers and tears of gratitude. On the same day, the King was greeted with hisses, his Queen spat at. Six days later, the monarch, who had kept the loyalty of many in the police and the military, invited Mussolini to his villa. Il Duce's son-in-law, Count Ciano, and other members of the Fascist Grand Council had already voted to strip Mussolini of his powers, but he refused to accept their decision, and expected to receive the customary royal blessing. Instead, the King quietly informed him he would be replaced as *Capo del Governo* by a hoary veteran of the First World War, Marshal Badoglio. In the villa's courtyard, he was taken into custody by a squad of armed *carabinieri*, who whisked him off to imprisonment in a military hospital. (According to one eyewitness, when he saw the ambulance that was waiting for him, Il Duce pissed his rumpled blue suit.)

Though Fascism would survive for a time in Italy, its over twenty years of supremacy in Rome came to an end on that morning. Learning the news that evening, Romans, many in their pyjamas, left their homes to parade through the streets. The offices of the arch-Fascist newspaper *Il Tevere*, in whose pages Lauro de Bosis had been mocked as *"una carogna,"* were set ablaze—as so many Liberal and Socialist newspaper offices had been burnt by the *squadristi*—and the doors of the Regina Coeli prison, where Lauro's comrades Rendi and Vinciguerra had been tortured, were thrown open, the regime's political prisoners freed. As firemen pried metal fasces from the sides of buildings, portraits of Mussolini were thrown out of shops, schools, and offices, to be trampled underfoot on the cobblestones.

Though Marshal Badoglio announced an armistice with the Allies, the war was not yet over for Rome. As British and American forces, following their successful invasion of Sicily, fought their way up the peninsula, German columns marched up the Via dell'Impero, following the same route Hitler had taken on his

1938 visit. By that time, the King and his retinue had already abandoned his subjects to their fate, fleeing eastwards along the Via Tiburtina to the Adriatic Sea.

At the time, Wilder, who had been promoted to lieutenant-colonel and transferred to Caserta, two hundred kilometres to the southeast, dreaded what the Nazis would do to Rome. It was the city, after all, that had launched his literary career by providing the subject matter for his first novel, *The Cabala*. The Germans had declared that their erstwhile Axis partners were in fact a "gypsy people gone to rot," and would be forced to pay for their treachery. There were rumours of torture, reprisals against civilians, and atrocities in the Jewish ghetto on the left bank of the Tiber. (It was only after the war that full details of the round-up on October 16, 1943, would be revealed: over 1,200 Jews, most of them women and children, were sent by train to Auschwitz, where all but 196 died.)

Rome's official status as an "Open City," a demilitarized zone, spared it the bombing that reduced much of Berlin and other Axis strongholds to rubble. The beleaguered Nazis—who had in fact turned the centre of the city into a parking lot for their guns and tanks—began a disorderly withdrawal. During their retreat, the Germans revived the vandalism of the barbarian hordes by cutting several aqueducts, thus flooding the Pontine Marshes and undoing one of the regime's most persistent boasts: that Fascism had eliminated malaria from Italy. On June 4, 1944, Wilder, billeted in a tent in Caserta, learned that the main body of General Mark Clark's Fifth Army had entered Rome, and that Jeeps and American half-tracks were parked beneath Mussolini's balcony.

It was thus, in the first days of December, that Wilder found himself back in Rome, amazed that the city he had first discovered in his "wild wandering" as a visiting scholar at the American Academy was still intact. The ribbed Baroque domes, the listing Corinthian columns, the towering umbrella pines silhouetted against the bluest of skies—all were there, as he'd first seen them, seemingly untouched by war. Finding a gate unlocked next to the Cancellaria, the old papal palace on the Corso Vittorio Emanuele ii, he entered an elegant palazzo, whose greenery-filled courtyard, bracketed by tiers of wrought-iron latticework, looked like it hadn't been altered since the Renaissance. In the Palazzo Venezia, where Mussolini's offices had been, he found an exhibit of paintings hastily gathered from collections in Naples, Rome, and Florence. He took a nostalgic drive to the Janiculum Hill, and once again gazed out over the rooftops of Rome, enjoying the view that had excited his wonder as a young man. Leaving the Albergo Maestoso at night, he used a flashlight to illuminate his way in a city where no street lights shone, letting the beam dance over the facades of the Villa Medici and the Quirinal Palace. By day, he carried out errands, bringing money to an aged writer, and paying visits to some of the ladies with whom he'd enjoyed cakes and tea as a student.

But the city, traumatized by years of dictatorship and conflict, had lost its old insouciance. Ill-fed Romans walked around in threadbare coats and perforated shoes. On the Via Veneto, demobilized Italian soldiers begged him for money, and prostitutes offered him their time. On his last night of leave, he invited some Roman acquaintances for a slap-up meal at a black-market restaurant: an actress who had performed in the Italian premiere of *Our Town*, an English music-hall performer angling for a part, the son of the Austrian novelist Hermann Broch. But the laughter was forced and the frivolity as simulated as the coffee. After picking up the bill, Wilder walked out on the party early.

His thoughts were elsewhere. One of his most vivid memories of his student year in Rome was of the young poet who had invited him to read his plays in his studio in the Aurelian Walls, with whom he'd walked the ancient paving stones of the Via Appia Antica. At the time, he'd outlined the plot of a novel based on the life of Julius Caesar. Now, in his rambles through the city where he'd first met Lauro de Bosis, the idea came back to him.

As Wilder left Rome to return to his duties in Caserta, he was already mapping out a new version of the novel, one that would meld ancient and modern, in which the words of an idealistic poet would challenge and undermine the authority of an all-powerful dictator.

Mussolini hadn't finished with Rome, but Rome was finished with him.

After his arrest, he would never again see the city that had embodied all his provincial ambitions. After being arrested at the King's Roman villa, he was transferred to the heights of the Apennine mountains, a ski resort he bitterly referred to as "the highest prison in the world." Amidst the chaos of the Victor Emmanuel's flight from Rome, Hitler dispatched an ss glider team to the mountaintop to rescue his old friend. After being flown to Munich, Mussolini was restored by the Nazis to a semblance of power as the head of the *Repubblica Sociale Italiana*, known as Salò after the northern Italian town which, for nineteen months, the doomed German puppet state turned into its headquarters. Living with his family in the Villa Feltrinelli on the shores of Lake Garda, Mussolini was heard pathetically asking a Fascist henchman if he thought the people of Rome had already forgotten their Duce.

Though Romans had ceased to honour Mussolini with parades, hymns, and salutes, they would never be able to forget him. He had approved the slaughter of Africans with aerial bombs and poison gas, building—and by 1943, losing—what would prove to be one of history's most fleeting empires. By consenting to join in the total war of the Nazis, he bore responsibility for the deaths of 400,000 Italians. He had approved, belatedly but fatally, participation in the Holocaust, dispatching 7,500 Italian Jews to the concentration camps, only 610 of whom survived. Over twenty years, his Fascist dictatorship was responsible for sending—by conservative estimate—a million people to an early grave.

For those responsible for the regime, and for those who had embraced it, the end had either come, or was fast approaching. Gabriele d'Annunzio, who had conjured to life the bellicose aesthetic of Fascism from the trenches of the First World War, had died in 1938, overcome by a brain hemorrhage while sitting at a desk in his eccentric aerie overlooking Lake Garda. The gluttonous Arturo Bocchini, whose OVRA spies had trailed Lauro de Bosis and assassinated anti-Fascists in exile, had died of overeating in 1940 after a lavish feast in a Roman restaurant. (Thomas Lamont of the House of Morgan, who had secured the loans that underwrote the early years of the dictatorship, died in the same year, shortly after the Italy America Society was finally dissolved.) Filippo Marinetti, the Futurist who had fantasized about driving his car into the ruins of Rome, died of a heart attack while fleeing partisans in Salò. The unlucky Count Ciano would be dispatched by firing squad in 1944, along with four other Fascist *gerarchs*, for daring to vote to end his father-in-law's rule. Eugénie Sellers Strong, who had exulted as Mussolini promised to revive Augustus's empire and secure Italy from barbarism, succumbed to cancer in a clinic six days after the Nazis marched into Rome. Ezra Pound, who had begun broadcasting shortwave rants excoriating Roosevelt and "Anglo-Jewish" capitalism over Rome Radio before the attack on Pearl Harbor, was arrested for treason and imprisoned outdoors in a floodlit, two-by-two-metre cage at the Disciplinary Training Center outside Pisa, alongside some of the worst criminals in the American army. His jailors threw the poet, who was then nearly sixty, scraps of meat through the wires of his cage. Deemed unfit to stand trial in the United States, the poet who exalted Mussolini would spend a dozen years confined in a

Washington, D.C. psychiatric hospital.

Those who hadn't given up on liberty and democracy—those who had the courage *not* to change when the world around them did—found their faith rewarded. During the German occupation, Lillian de Bosis allowed the family's palazzo on Via dei Due Macelli to be used for clandestine meetings of the Central Committee of National Liberation, which brought together leading anti-Fascists to organize the resistance. A secret room was outfitted with supplies in a narrow passage, and a bomb was hidden in a potted geranium in the event the gathering was discovered. The meetings included men who would go on to plot the course of the post-war Italian Republic, among them future prime ministers Alcide de Gasperi and Ivanoe Bonomi. Against great odds, the institutions of a free society—and Italy had existed as a modern democracy for only four and a half decades before the March on Rome—had survived the dark years of dictatorship and war, to be kindled back to life by those who had never given up on them.

For those people, Lauro de Bosis would always be a hero, a light, and an inspiration. Though his National Alliance was derided by left-wing anti-Fascists for its support of the King, Lauro had made it clear to the confidants he most respected—La Piana, Sturzo, and most of all Salvemini, who would be able to return, in triumph, to his old history-teaching position in Florence in 1949—that his monarchism was strictly tactical. In a series of unpublished essays, he set out a vision of a post-war Italy as an independent republic, and imagined a future in which democracy, shorn of the corruption and colonialism that had discredited nineteenth-century Liberalism, would trump blood and race in a united Europe. In the end, his instincts proved well-founded: it was the King who would ultimately depose the dictator, before discrediting himself—along with the entire institution of the monarchy—by putting his own self-preservation before the fate of his people. And Liberal democracy, rather than Communism, Socialism, Fascism, or Anarchism, would prevail— albeit shakily, and never purged of corruption—in an Italy whose borders would eventually blur into a European Union.

Giorgio de Santillana, who more than anyone understood his childhood friend's convictions and complexities, tried to imagine how Lauro would be remembered by generations to come.

"His enemies have done all that was expected of them," de Santillana wrote, a dozen years after Lauro's disappearance. "His action was ridiculed, his sacrifice hushed up, even now Italians are sedulously kept under a vague impression that he is still alive somewhere...

"In the years to come, he shall come to life again, and then perhaps we shall not know him. He is, up to now, the only man who has given his life purely and simply for Italian freedom... I think that it is his deed, more than his words, that will inspire the youth of tomorrow. He will dissolve in the halo of legend. For among the many sides of his nature, there was that which the Latin mind cannot really assimilate: the unwavering devotion to an abstract principle, which is part of his Puritan ancestry."

In Lauro's sacrifice, de Santillana discerned the wit, wisdom, and self-devotion of such historic martyrs to an ideal as Sir Thomas More. It was a characteristic that put him at odds with the pragmatic malleability of many of his fellow Italians, who, as the English-born writer Iris Origo observed, "are prepared to yield in principle, where they can gain in practice." But, in the final gesture of this child of the Eternal City, there was also something distinctly Roman, a sense of civility that predated the nineteenth century, or even citizenship as it was understood under the ancient Empire.

For his friend, Lauro was "the flower of a line that goes back through the Renaissance and the Feudal Ages to the majesty of Rome... back still to the very dawn of our race: that quality which our Latin fathers had in mind when they coined that beautiful term, *vir liberalis et ingenuus."*

Lauro was indeed a *vir ingenuus*, a man both "free-born" and "noble-minded." But he was also a *vir liberalis*—a "liberal man." Not in the modern political definition, but in a sense intended by Cicero and Seneca, who contrasted it with the slavish obsession with private profits and pleasures.

When to be "liberal" was to be generous, devoted to the common good, and—above all—a lover of liberty.

Italy's dictator died trying to flee the country he had brought to ruin. On the morning of April 27, 1945, Mussolini was found by members of the 52nd Garibaldi brigade in the back of a truck bound for Switzerland, ignominiously disguised in the greatcoat of one of the retreating Nazis whose convoy he'd joined. The following day, he and the last of his mistresses, Claretta Petacci, were taken to a villa outside the hamlet of San Guilino di Mezzegra and executed by partisans. Their bullet-ridden bodies were driven to a piazza in Milan, where a large mob pummelled them with sticks and their bare hands.

At the height of his power, Mussolini had envisioned a glorious interment in an Eternal City purged of all foreign influence, and eternal rest in the newly restored Mausoleum of Augustus. Instead, his mutilated corpse was hoisted up on a meat hook, to be displayed for all to see, where it dangled upside from the girder of an unfinished Standard Oil gas station.

EPILOGUE

"If the main pillar of the system is living a lie, then it is not surprising that the fundamental threat to it is living in truth."
—Vaclav Havel

THE OBELISK

The American Academy, though long since overtaken by the city whose outskirts it once dominated, remains an oasis of serenity and scholarship on the Janiculum Hill.

The institution survived its first century of existence with difficulty. During the Second World War, it was kept running by its librarian Albert Van Buren (Fellow in Classical Studies and Archaeology, 1906), who escaped internment as an enemy alien thanks to a group of Italian scholars who served as his guarantor during the Nazi occupation. As the Allies were liberating the city, a former student, wearing the uniform of a lieutenant-colonel, found Van Buren in his office, absorbed in a volume of Latin inscriptions as Italians cheered the American tanks rolling past outside his window. ("The professor said hello to me and he was very nice," the student told a reporter. "But I think I made him lose his place.") After being reopened in 1947, the privately funded Academy suffered from periodic budgetary shortfalls, and by the late eighties had fallen into disrepair. Fellows recall having to stay warm by sleeping in their coats, cooking meals on a stove with only one burner, and carrying flashlights on nighttime visits to the communal bathrooms.

Since revitalized by donations, the Academy has benefited from a thorough renovation. In front of a studio once occupied by the novelist Ralph Ellison, rows of kale, cabbage, and broccoli are harvested from an organic kitchen garden first planted by the chef Alice Waters. In the Main Building, where a billiard table is overlooked by an excruciatingly detailed Chuck Close portrait, middle-aged waiters carry espressos to young classicists in chinos and button-down shirts. Don Delillo was a recent guest, joining a list of creators—Aaron Copland, Mary McCarthy, Joseph Brodsky, William Styron, Elizabeth Bowen, Anthony Doerr—who have, for a time, made the Academy their home in Rome.

The Academy's tranquil heart remains the reading rooms of the Arthur and Janet C. Ross library, where wrought-iron staircases spiral upwards to lofty mezzanines. Among the over hundred thousand volumes on the library's shelves is a novel by a former student, a visiting scholar in Classical Studies, 1921. Opening the title page of Thornton Wilder's *The Ides of March* reveals a dedication to:

LAURO DE BOSIS
Roman poet, who lost his life
marshaling a resistance against
the absolute power of Mussolini;
his aircraft pursued by those of the Duce
plunged into the Tyrrhenian Sea.

Wilder was misinformed about Lauro's fate. No evidence ever emerged that *Pegasus* was pursued by Italian planes. Ruth Draper was nonetheless delighted by the tribute from her lover's old friend. In the novel, written in the form of documents purported to have been rescued from antiquity, Lauro is discernible as the poet Catullus, who opposes Julius Caesar's growing power by organizing "The Broadsides of Conspiracy," chain letters like those the National Alliance directed against Mussolini. (In a preface, Wilder wrote that the idea had been suggested to Lauro by George Bernard Shaw; Ruth sent him a letter pointing out that this was not the case, and Shaw had long persisted in expressing his admiration for the dictator.) Wilder's Caesar is less recognizable as a surrogate Duce. Though portrayed as an aspirant dictator intent on ending the Roman Republic, he also grapples with his lack of faith in the old Roman gods. He is less ancient tyrant than doubt-ridden modern, a portrait in part based on Wilder's friendship with the French existentialist Jean-Paul Sartre.

On its publication in 1948, the book was ignored by the critics, who had long-since consigned Wilder to middlebrow status. But it sold well, and the author judged it his best novel. And *The Ides of March* served another purpose. Just a decade after Mussolini had mounted elaborate celebrations of the cult of Augustus, Wilder reclaimed the ancient Romans from the Fascist myth-making machine, portraying not caricatures of empire-builders in togas, but complex human beings riven by worldly passions and philosophical doubts.

There are two volumes missing from the Academy's library. In 1936, Ruth sent Amey Aldrich personally inscribed copies of her translations of *Icaro* and *The Story of My Death*, which she promised to place in the collections. They are no longer on the shelves, and there is no record of the name "Lauro de Bosis"—the Italian-American poet whose portrait once hung on the Academy's walls—anywhere in the catalogue.

To find a memorial to Lauro in the city of his birth, you must turn left out of the main gate of the Academy, and stroll for a few minutes down the tree-shaded Passeggiata del Gianicolo. The promenade at the top of the Janiculum, lined with statues of those who fought to unify the nation in the nineteenth century, has been turned into an open-air shrine to the heroes of the Italian Risorgimento. Just past a piazza dominated by an impressive statue of Garibaldi—the anti-clerical general is mounted on a horse whose backside is directed at the Vatican—a bust of Lauro de Bosis, a larger version of Nancy Cox McCormack's 1922 bronze, is poised on a white plinth. Unlike the Risorgimento patriots around him, most of whom are portrayed with long beards, Lauro's bust wears only a wispy moustache. His head is turned away from the panorama of Rome's rooftops, the heart of a metropolis whose population now exceeds three million. Instead, his intelligent, inquisitive gaze is directed towards the west, as though he is scanning the sky for another dot to appear from over the Tyrrhenian Sea.

Or perhaps expecting an ambush. A dark line circles Lauro's neck, as though he has been garroted. The bust was dedicated in 1954, the year that also marked the last time Ruth Draper performed her monologues. Two years earlier, Lillian de Bosis had died in Rome at the age of 87. Two years later, Ruth would die in her sleep, at the age of 72. Her ashes were scattered over the sea, to mingle with Lauro's remains in their final resting place. In the years that followed, Lauro's statue on the Janiculum has frequently been the target of vandalism by Fascists and neo-Fascists. The latest damage suggests a complete decapitation, followed by a hasty and incomplete repair.

The legacy of Fascism remains contested in Italy, a fact that continuing a stroll in its erstwhile capital makes clear. While Berlin rapidly purged itself of the symbols of Nazism, traces of twenty years of Fascist rule are to be found all over Rome. East of Termini Station, multiple helmeted heads of Il Duce glower over Roman eagles on the facade of the Senior Judicial Advisory Office, just across the street from the German embassy. Four of the Fascist-erected marble maps showing the spread of Italian

power in the Mediterranean still stand on the Via dei Fori Impe-
riali, as the Via dell'Impero is now known (the fifth, showing
Mussolini's short-lived African empire, was vandalized during the
war and removed). In the Sala della Mappamondo of the Palazzo
Venezia, tourists from around Italy line up to take selfies giving
straight-armed salutes from Mussolini's famous balcony. In EUR,
the most Fascist district of them all, the Museo della Civiltà
Romana houses the centrepiece of Mussolini's 1937 celebration
of Romanità and Augustan imperialism, the vast scale-model of
Imperial Rome. A sculptured relief on one of EUR's government
buildings portrays Il Duce, helmeted and on horseback, as the
culmination of Roman civilization. His face, which was chiselled
off after the war, has recently been restored.

The politicians who lived through the dictatorship tried to
make it impossible for Fascism to ever take root in Italy again. A
1946 referendum ended the monarchy that had enabled Mussolini's rise to power, and the constitution of the new Italian Republic
made the Fascist Party illegal. Decades of rule by centrist Christian
Democrats, during which Communists and leftist intellectuals
exerted a strong influence on the nation's cultural life, meant that
anything that smacked of Fascism was subject to ritual denunciation. Yet in Rome, the material remains of the regime are
everywhere. And a society that tolerates and accommodates the
symbols of a shameful past risks seeing the memory of violence
and repression—and all the sacrifices required to end them—forgotten. Mussolini's cadaver now occupies an honoured place in a
crypt in his birthplace of Predappio, where visitors can file by an
eternal flame and an altar inscribed with a giant letter "M." In cities
throughout Italy, the media-savvy neo-Fascist group CasaPound—
named after Ezra Pound—terrorizes the Roma population and
stages stunts like planting hills with pine trees that spell out the
word "DUX." (Its leader has d'Annunzio's slogan *Me ne frego*—"I
don't give a damn" tattooed on the back of his neck.) In spite of

the constitutional ban, a neo-Fascist party has been a presence in Italian politics since the nineteen-fifties, first as the Movimento Sociale Italiano (with its suggestive initials "MSI"), then as the Alleanza Nazionale, which enjoyed a long power-sharing coalition with Silvio Berlusconi. The party's leaders forgot—if they ever knew—that "National Alliance" was also the name of an anti-Fascist group whose propaganda campaign maddened Mussolini and his chief of police at the height of the dictatorship.

Reassuringly, the contemporary map of the city is dotted with the names of Second World War partisans and heroes of the resistance. Rome's first Fascist-built bridge, the Littorio, is now the Ponte Giacomo Matteotti, in honour of the Socialist deputy who was kidnapped and stabbed to death on the nearby banks of the Tiber. The park across from Ostiense Station, built to welcome Hitler, is now the Parco della Resistenza 8 Settembre, commemorating a doomed 1943 battle to drive the advancing Nazis out of Rome. And, on a bend in the river south of the ancient Ponte Milvio, a square at the foot of Monte Mario bears the name "Lauro de Bosis."

The piazza is bordered to the east by a busy riverfront drive alive night and day with the buzz of Vespas. To the west, it provides an entrance to the Foro Italico, the vast sporting complex formerly known as the Foro Mussolini. Originally built for choreographed displays of Fascist athletics, it is now home to a stadium that hosts raucous matches between the arch-rival soccer teams, Roma and Lazio. The Foro's expanses of concrete are now favoured by skateboarders, whose polyurethane wheels roll over mosaic tiles that reiterate Fascist slogans: MOLTI NEMICI MOLTO ONORE ("Many Enemies Much Honour"); NECESSARIO VINCERE PIV NECESSARIO COMBATTERE ("You Must Win But Above All You Must Fight").

It is easy for a stroller to miss the square's name, which is written in lower-case letters on a standard municipal street sign. One's attention is instead monopolized by the monumental structure, as tall as a six-storey building, at the centre of the piazza. It is a stylized version of an Egyptian obelisk—a modernist take on the ones the Roman emperors and Fascist colonizers stole from Africa—carved from three hundred tons of Carrara marble, terminating in a four-sided pyramid. During the Allied occupation, when the Foro was turned into a U.S. Army Rest Center, Italian partisans tried to topple the monument, but their efforts were blocked by American forces.

The obelisk's shaft, which thrusts upwards from the "piazza l. de bosis" into the sky of Rome, is inscribed in block capitals with the words:

"MUSSOLINI DUX."

It is true that Il Duce succeeded in staking his claim to the ground of Rome. The city as we see it today was largely rebuilt in his image. But mastery of the sky, and with it the irreverent and indomitable spirit of the people of Rome, always eluded him.

For all his bluster, Mussolini was never able to possess the air.

FURTHER READING

PRIMARY SOURCES

Baedeker, Karl. *Rome and Central Italy Handbook for Travellers*. Leipzig: Karl Baedeker, 1930.

Bagnani, Gilbert. *The Roman Campagna and Its Treasures*. New York: Charles Scribner's Sons, 1930.

Bagnani, Gilbert. *Rome and the Papacy: An Essay on the Relations Between Church and State*. London: Methuen & Co., 1929.

Cox McCormack, Nancy. "La Famiglia de Bosis and Other Memoirs," 1953, unpublished memoir in Lauro de Bosis Papers, Houghton Library, Harvard University, Cambridge, MA.

Deakin, Richard. Flora of the Colosseum of Rome. London: Groombridge and Sons, 1873.

De Bosis, Lauro. *The Golden Book of Italian Poetry*. London and New York: Oxford University Press, 1932.

De Bosis, Lauro. *Icaro*. London: Oxford University Press, 1933.

De Bosis, Lauro. *Storia della mia morte*. Florence: Passigli Editori, 2009.

De Bosis, Lillian Vernon. "Lilian [sic] Goes to Rome: A XIX Century Memoir," translated by Arturo Vivante, Lauro de Bosis Papers, Houghton Library, Harvard, Cambridge, MA.

De Santillana, Giorgio. Lauro de Bosis, unpublished, undated memoir, Lauro de Bosis Papers, Houghton Library, Harvard, Cambridge, MA.

Ezekiel, Moses-Jakob. *Memoirs from the Baths of Diocletian*. Detroit: Wayne State University Press, 1975.

Hare, Augustus J.C. *Walks in Rome: Volume 1 (14th edition)*. London: George Allen, 1897.

Hare, Augustus J.C. *Walks in Rome: Volume 2*. London: Smith, Elder & Co, 1871.

Lewis, Sinclair. *It Can't Happen Here*. New York: Signet, 2014.

Mowrer, Edgar Ansel. *Immortal Italy*. New York: D. Appleton and Company, 1922.

Mowrer, Edgar Ansel. *Triumph and Turmoil: A Personal History of Our Time*. London: Allen & Unwin, 1970.

Mowrer, Lilian T. *Journalist's Wife*. New York: William Morrow & Co., 1937.
Mussolini, Benito. *My Diary, 1915–1917*. Whitefish: Kessinger Publishing, 2004.
Mussolini, Benito. *Opera Omnia*, 44 vols. Florence: La Fenice, 1951.
Origo, Iris. *A Chill in the Air: An Italian War Diary, 1939–40*. New York: New York Review Books, 2017.
Ovid. *Metamorphoses v–viii*. (translated by D.E. Hill). Warminster: Aris & Phillips, 1992.
Prezzolini, Giuseppe. *L'Italiano inutile*. Milan: Rusconi, 1983.
Salvemini, Gaetano. *Scritti sul fascismo, volume II*. Milan: Feltrinelli Editore, 1966.
Salvemini, Gaetano. *Under the Axe of Fascism*. London: Victor Gollancz, 1936.
Scrivener, Jane. *Inside Rome with the Nazis*. New York: Macmillan, 1945.
Seldes, George. *Sawdust Caesar: The Untold History of Mussolini and Fascism*. New York: AMS Press, 1978.
Seldes, George. *Witness to the Century: Encounters with the Noted, the Notorious, and the Three SOBs*. New York: Ballantine, 2011.
Seldes, George. *You Can't Print That! The Truth Behind the News 1918–1928*. New York: Payson & Clarke, 1929.
Shelley, Percy Bysshe. Poems of Percy Bysshe Shelley. Hoboken: Bibliobytes, 199–?.
Warren, Neilla, ed. *The Letters of Ruth Draper: A Self-Portrait of a Great Actress*. London, Hamish Hamilton, 1979.
Wilder, Thorton. *The Cabala*. New York: Carroll & Graf, 1987.
Wilder, Thornton. *The Ides of March*. Cutchoge, N.Y.: Buccaneer, 1976.

SECONDARY SOURCES

Aicher, Peter J. *Guide to the Aqueducts of Rome*. Wauconda: [S.I.], 1995.
Amfitheatrof, Erik. *The Enchanted Ground: Americans in Italy, 1760–1980*. Boston: Little, Brown and Company, 1980.
Arendt, Hannah. *The Origins of Totalitarianism*. London: Penguin, 2017.
Arthurs, Joshua. *Excavating Modernity: The Roman Past in Fascist Italy*. Ithaca: Cornell University Press, 2016.
Barzini, Luigi. *The Italians*. New York: Touchstone, 1996.
Barzini, Luigi. *O America, When You and I Were Young*. New York: Harper & Row, 1985.
Baxa, Paul. *Roads and Ruins: The Symbolic Landscape of Fascist Rome*. Toronto: University of Toronto Press, 2010.
Beard, Mary. *SPQR: A History of Ancient Rome*. New York: W.W. Norton, 2015.
Bonsaver, Guido. *Censorship and Literature in Fascist Italy*. Toronto: University of Toronto Press, 2007.
Bosworth, R.J.B. *Mussolini*. New York: Oxford University Press, 2002.
Bosworth, R.J.B. *Mussolini's Italy: Life Under the Fascist Dictatorship*. New York: Penguin, 2006.
Bosworth, R.J.B. *Whispering City: Rome and Its Histories*. New Haven: Yale University Press, 2011.
Bowen, Elizabeth. *A Time in Rome*. New York: Penguin, 1960.
Brooks, Van Wyck. *The Dream of Arcade: American Writers and Artists in Italy 1760–1915*. New York: E.P. Dutton, 1958.
Bryer, Jackson R. *Conversations with Thornton Wilder*. Jackson: University Press of Mississippi, 1992.
Cameron, Garth. *Umberto Nobile and the Arctic Search for the Airship Italia. UK: Fonthill, 2017.
Cathcart-Jones, Owen. *Aviation Memoirs*. London: Hutchinson, 1934.

Cederna, Antonio. *Mussloni urbanista. Lo sventramento di Roma negli anni del consenso.* Rome: Laterza, 1981.

Chernow, Ron. *The House of Morgan: An American Banking Dynasty and the Rise of Modern Finance.* New York: Grove, 2001.

Clark, Eleanor. *Rome and a Villa.* South Royalton: Steerforth Italia, 1992.

Cohen, Rachel. *Bernard Berenson: A Life in the Picture Trade.* New Haven: Yale University Press, 2013.

Cortese de Bosis, Alessandro, ed. *Storia della mia morte: il volo antifascista su Roma.* Rome: Mancosu editore, 2002.

D'Annunzio, Gabriele. *Il piacere.* Rome: Newton Compton, 1995.

Davidson, Jo. *Between Sittings: An Informal Autobiography.* New York: The Dial Press, 1951.

Delzell, Charles F. *Mussolini's Enemies; the Italian Anti-Fascist Resistance.* Princeton: Princeton University Press, 1961.

Diggins, John P. *Mussolini and the Fascism: The View from America.* Princeton: Princeton University Press.

Duggan, Christopher. *Fascist Voices: An Intimate History of Mussolini's Italy.* London: The Bodley Head, 2012.

Duggan, Christopher. *The Force of Destiny: A History of Italy Since 1796.* London: Penguin, 2008.

Dyson, Stephen L. *Eugénie Sellers Strong: Portrait of an Archaeologist.* London: Duckworth, 2004.

Dyson, Stephen L. *In Pursuit of Ancient Pasts: A History of Classical Archaeology in the Nineteenth and Twentieth Centuries.* New Haven: Yale University Press, 2006.

Ebner, Michael R. *Ordinary Violence in Mussolini's Italy.* Cambridge: Cambridge University Press, 2011.

Eco, Umberto. *Il fascismo eterno.* Milan: La Nave di Teseo, 2017.

Fawcett, Edmund. *Liberalism: The Life of an Idea.* Princeton: Princeton University Press, 2018.

Fucci, Franco. *Ali contro Mussolini: I raid aerei antifascisti degli anni trenta.* Milan: Mursia, 1978.

Geffcken, Katherine A. and Goldman, Norma W., eds. *The Janus View from the American Academy in Rome: Essays on the Janiculum.* New York: American Academy in Rome, 2007.

Gilmour, David. *The Pursuit of Italy: A History of a Land, Its Regions and their Peoples.* London: Penguin, 2011.

Gleason, Abbott. *Totalitarianism: The Inner History of the Cold War.* New York: Oxford University Press, 1995.

Goldstone, Richard Henry. *Thornton Wilder, an Intimate Portrait.* New York: Saturday Review Press, 1975.

Harrison, Gilbert A. *The Enthusiast: A Life of Thornton Wilder.* New Haven: Ticknor & Fields, 1983.

Hertog, Susan. *Anne Morrow Lindbergh: Her Life.* New York: Anchor, 2010.

Hibbert, Christopher. *Rome: The Biography of a City.* New York: W.W. Norton, 1985.

Hodges, Richard. *Visions of Rome: Thomas Ashby, Archaeologist.* London: British School at Rome, 2000.

Hooper, John. *The Italians.* New York: Viking, 2015.

Hughes, Robert. *Rome: A Cultural, Visual, and Personal History.* New York: Vintage, 2011.

Hughes-Hallett, Lucy. *The Pike: Gabriele d'Annunzio, Poet, Seducer and Preacher of War.* London: HarperCollins, 2013.

Hutchisson, James M. *The Rise of Sinclair Lewis 1920–1930*. University Park: Pennsylvania University Press, 1997.

Johnson, Bruce, ed. *Jazz and Totalitarianism*. New York: Routledge, 2017.

Kargon, Robert H. *Invented Edens: Techno-Cities of the Twentieth Century*. Cambridge, MA: The MIT Press, 2008.

Katz, Robert. *The Battle for Rome: the Germans, the Allies, the Partisans, and the Pope*. New York: Simon & Schuster, 2003.

Killinger, Charles. *Gaetano Salvemini: A Biography*. Westport: Praeger, 2002.

Kneale, Matthew. *Rome: A History in Seven Sackings*. New York: Simon & Schuster, 2017.

Kostof, Spiro. *The Third Rome 1870–1950 Traffic and Glory*. Berkeley: University Art Museum, 1973.

Lamont, Edward M. *The Ambassador from Wall Street: The Story of Thomas W. Lamont, J.P. Morgan's Chief Executive*. Lanham: Madison Books, 1994.

Larson, Erik. *In the Garden of Beasts: Love, Terror, and an American Family in Hitler's Berlin*. New York: Random House, 2011.

Lazzaro, Claudia and Crum, Roger J., eds. *Donatello Among the Blackshirts: History and Modernity in the Visual Culture of Fascist Italy*. Ithaca: Cornell University Press, 2005.

Ledeen, Michael A. *D'Annunzio: The First Duce*. New Brunswick: Transaction Publishers, 2002.

Levi, Carlo. *Fleeting Rome: In Search of la Dolce Vita*. London: John Wiley & Sons, 2005.

Lewis, Grace Hegger. *With Love from Gracie, Sinclair Lewis: 1912–1925*. New York: Harcourt, Brace and Company, 1956.

Lindbergh, Anne Morrow. *The Flower and the Nettle: Diaries and Letters 1936–1939*. San Diego: Harcourt Brace, 1994.

Lingeman, Richard. *Sinclair Lewis: The Rebel from Main Street*. New York: Random House, 2002.

Lussu, Emilio. *Marcia su Roma e dintorni*. Rome: Einaudi, 1945.

Macmillan, Margaret. *Paris 1919: Six Months that Changed the World*. New York: Random House, 2003.

Matthews, Herbert L. *The Education of a Correspondent*. New York: Harcourt, Brace and Company, 1946.

Meier, Jessica. *Rome Measured and Imagined: Early Modern Maps of the Eternal City*. Chicago: The University of Chicago Press, 2015.

Migone, Gian Giacomo. *The United States and Fascist Italy: The Rise of American Finance in Europe*. Cambridge: Cambridge University Press, 2015.

Milton, Joyce. *Loss of Eden: A Biography of Charles and Anne Morrow Lindbergh*. New York: HarperCollins, 1993.

Moorehead, Caroline. *A Bold and Dangerous Family: The Remarkable Story of an Italian Mother, Her Two Sons, and Their Fight Against Fascism*. New York: Harper, 2017.

Moravia, Alberto. *Il Conformista*. Milan: Tascabili Bompiani, 2010.

Morena, Antonio. *Mussolini's Decennale: Aura and Mythmaking in Fascist Italy*. Toronto: University of Toronto Press, 2015.

Moseley, Ray. *Mussolini's Shadow: The Double Life of Count Galeazzo Ciano*. New Haven: Yale University Press, 1999.

Mudge, Jean. *The Poet and the Dictator: Lauro de Bosis Resists Fascism in Italy and America*. Westport: Praeger, 2002.

Niven, Penelope. *Thornton Wilder: A Life*. New York: HarperCollins, 2012.

Olla, Roberto. *Il Duce and His Women: Mussolini's Rise to Power*. London: Alma, 2011.

Origo, Iris. *A Need to Testify: Portraits of Lauro de Bosis, Ruth Draper, Gaetano Salvemin, Ignazio Silone*. New York: Harcourt, 1984.

Packard, Reynolds and Eleanor. *Balcony Empire: Fascist Italy at War*. London: Chatto and Windus, 1943.

Painter, Jr., Borden W. *Mussolini's Rome: Rebuilding the Eternal City*. New York: Palgrave Macmillan, 2005.

Paxton, Robert O. *The Anatomy of Fascism*. New York: Vintage, 2004.

Pugh, Martin. *"Hurrah for the Blackshirts!": Fascists and Fascism in Britain Between the Wars*. London: Vintage, 2006.

Rosenblatt, Helena. *The Lost History of Liberalism: From Ancient Rome to the Twenty-First Century*. Princeton: Princeton University Press, 2018.

Salvemini, Gaetano. *Italian Fascist Activities in the United States*. New York: Center for Migration Studies, 1977.

Santomassimo, Gianpasquale. *La Marcia su Roma*. Florence: Giunti Gruppo Editoriale, 2000.

Saunders, Frances Stonor. *The Woman Who Shot Mussolini*. London: Faber & Faber: 2010.

Segrè, Claudio. *Italo Balbo: A Fascist Life*. Berkeley: University of California Press, 1990.

Simon, Linda. *Thornton Wilder: His World*. Garden City: Doubleday & Company, 1979.

Smith, Harrison. *From Main Street to Stockholm: Letters of Sinclair Lewis, 1919–1930*. New York: Harcourt, Brace and Company, 1952.

Snyder, Timothy. *On Tyranny: Twenty Lessons from the Twentieth Century*. New York: Tim Duggan Books, 2017.

Sturgis, Matthew. *When in Rome: 2000 Years of Roman Sightseeing*. London: Frances Lincoln, 2011.

Talbot, David. *Devil Dog: The Amazing True Story of the Man Who Saved America*. New York: Simon & Schuster, 2010.

Talbot, George. *Censorship in Fascist Italy 1922–43*. Basinstoke: Palgrave Macmillan, 2007.

Taylor, Rabun M. *Rome: An Urban History from Antiquity to the Present*. New York: Cambridge University Press, 2016.

Tytell, John. *Ezra Pound: The Solitary Volcano*. New York: Doubleday, 1987.

Valentine, Lucia, and Valentine, Alan. *The American Academy in Rome 1894–1969*. Charlottesville: University Press of Virginia, 1973.

Vance, William L. *America's Rome II: Catholic & Contemporary Rome*. New Haven: Yale University Press, 1989.

Vivante, Arturo. *Trulove Knot: A Novel of World War II*. Notre Dame: University of Notre Dame Press, 2007.

Warren, Dorothy. *The World of Ruth Draper: A Portrait of an Actress*. Carbondale: Southern Illinois University Press, 1999.

Wilder, Robin G. and Bryer, Jackson R. *The Selected Letters of Thornton Wilder*. New York: Harper Perennial, 2009.

Wiseman, T.P. *A Short History of the British School at Rome*. London: British School at Rome, 1990.

Yegül, Fikret K. *Gentlemen of Instinct and Breeding: Architecture at the American Academy in Rome 1894–1940*. Oxford: Oxford University Press, 1991.

ARTICLES ON WEBSITES OR IN JOURNALS, NEWSPAPERS, AND EDITED VOLUMES

Bagnani, Gilbert. "The Great Egyptian Crocodile Mystery," *Archaeology*, Vol. 5, No. 2 (June 1952).

Bagnani, Gilbert. "On Fakes and Forgeries," *Phoenix*, Vol. 14, No. 4 (Winter, 1960).

Begg, D.J. Ian. "Fascism in the Desert: A Microcosmic View of Archaeological Politics," in Galaty, Michael L., ed. *Archaeology Under Dictatorship*. New York: Kluwer Academic, 2004.

Begg, D.J. Ian. "Greece 1921–1924 in the Bagnani Archives," *Scripta Mediterranea*, Vol. XXIII, 2002.

Begg, D.J. Ian. "Papyrus Finds at Tebtunis from the Bagnani Archives, 1931–1936," *Bulletin of the American Society of Papyrologists* 35 (1998).

Bergmann, Bettina. "What a Task for a Lady! Marion Blake at Work," *Musivia & Sectilia*, 7, 2010.

Consolato, Sandro. "Giacomo Boni, l'archeologo-vate della Terza Roma," in De Turris, Gianfranco, *Esoterismo e fascismo*, Rome: Edizioni meditarenee, 2006.

Cox McCormack, Nancy. "Giacomo Boni, Humanist-Archaelogist of the Roman Forum and the Palatine," *Art and Archaeology* 28, nos. 1 and 2, July–August 1929.

Della Terza, Mollie. "Lauro de Bosis (1901–1931)," *Harvard Library Bulletin*, xxx, No. 3, July 1982.

Einaudi, Karin. "Esther Van Deman and the Roman Forum," *Places*, 5 (1), 1988.

Farell, Joseph. "Icarus as Anti-Fascist Myth: The Case of Lauro de Bosis," *Italica*, Vol. 69, No. 2, 1992.

Genêt. "Letter from Rome," *The New Yorker*, Nov. 4, 1950.

Gottlieb, Robert. "Man of Letters: The Case of Thornton Wilder," *The New Yorker*, Dec. 30, 2012.

Greenberg, Mark. "Interview with George Seldes, October 29, 1987," accessed at vermonthistory.org.

McCarthy, Pearl. "Boldness, Unerring Taste Create a Splendid Art Collection," *The Globe and Mail*, Oct. 26, 1957.

Rainey, Lawrence. "Ezra Pound's Odyssey," in *Institutions of Modernism: Literary Elites and Public Culture*. New Haven: Yale University Press, 1998.

Ricciardi, Caterina. "Nancy Cox McCormack scultrice a Roma, fra eventi artistici e vita sociale (1922–1924)," accessed at uniroma3.academia.edu/CaterinaRicciardi.

Richet, Isabelle. "'The Irresponsibility of the Outsider'? American Expatriates and Italian Fascism," in *Transatlantica*, accessed at journals.openedition.org/transatlantica/.

Salvemini, Gaetano. "Mussolini Chokes the Press," *The Nation*, Vol. 124, No. 3210.

Sprigge, Sylvia. "A Statue on the Janiculum," *Encounter*, Feb. 1958.

Visser, Romke. "Fascist Doctrine and the Cult of the Romanità," in *Journal of Contemporary History*, Vol. 27 (1992).

Vivante, Arturo. "The Visit," *The New Yorker*, July 3, 1965.

Welch, Katherine. "Esther B. Van Deman (1862–1937)," in Cohen, Getzel M., ed. *Breaking Ground: Pioneering Women Archaeologists*. Ann Arbor: University of Michigan Press, 2010.

NOTES

ABBREVIATIONS

ACS Archivio Centrale dello Stato (Rome)

AGO E.P. Taylor Library and Archives, Art Gallery of Ontario (Toronto, Ontario)

AHT Andover Harvard Theological Library, Harvard University (Cambridge, MA)

BLH Baker Library, Harvard Business School (Cambridge, MA)

BNL Beinecke Rare Book Library, Yale University (New Haven, CT)

CDS *Corriere della Sera* Newspaper (Rome)

GAM *Globe and Mail* (Toronto)

HLH Houghton Library, Harvard University (Cambridge, MA)

NYH New York Historical Society (New York)

NYT *The New York Times* (New York)

TUA Trent University Archives (Peterborough, Ontario)

PROLOGUE: THE VIEW FROM THE JANICULUM

page

2   "mock naval battles": Katherine A. Geffcken, ed., *The Janus View from the American Academy in Rome*, xvii.

2   "'seven lordly hills'": quoted in Jessica Meier, *Rome Measured and Imagined*, 116.

3   "the day's newspapers": CDS, October 3, 1931.

CHAPTER 1: THE BLACK DEVILS

page

7   "called themselves *Fascisti*": Lilian Mowrer, *Journalist's Wife*, 92.

8   "'Saint Bludgeon'": Christopher Duggan, *The Force of Destiny*, 425.

8   "top-floor apartment": Edgar Mowrer, *Triumph and Turmoil*, 145.

9 "pitched her into the street": Lilian Mowrer, *Journalist's Wife*, 171.

CHAPTER 2: TRAIN 112 FROM NAPLES

Quotes from Thornton Wilder's letters are from the Thornton Wilder Papers (TWP), the Yale Collection of American Literature, BNL. Details on Train 112 from Naples are from *Orario Generale*, Ferrovie-Tramvie, Navigazione e Servizi Automobilistici, Linee Ferroviarie e Marittime, Marzo 1920.

page

10 "middle of Via Cavour": Thornton Wilder, *The Cabala*, 7.

11 "lyrical Roman dispatches": Stark Young, "Miserable Innocents," *The New Republic*, August 25, 1920.

11 "missives from his father": details on Wilder's early life before coming to Rome are from Penelope Niven, *Thornton Wilder, a Life*, pp. 106–184.

12 "'peculiar gait'": ibid, p. 110.

13 "'Outside in wonderful Rome'": Thornton Wilder to family, Oct. 14, 1920, TWP, BNL.

14 "'rum in their tea'": Thornton Wilder to family, Oct. 15 (2), 1920, TWP, BNL.

CHAPTER 3: A VILLA IN ROME

The description of the contemporary appearance of the American Academy in Rome is drawn from the author's guided tour of the campus, led by external affairs officer Tina Cancemi, on January 9, 2017.

page

16 "long period of uncertainty": details of the early years of the American Academy are drawn from Lucia and Alan Valentine, *The American Academy in Rome*, pp. 1–76, and Katherine A. Geffcken, ed., *The Janus View from the American Academy in Rome*.

17 "'true leaven in America'": Lucia and Alan Valentine, *The American Academy in Rome*, p. 6.

18 "'never felt so modern'": ibid, 54.

19 "'that enormous vampire city'": Benito Mussolini, *Opera Omnia*, vol. 3, 190–191.

19 "surrounded by pig farmers": R.J.B. Bosworth, *Mussolini*, pp. 78–82.

20 "'on a blue satin sofa'": Katherine A. Geffcken, ed., *The Janus View from the American Academy in Rome*, 115.

21 "stripped the villa": ibid, 161.

21 "'a tiny darling house'": Thornton Wilder to family, Oct. 21, 1920, TWP, BNL.

22 "'hats for twenty lire'": Stark Young, "Miserable Innocents," *The New Republic*, August 25, 1920.

CHAPTER 4: A BEAUTIFUL BACKWATER

page

23 "'swaddling clothes'": Goethe, quoted in Matthew Sturgis, *When in Rome*, p. 210.

23 "'sacred to eternity'": ibid, p. 217.

24 "only 25,000 remained": Robert Hughes, *Rome*, 242.

24 "420 species": Richard Deakin, *Flora of the Colosseum of Rome*, vi.

25 "high embankments": Rabun M. Taylor, *Rome: An Urban History from Antiquity to the Present*, 319.

25 "'the Goths and the Vandals'": Augustus J.C. Hare, *Walks in Rome I*, 10.

26   "'National Urinal'": Robert Hughes, *Rome*, 373.
26   "only eight thousand": Lucy Hughes-Hallett, *The Pike*, 428.
27   "'son of Wilson'": Lilian Mowrer, *Journalist's Wife*, 77.
27   "gobbled up everything": Stark Young, "Dogfish," *The New Republic*, August 11, 1920.
28   "'incredibly stirring'": Thornton Wilder to family, [undated], TWP, BNL.
28   "'whooping centerpiece'": Thornton Wilder to family, Oct. 15, 1920, TWP, BNL.

CHAPTER 5: MORTAL ITALY
Background on the Mowrers' experiences in Italy is from Lilian Mowrer's *Journalist's Wife* (1937), and Edgar Mowrer's *Immortal Italy* (1922) and *Triumph and Turmoil* (1970). Many of the details of Gabriele d'Annunzio's extraordinary career come from Michael Ledeen's *D'Annunzio: The First Duce* (2002) and Lucy Hughes-Hallett's exhaustive biography *The Pike* (2013).

page
29   "met on a Liverpool-bound train": Lilian Mowrer, *Journalist's Wife*, 3.
30   "'a crusade of liberty!'": ibid, 31.
31   "a half million Italians": R.J.B. Bosworth, *Mussolini*, 121.
31   " 400,000 workers": Christopher Duggan, *The Force of Destiny*, 423.
31   "level of the streets": Lilian Mowrer, *Journalist's Wife*, 77.
32   "ready for a long siege": ibid, 83.
32   "one disgusted priest": quoted in Christopher Duggan, *The Force of Destiny*, 428.
33   "'a hundred against one'": Edgar Mowrer, *Immortal Italy*, 357.
33   "fifty of them": ibid, 356.
33   "tens of thousands of people wounded": Michael R. Ebner, *Ordinary Violence in Mussolini's Italy*, 9.
34   "'*the new face of Rome*'": quoted in Lucy Hughes-Hallett, *The Pike*, 54.
35   "'frightful gnome'": ibid, 271.
36   "'dropping bombs on you'": ibid, 443.
38   "black tunics of the *Arditi*": R.J.B. Bosworth, *Mussolini*, 145.
39   "considered it bad luck": Lilian Mowrer, *Journalist's Wife*, 36.
39   "included it in the novel": ibid, 99.
39   "'white Carrara marble'": Edgar Mowrer, *Immortal Italy*, 12.
40   "'normal anarchy'": ibid, 373.
40   "translated Shelley as he rode": Edgar Mowrer, *Triumph and Turmoil*, 149.

CHAPTER 6: THE BRICK-LICKING BARBARIANS
page
41   "hard brown bread with jam": Thornton Wilder to family, Nov. 22, 1920, TWP, BNL.
42   "'wild wandering'": Thornton Wilder to family, (undated, sent from Hotel Contenintale), TWP, BNL.
42   "adventures of Heinrich Schliemann": Linda Simon, *Thornton Wilder: His World*, 33.
43   "'street-cars of today rushed by'": Thornton Wilder to family, Oct. 21, 1920, TWP, BNL.
43   "'you look at Times Square'": quoted in Gilbert A. Harrison, *The Enthusiast*, 68.
44   "'What does the Pope do?'": Harold Norse, "Translations from G.G. Belli," *The Hudson Review*, Spring 1956.
44   "real archaeological scholarship": Matthew Sturgis, *When in Rome*, 214.
45   "'without seeing a single thing'": quoted in Christopher Hibbert, *Rome: The Biography of a City*, 243.

45 "use of balloon photography": Stephen L. Dyson, *Eugénie Sellers Strong*, 114.

46 "discovered a broad fissure": Lucia and Alan Valentine, *The American Academy in Rome*, 90.

46 "'the taste of its mortar'": Getzel M. Cohen, ed., *Breaking Ground*, 76.

47 "'misprision of remote peoples'": Thornton Wilder to family, Nov. 11, 1920, TWP, BNL.

47 "'neck of an exhausted people'": Thornton Wilder to family, Nov. 11, 1920, TWP, BNL.

47 "'Viva Lenin!'": Thornton Wilder to family, (undated, sent from Hotel Continentale), TWP, BNL.

48 "'their conceit and phlegm'": Thornton Wilder to father, Jan. 21, 1921, TWP, BNL.

48 "invited him to her parlour": Thornton Wilder to mother, Apr. 7, 1921, TWP, BNL.

48 "upper levels of the Baths of Diocletian": Regina Soria, "Moses Ezekiel's Studio in Rome," *Archives of American Art Journal*, Apr. 1964.

49 "third act of his play *Villa Rhabini*": Thornton Wilder to mother, Apr. 13, 1921, TWP, BNL.

49 "'urging me to read'": Thornton Wilder to mother, Apr. 7, 1921, TWP, BNL.

49 "reddish-yellow villa": Maria Delgado, "Memoirs of Villa Diana, Rome, 1913–1920," Lauro de Bosis Papers (LBP), HLH.

CHAPTER 7: THE NEXT SHELLEY

Many of Nancy Cox McCormack's experiences in Italy are recounted in the unpublished typescript manuscript "La Famiglia de Bosis and Other Memoirs, 1922–1933," (1953), a copy of which is held in the Lauro de Bosis Papers (LBP) at Harvard's Houghton Library.

page

51 "marriage of convenience": Caterina Ricciardi, "Nancy Cox McCormack scultrice a Roma, fra eventi artistici e vita sociale (1922–1924), 104.

53 "'flavor of adventure'": Nancy Cox McCormack, "La Famiglia de Bosis," 1.

54 "winged horse Pegasus": Giorgio de Santillana, "Lauro de Bosis memoir," 4.

54 "'ooze-covered Latium lake-god'": Giuseppe Prezzolini, *L'Italiano inutile*, 347.

55 "shot himself with a revolver": Lillian Vernon de Bosis, "Lilian [sic] Goes to Rome," 69.

55 "convinced de Bosis to sail": Lucy Hughes-Hallett, *The Pike*, 171.

56 "'beautiful as a naked blade'": ibid, 172.

56 "'you liked it?'": Lillian Vernon de Bosis, "Lilian [sic] Goes to Rome," 78.

57 "'never came near me'": ibid, 42.

58 "'I kiss your hands'": Lauro de Bosis to Nancy Cox McCormack, [Spring 1922], LBP, HLH.

59 "'my likeness in enduring bronze'": Nancy Cox McCormack, "La Famiglia de Bosis," 15.

59 "somewhat fantastic—but Roman'": ibid, 15.

59 "'a positively glowing youth'": Nancy Cox McCormack, "Giacomo Boni: Humanist—Archaeologist of the Roman Forum and the Palatine," *Art and Archaeology*, July–Aug. 1929, 37.

61 "offered a panorama from the dome": Nancy Cox McCormack, "La Famiglia de Bosis," 10.

61 "his usual smile!": Lauro de Bosis to Jean Loyson, March 15, 1919, LDP, HLH.

62 "'LEARN FRENCH'": Linda Simon, *Thornton Wilder: His World*, 34.

63 "'This is no joke'": Thornton Wilder to family, May 1, 1921, TWP, BNL.

63 "attended the second performance": Thornton Wilder to family, May 26, 1921, TWP, BNL.

64 "'all so easy and joyous'": quoted by Selden Rodman, Oct. 27, 1941, TWP, BNL.

64 "'with her amazing mind'": Thornton Wilder to family, May 10, 1921, TWP, BNL.

64 "'took me out to the tombs'": quoted by Selden Rodman, Oct. 27, 1941, TWP, BNL.

CHAPTER 8: THE MARCH ON ROME

page

67 "old hunting rifles": Gianpascuale Santomassimo, *La Marcia su Roma*, 74.

68 "'the galvanizing spirit'": quoted in Christopher Duggan, *The Force of Destiny*, 471.

68 "only sixteen thousand Fascists": ibid, 431.

68 "reinforced by five battalions": Gianpascuale Santomassimo, *La Marcia su Roma*, 76.

68 "'government that will govern'": Lilian Mowrer, *Journalist's Wife*, 168.

69 "fourteen hours to reach Rome": Roberto Olla, *Il Duce and His Women*, 223.

69 "implored him to send his followers": Christopher Duggan, *Fascist Voices*, 60.

70 "at the Pensione Rocchi": Nancy Cox McCormack, "La Famiglia de Bosis," 19.

70 "'driven by curiosity'": Nancy Cox McCormack, in the preface to *Benito Mussolini, My Diary*, 1915–1917.

71 "burst into the home of former prime minister": Christopher Duggan, *The Force of Destiny*, 432.

71 "'almost mystical intensity'": quoted in Roberto Olla, *Il Duce and His Women*, 225.

71 "'step forward for civilization'": Nancy Cox McCormack, in the preface to *Benito Mussolini, My Diary*, 1915–1917.

72 "'the king's expedient'": Nancy Cox McCormack, "La Famiglia de Bosis," 19.

72 "'hopes in the new regime'": Giorgio de Santillana, "Lauro de Bosis memoir," 49.

73 "seriously fracturing his skull": Lucy Hughes-Hallett, *The Pike*, 594.

73 "'he is a pig'": Giorgio de Santillana, "Lauro de Bosis memoir," 30.

74 "'a well-trained fist'": ibid, 48.

74 "'he devoured Plato'": Giorgio de Santillana on Lauro's literary and philosophical influences, "Lauro de Bosis memoir," 14–22.

74 "Lauro was imprisoned": ibid, 9.

75 "watching from the front row": "'Edipo Re' allo stadio del Palatino alla presenza del Soverano," *CDS*, May 18, 1923.

75 "'a corpse in our midst'": Lilian Mowrer, *Journalist's Wife*, 173.

76 "'fascinating baby daughter'": Edgar Mowrer, *Triumph and Turmoil*, 152.

CHAPTER 9: TRAMPING THE CAMPAGNA

Much of the background on Gilbert Bagnani's life comes from my research on the archaeologist's papers (GBP), which are shared between the Trent University Archives (Peterborough, Ontario) and the E.P. Taylor Library and Archives, Art Gallery of Ontario (Toronto). I'm particularly grateful to Bagnani's biographer, Ian Begg, for sharing the unpublished text of a talk presented at the University of Padua entitled "Gilbert Bagnani: A Life in Focus," which provides a crucial chronology of Bagnani's life and work.

page

78 "'we went climbing'": quoted in Richard Hodges, *Visions of Rome*, 33.

78 "he was born in Rome": Ian Begg, "Gilbert Bagnani: A Life in Focus," 1.

79 "'to think of the time'": Gilbert Bagnani to mother, Feb. 13, 1919, GBP, AGO.

79 "and briefly arrested": Gilbert Bagnani to mother, March 11, 1919, GBP, AGO.

80 "'those harmless drudges'": Gilbert Bagnani, untitled typescript "Twenty-five years ago to day," GBP, TUA.

80 "son of an engineer": Richard Hodges, Visions of Rome, 31.

80 "'pathetically tender-hearted'": ibid, 5.

81 "celebrated architect Edwin Lutyens": Stephen L. Dyson, Eugénie Sellers Strong, 119.

81 "heating and basic maintenance": Richard Hodges, Visions of Rome, 53.

81 "500-kilometer network": Peter J. Aicher, Guide to the Aqueducts of Rome, ix.

82 "just 2.5 meters per kilometre": Robert Hughes, Rome, 66.

82 "eleven public baths": Matthew Kneale, Rome: A History in Seven Sackings, 53.

82 "by the Middle Ages": ibid, 133.

82 "flaming red beard": Richard Hodges, Visions of Rome, 2.

83 "eventually master Latin": E.T. Salmon, "Gilbert Bagnani 19000–1985," Proceedings of the Royal Society of Canada, Vol. XXIII, 1985.

83 "'I have met Cortese'": Gilbert Bagnani to mother, Nov. 10, 1918, GBP, AGO.

83 "engaged in espionage": Ian Begg, "Gilbert Bagnani: A Life in Focus," 7.

84 "'marble sepulchres'": ibid, 3.

84 "'charm of the Campagna'": Gilbert Bagnani, The Roman Campagna and its Treasures, vii.

84 "'Caligula was learning to drive'": Gilbert Bagnani to mother, July 9, 1926, GBP, TUA.

85 "'drowned in one of the volcanic lakes'": quoted in Richard Hodges, Visions of Rome, 87.

85 "Oscar Wilde once rhapsodized": Stephen L. Dyson, Eugénie Sellers Strong, 13.

86 "'small wire-haired terrier'": quoted in Richard Hodges, Visions of Rome, 54.

86 "dispute over sleeping quarters": ibid, 72.

86 "'damnable silly wife's'": ibid, 90.

86 "'long and inspiring relationship'": Gilbert Bagnani, Rome and the Papacy,(dedication page).

87 "'in power for a year'": Gilbert Bagnani, Dictators versus Parliaments, undated [1923?] typescript, GBP, TUA.

88 "'I almost fainted!'": Gilbert Bagnani to Stewart Houston, undated letter, 1929, GBP, AGO.

CHAPTER 10: SCULPTING IL DUCE

page

89 "battalion of ss police": Robert Katz, The Battle for Rome, 3.

89 "second week of May 1923": Lawrence Rainey, Institutions of Modernity, 134.

90 "cruising through the gardens": Roberto Olla, Il Duce and His Women, 196.

90 "new bachelor's quarters": R.J.B. Bosworth, Mussolini, 175.

90 "'guardian of the threshold'": Roberto Olla, Il Duce and His Women, 257.

90 "'glad to welcome you'": Nancy Cox McCormack, in the preface to Benito Mussolini, My Diary, 1915–1917.

91 "began to cultivate Rismondo": Lawrence Rainey, Institutions of Modernity, 133.

91 "'useful-looking hands'": Nancy Cox McCormack, in the preface to Benito Mussolini, My Diary, 1915–1917.

93 "Pound hounded her with requests": Lawrence Rainey, Institutions of Modernity, 140.

93 "'Germany is busted'": ibid, 140.

93 "'divinely brave swashbuckler'": Ernest Hemingway, "Mussolini, Europe's Prize Bluffer," Toronto Daily Star, Jan. 27, 1923.

94   "Hemingway led his hosts": John Tytell, *Ezra Pound: The Solitary Volcano*, 182.
94   "Council's first act": R.J.B. Bosworth, *Mussolini*, 181.
94   "'Italy wants peace'": Nancy Cox McCormack, in the preface to *Benito Mussolini, My Diary*, 1915–1917.
95   "'We must stop this!'": Lilian Mowrer, *Journalist's Wife*, 177.
95   "sixteen were killed": R.J.B. Bosworth, *Mussolini*, 186.
96   "'devised the Acerbo Law'": Christopher Duggan, *The Force of Destiny*, 441.
96   "'hurl the country backwards'"; ibid, 443.
96   "stabbed him to death": Christopher Duggan, *Fascist Voices*, 90.
97   "Sinclair Exploration Company": John P. Diggins, *Mussolini and Fascism*, 150.
97   "'trying my fortune in America'": quoted in George Seldes, *Witness to a Century*, 216.
98   "cleaning out the desk": ibid, 217.
98   "'American-born Jessie Williams": ibid, 219.
99   "with its well-stocked bar": Reynolds and Eleanor Packard, *Balcony Empire*, 1.
99   "joined the crowds welcoming Mussolini": Nancy Cox McCormack, "La Famiglia de Bosis," Part 2, 9.
100   "'impossible ruffian'": ibid, Part 2, 13.
100   "had put his name forward": Giuseppe Prezzolini, *L'Italiano inutile*, 267.
101   "'wear out with old age'": Nancy Cox McCormack, "La Famiglia de Bosis," Part 6, 4.
101   "boycotting parliament": Christopher Duggan, *The Force of Destiny*, 445.
101   "carried the dollars Thornton Wilder": Lillian Vernon de Bosis to Thornton Wilder, March 26, 1949, TWP, BNL.
101   "'the greatest of all cities'": Thornton Wilder, *The Cabala*, 148.

CHAPTER 11: WOOING STEWART

page

102   "knee-breached attendants": Mary Augusta Stewart (Houston) Bagnani, "Diary," Feb. 6, 1925, GBP, TUA.
102   "descendant of the Family Compact": "Lives Lived: Stewart Bagnani," *Globe and Mail*, May 8, 1996.
103   "when Stewart was only seven": Ian Begg, "Gilbert Bagnani: A Life in Focus," 8.
103   "the maid to Mrs. Malaprop": playlist for Sheridan's The Rivals, Hart House Theatre, April 1923, GBP, TUA.
103   "'the Year of Experience'": Mary Augusta Stewart (Houston) Bagnani, "Diary," Oct. 16, 1924, GBP, TUA.
103   "'I was never Italian": ibid, Dec. 29, 1924.
104   "'such a queer mixture'": ibid, Mar. 29, 1925.
104   "identified with the Black Nobility": ibid, Mar. 14, 1925.
105   "offering his benediction": ibid, Dec. 29, 1925.
105   "'woman with an untidy mind'": ibid, Feb. 24, 1925.
105   "'as we drove home'": ibid, Apr. 16, 1925.
105   "young doctor of Rome'": ibid, Mar. 21, 1925.
106   "list more than three dozen churches": ibid, list "Churches Seen in Rome."
106   "something to have seen!": ibid, Apr. 23, 1925.
107   "'the first sight of N.Y.'": Gilbert Bagnani to mother, Jan. 23, 1926, GBP, TUA.
107   "'Americans are good at mathematics'": ibid, Jan. 31, 1926, GBP, AGO.
107   "'staple piece of conversation'": ibid, Feb 8, 1926.
108   "'Foffino there, quite amusing'": ibid, Jan. 31, 1926.
108   "'the scenery strikes me'": ibid, Jan. 31, 1926.

108 "'the finest building I have seen'": ibid, Jan. 18, 1926.
108 "'they are in a backwater'": ibid, March 31, 1926.
109 "'it is all covered with snow'": ibid, Feb. 8, 1926.
109 "'the Wild and Woolly West'": Gilbert Bagnani to Stewart Bagnani (undated, 1927), GBP, AGO.
110 "'people of a certain class'": Augusta Stewart Houston (Stewart's mother) to Gilbert Bagnani, July 20, 1926, GBP, TUA.
110 "'A most frightful row!'": Gilbert Bagnani to mother, (undated, 1927), GBP, AGO.
110 "'on principle I black-balled'": Gilbert Bagnani to mother, Jan. 29, 1931, GBP, AGO.
111 "'allusions to the present Italian state'": Gilbert Bagnani, *Rome and the Papacy*, x.

CHAPTER 12: A GILT-EDGED TRAP

page

112 "seven-storey Renaissance palazzo": Olga Ragusa, "Italian Department and Casa Italiana at Columbia University," *Italian Americana*, Winter 1995, 60.
112 "leading cultural outpost": John P. Diggins, *Mussolini and Fascism*, 255.
113 "daughter of a First World War general": Frances Toor, *Festivals and Folkways of Italy*, 201.
113 "twenty-two branch offices": Jean McClure Mudge, *The Poet and the Dictator*, 44.
113 "praise from the archaeologist Giacomo Boni": "Dr. Lauro de Bosis," brochure, Italy America Society, p. 2, LBP, HLH.
113 "a handsome four thousand dollars": "Lecture Tour Conducted by Lauro de Bosis, 1924–25," report by Irene di Robilant, Thomas Lamont Papers (TLP), BLH.
114 "reputation for being a staunch liberal": Iris Origo, *A Need to Testify*, 42.
114 "founded by an Italian banker": Jean McClure Mudge, *The Poet and the Dictator*, 42.
114 "feted with the Blackshirt marching song": Olga Ragusa, "Italian Department and Casa Italiana at Columbia University," *Italian Americana*, Winter 1995, 73.
115 "bomb throwers and organ-grinders": John P. Diggins, *Mussolini and Fascism*, 12.
115 "one million Italians a year": R.J.B. Bosworth, *Mussolini*, 251.
116 "'a gluttonous worker'": quoted in John P. Diggins, *Mussolini and Fascism*, 17.
116 "he had a dimple": ibid, 63.
116 "'if you have the right Dictator'": Will Rogers, "Letters of a Self-Made Diplomat to His President," *Saturday Evening Post*, July 31, 1926.
117 "d'Annunzio's third son Ugo Veniero": Luigi Barzini, *O America When You and I Were Young*, 186.
117 "around his flower-wreathed casket": John P. Diggins, *Mussolini and Fascism*, 127.
117 "Sforza accused Mussolini": ibid, 121.
118 "'head of that criminal organization!'": quoted in R.J.B. Bosworth, *Mussolini*, 203.
118 "friends that included H.G. Wells": Ron Chernow, *The House of Morgan*, 278.
118 "signed photo of Benito Mussolini": Edward M. Lamont, *The Ambassador from Wall Street*, 278.
119 "'most formidable financial combine'": Ron Chernow, *The House of Morgan*, xi.
119 "take tea with Bernard Berenson": Edward M. Lamont, *The Ambassador from Wall Street*, 216.
119 "her $2 billion in war debts": Ron Chernow, *The House of Morgan*, 281.
119 "'that impressive figure'": Edward M. Lamont, *The Ambassador from Wall Street*, 215.
120 "strictly for his 'health'": John P. Diggins, *Mussolini and Fascism*, 151.
120 "Lamont's palatial upper east side townhouse": Jean McClure Mudge, *The Poet and the Dictator*, 45.

120 "a 'very attractive *signorino*'": Nancy Cox McCormack, "La Famiglia de Bosis," Part 3, p. 7.

121 "Lippmann called out the Fascists": Ron Chernow, *The House of Morgan*, 283.

121 "says Bosis of Mussolini": "Says Bosis of Mussolini: 'He Saved Italy,'" *Toronto Daily Star*, Apr. 22, 1925.

122 "'free as cattle on a range'": Luigi Barzini, *O America When You and I Were Young*, 137.

123 "four hundred leading artists": R.J.B. Bosworth, *Mussolini*, 216.

123 "would die in exile": Caroline Moorehead, *A Bold and Dangerous Family*, 143.

123 "'refused to utter one single word'": Lauro de Bosis, preface to National Alliance newsletter ii, ACS.

123 "'as a result of his journey'": report by Irene di Robilant, TLP, BLH.

123 "'between this great nation and Italy'": Lauro de Bosis to Thomas Lamont, May 20, 1925, TLP, BLH.

124 "a credit line of $50 million": Edward M. Lamont, *The Ambassador from Wall Street*, 221.

124 "'seemed to me exaggerated'": Ron Chernow, *The House of Morgan*, 281.

124 "to four-tenths of one percent": ibid, 282.

CHAPTER 13: *I PICCONI DI ROMA*

page

125 "'*Evivva il fascismo!*'": CDS, "Il primo Governatore di Roma insediato da Mussolini," Dec. 31, 1925.

126 "'Within five years Rome'": quoted in Joshua Arthurs, *Excavating Modernity*, 51.

127 "made an honorary citizen": Spiro Kostof, *The Third Rome 1870–1950*, 9.

127 "template for the new city": Joshua Arthurs, *Excavating Modernity*, 88.

128 "clambering atop a roof": ibid, 69.

128 "'with their accursed Baedekers'": ibid, 26.

128 "'glories of the past'": ibid, 51.

128 "'escapes his watchful eye'": ibid, 55.

128 "arches of the Theatre of Marcellus": Borden W. Painter, Jr., *Mussolini's Rome*, 12.

129 "twelve-storey-tall bronze of Nero": Joshua Arthurs, *Excavating Modernity*, 63.

129 "standing alongside Mussolini": ibid, 28.

129 "most powerful archaeologist in Fascist Italy": Stephen L. Dyson, *Eugénie Sellers Strong*, 181.

130 "'from which she never wavered'": Getzel M. Cohen, ed., *Breaking Ground*, 98.

130 "'were christened 'Mussolinia'": Robert H. Kargon, *Invented Edens*, 50.

130 "surpassing its maximum": Joshua Arthurs, *Excavating Modernity*, 64.

130 "'the city is spreading rapidly'": quoted in Getzel M. Cohen, ed., *Breaking Ground*, 93.

131 "'cataloguing errors": Stephen L. Dyson, *Eugénie Sellers Strong*, 152.

131 "shutter its doors after Italy's invasion": T.P. Wiseman, *A Short History of the British School at Rome*, 18.

131 "'as regards building Vandals'": Stephen L. Dyson, *Eugénie Sellers Strong*, 183.

131 "were relocated to the *borgate*": Spiro Kostof, *The Third Rome 1870–1950*, 9.

132 "large families were crowded": Borden W. Painter, Jr., *Mussolini's Rome*, 97.

132 "inaugural address at a congress": Frances Stonor Saunders, *The Woman Who Shot Mussolini*, 9.

133 "Within Italy's borders": lyrics from http://www.nationalanthems.info/it-gio.htm

133 "a divot off the bridge of his nose": Frances Stonor Saunders, *The Woman Who Shot Mussolini*, 13.

133 "Mussolini's chauffeur-driven Lancia": ibid, 218.

134 "'All would be for the state'": R.J.B. Bosworth, *Mussolini*, 216.

134 "'Believe, fight, obey'": ibid, 294.

134 "handshakes had been banned": ibid, 314.

134 "forced to join the *Balilla*": Arturo Vivante, "The Rally," *New Yorker*, July 27, 1963.

135 "his ministers were recruited": Ron Chernow, *The House of Morgan*, 284.

135 "forced to print the word 'DUCE'": Frances Stonor Saunders, *The Woman Who Shot Mussolini*, 8.

135 "forced to step down": R.J.B. Bosworth, *Mussolini*, 215.

135 "2,500 poses in circulation": ibid, 211.

135 "Mussolini ha sempre ragione": ibid, 215.

136 "used as an expression of scorn": ibid, 218.

136 "'ideals they are betraying'": Iris Origo, *A Chill in the Air*, 148.

136 "agreed to chaperone": Jean McClure Mudge, *The Poet and the Dictator*, 51.

137 "grave danger of marriage": Lauro de Bosis to Giorgio La Piana, Sept. 1 1927, Giorgio La Piana Papers (GLP), AHT.

137 "helped save Mussolini's life": Nancy Cox McCormack, "La Famiglia de Bosis," part 2, pg. 14.

138 "'the same old bag of tricks'": Giorgio de Santillana, "Lauro de Bosis memoir," 51.

138 "fifteen thousand Italians into internal exile": Michael R. Ebner, *Ordinary Violence in Mussolini's Italy*, 47.

139 "'prevent his mind working'": quoted in Caroline Moorehead, *A Bold and Dangerous Family*, 162.

139 "not-so-distant better future": Giorgio de Santillana, "Lauro de Bosis memoir," 52.

139 "fought from within the nation": ibid, 63.

140 "greeted by a crowd of one hundred thousand": Jean McClure Mudge, *The Poet and the Dictator*, 66.

140 "had been sketching Pegasus": Giorgio de Santillana, "Lauro de Bosis memoir," 4.

140 "'wicked and powerful hands'": Jean McClure Mudge, *The Poet and the Dictator*, 64.

140 "'possess the air'": Ovid, Metamorphoses V VIII (trans., D.E. Hill.)

CHAPTER 14: APPARITION IN ROME

The description of Ruth Draper's performance of "An Italian Church" at Rome's Palazzo Odescalchi is adapted from Dorothy Warren's *The World of Ruth Draper* (1999).

page

142 "'oceanic' rallies that steered": Borden W. Painter, *Mussolini's Rome*, 2.

143 "performance by a foreign visitor": Dorothy Warren, *The World of Ruth Draper*, 56.

143 "frescoed with scenes from Genesis": from http://www.governo.it/palazzo-chigi-la-storia-le-immagini-e-il-restauro/gli-interni-del-palazzo/la-galleria-deti/2901

143 "aiming a sniper's rifle": Robert Olla, *Il Duce and His Women*, 302.

143 "'sorry for the poor little man'": Dorothy Warren, *The World of Ruth Draper*, 56.

144 "'Flowers from Mussolini'": Dorothy Warren, *The Letters of Ruth Draper*, 96.

144 "given by the Marchesa Presbitero": Katherine Presbitero to Ruth Draper, March 14, 1928, Ruth Draper Papers (RDP), NYH.

144 "drive to the town of Frascati": Ruth Draper to Lauro de Bosis, April 20, 1928, RDP, NYH.

144 "woman wearing a smock": Dorothy Warren, *The World of Ruth Draper*, 2.

146   "first time eighteen years earlier": ibid, 3.
146   "Henry James crafted a monologue": Iris Origo, *A Need to Testify*, 91.
146   "eight to ten years": ibid, 87.
147   "'That's not acting. That's life": ibid, 89.
147   "'mass hypnotism'": Dorothy Warren, *The World of Ruth Draper*, 24.
147   *"la grande passion"*: Iris Origo, *A Need to Testify*, 90.
147   "twenty days in a row": Ruth Draper to Lauro de Bosis, April 20, 1928, RDP, NYH.
147   "'drunk the milk of Paradise'": Lauro de Bosis to Ruth Draper, April 18, 1928,
       RDP, NYH.
148   "to meet his mother": Dorothy Warren, *The Letters of Ruth Draper*, 96.
148   "best of a mediocre lot": Giuseppe Prezzolini, *L'Italiano inutile*, 349.
149   "accepted the title of the Society's executive secretary": *Trade Bulletin of the Italy
       America Society*, 1928, p. 210, TLP, BLH.
149   "di Robilant had been working": Jean McClure Mudge, *The Poet and the Dictator*, 75.
149   "Percy Winner of the *Associated Press*": Ron Chernow, *The House of Morgan*, 284.
150   "'go through with such hypocrisy'": quoted in Lauro de Bosis, *Storia della mia
       morte*, 16.
150   "awarded a lucrative Westinghouse": Irene di Robilant to Thomas Lamont, Sept.
       22, 1928, TLP, BLH.
151   "featured a translation of Mussolini's speech": *Trade Bulletin of the Italy America
       Society*, Nov. 1928, p. 213, TLP, BLH.
151   "supporting a lecture series on Fascism": John P. Diggins, *Mussolini and Fascism*, 255.
151   "'I need you ferociously!'": Lauro de Bosis to Ruth Draper, Dec. 5, 1928, RDP, NYH.
151   "a benefit for the Eleonora Duse Fellowship": Stark Young, "The Duse Memorial,"
       The New Republic, March 27, 1929.
152   "'a real school of style'": Lauro de Bosis to Thornton Wilder, Apr. 27, 1929, TWP, BNL.
152   "sharing rooms with Prezzolini": Giuseppe Prezzolini, *L'Italiano inutile*, 346.
153   "met Italy's most notorious exile": Gaetano Salvemini, *Scritti Vari*, 627.
153   "'wandering Jew of anti-Fascism'": Iris Origo, *A Need to Testify*, 164.
153   "one of nine children to a poor family": Caroline Moorehead, *A Bold and
       Dangerous Family*, 34.
154   "groping through the rubble": Iris Origo, *A Need to Testify*, 145.
154   "'I am a miserable wretch'": Stanislao G. Pugliese, *Carlo Rosselli*, 31.
154   "critic of the philosopher Benedetto Croce": Caroline Moorehead, *A Bold and
       Dangerous Family*, 36.
154   "challenged him to a duel": ibid, 75.
154   "thugs with truncheons": Iris Origo, *A Need to Testify*, 151.
155   "borrow his passport": ibid, 154.
155   "'go ahead, Fascists, and kill'": ibid, 155.
156   "emerged as the clear victor": Charles Killinger, *Gaetano Salvemini*, 210.
156   "shadowed by two men": ibid, 211.
156   "held up a book": ibid, 213.
156   "'insulted their personal dignity'": Iris Origo, *A Need to Testify*, 39.
156   "'get rid of their free institutions'": Robert O. Paxton, *The Anatomy of Fascism*, 191.
157   "'a perfect example of manly beauty'": "Icarus," *The New Yorker*, Oct. 2, 1943.
157   "power would have to revert": Lauro de Bosis, *Storia della mia morte*, 29.
157   "'assures me that it is possible'": Gaetano Salvemini, *Scritti sul fascismo*, 441.
158   "'challenging new horizon'": Nancy Cox McCormack, "La Famiglia de Bosis,"
       part 3, p. 18.

CHAPTER 15: THE BROADSIDES OF CONSPIRACY

page

161 "Esposizione Universale Roma": Rabun M. Taylor, *An Urban History from Antiquity to the Present,* 336.

161 "kilometre-long axial boulevards": Michael Z. Wise, "Walking Mussolini's Fascist Utopia," *NYT,* July 11, 1999.

162 "Himmler of Italy": R.J.B. Bosworth, *Mussolini,* 220.

162 "statues of naked girls": Caroline Moorehead, *A Bold and Dangerous Family,* 163.

162 "'Dictator of the Dictator'": R.J.B. Bosworth, *Mussolini,* 220.

163 "files on 130,000 Italians'": ibid, 222.

163 "'inciting rebellion'": "I compilatori dell''Alleanza Nazionale' al Tribunale Speciale," *CDS,* Dec. 23, 1930.

164 "within two years a million": R.J.B. Bosworth, *Mussolini,* 262.

164 "count on the usual delays": David Dudley, "The Problem with Mussolini and His Trains," *Citylab.com,* Nov. 15, 2016.

165 "'part romantic adventure'": Mario Vinciguerra, "'L'Alleanza Nazionale' e Lauro de Bosis,'" in Franco Antonicelli, ed., *Trent'Anni di Storia Italiana (1915–1945),* 171.

165 "forced out of Italy in 1924": Caroline Moorehead, *A Bold and Dangerous Family,* 261.

165 "'Got fifty lire?'": Giorgio de Santillana, "Lauro de Bosis memoir," 68.

166 "two hours in the Senate": Lauro de Bosis to Ruth Draper, [undated, June 9, 1930?], RDP, NYH.

166 "'not about Dante'": Lauro de Bosis to Ruth Draper, July 12, 1930, RDP, NYH.

166 "was soon recruited": Lauro de Bosis, *Storia della mia morte,* 22.

166 "at least six copies of each": Lauro de Bosis, Alleanza Nazionale, preface, Newsletter 1, ACS.

168 "'all the constitutional parties'": article published (in Italian) in Franco Fucci, *Ali contro Mussolini,* 228.

168 "'flooded with his little papers'": Giorgio de Santillana, "Lauro de Bosis memoir," 69.

168 "seized by the police as enemy": "Catene di Sant'Antonio e truffe telematiche," *Panorama,* Apr. 16, 2003.

168 "'Italy and of your own conscience'": Lauro de Bosis, Alleanza Nazionale, preface, Newsletter 1, ACS.

169 "six weeks of swimming": Dorothy Warren, *The World of Ruth Draper,* 62.

169 "'I have the Boss on toast'": Giorgio de Santillana, "Lauro de Bosis memoir," 69.

170 "'your life or your name undefiled'": ibid, 71.

170 "last time de Santillana saw him": ibid, 72.

170 "newsletters had originated in Paris": Lauro de Bosis to Giacomo de Martino, Nov. 5, 1930, ACS.

171 "'Permit me to address to His Excellency'": ibid, Nov. 15, 1930, ACS.

171 "the five o'clock sailing": "Outgoing Passenger and Mail Steamships," *New York Times,* Nov. 26, 1930.

172 "fitted out in the highest Edwardian style": Peter Newell, *Mauretania: Triumph and Resurrection,* 6.

172 "'He is really very nice'": Lauro de Bosis to Ruth Draper, Nov. 28, 1930, RDP, NYH.

173 "'She was stunned'": quoted in Dorothy Warren, *The World of Ruth Draper,* 65.

173 "received a cable from a friend": Lauro de Bosis, *Storia della mia morte,* 22.

CHAPTER 16: 40,000,000 SHEEP

page

174 " the 'Bagnani brothers'": "Lives Lived: Stewart Bagnani," *Globe and Mail*, May 8, 1996.

174 "Located on Via Pompeo Magno": Letter from Carlo Ferrari to Gilbert Bagnani, Dec. 31 1929, GBP, TUA.

174 "dome was picked out by oil lamps": Lives Lived: Stewart Bagnani," *GAM*, May 8, 1996.

175 "'admirably suited her fair hair'": Weddings, *The Mail and Empire* (Toronto), June 28, 1929.

175 "LOVE FROM BOTH CHILDREN": Telegram, Gilbert Bagnani to mother (Rome), June 28, 1929, GBP, AGO.

175 "second-hand motorboat": Gilbert Bagnani to mother, (undated; July 3, 1929?), GBP, AGO.

175 "'The changes in Rome are amazing'": Gilbert Bagnani to mother (undated, late 1929) GBP, AGO.

176 "avoid getting a Fascist *tessera*": Gilbert Bagnani to mother, Jan. 20, 1934, GBP, AGO.

176 "may be preying on his mind": Gilbert Bagnani to mother, July 7 (?), 1930, GBP, AGO.

176 "leisurely cruise down the Nile": Ian Begg, "Gilbert Bagnani: A Life in Focus," 9.

176 "'peaceful penetration of the Mediterranean'": Ian Begg, "Fascism in the Desert," in Michael L. Galaty, ed., *Archaeology Under Dictatorship*, 36.

176 "had allocated a half million lire": ibid, 22.

177 "Gilbert had first met in Athens": Ian Begg, "Gilbert Bagnani: A Life in Focus," 2.

177 "interested in the laying out of new towns": Ian Begg, "Fascism in the Desert," in Michael L. Galaty, ed., *Archaeology Under Dictatorship*, 23.

177 "was being eliminated to allow": Paul Baxa, *Roads and Ruins*, 83.

178 "surrounded by cars and trucks": ibid, 112.

178 "Via del Mare swept drivers": ibid, xii.

178 "a new *idroscalo*": ibid, xiv.

179 "beat his bodyguards by racing": ibid, xiii.

179 "swiftly marshalled to the center": ibid, 77.

179 "city-block-sized Palazzo di Giustizia": Frances Stonor Saunders, *The Woman Who Shot Mussolini*, 243.

179 "tortured by the agents of OVRA": "Denunzia a carico di Vinciguerra, Mario," Questura di Roma, Dec. 9, 1930, ACS.

180 "'the most stringent interrogations'": ibid, 2.

181 "left on the roof": Lauro de Bosis, *The Story of My Death*, 12.

181 "leaving him permanently deaf": Lauro de Bosis, *Storia della mia morte*, 49.

181 "gave the police the names": "Denunzia a carico di Vinciguerra, Mario," Questura di Roma, Dec. 9, 1930, ACS.

181 "watching a movie at the Cinema Imperiale": ibid, 3.

181 "Charis received them icily": Franco Fucci, *Ali contro Mussolini*, 156.

182 "'Because I am not a sheep'": Lauro de Bosis, *Storia della mia morte*, 24.

182 "'You know it is no bluff'": Lauro de Bosis to Ruth Draper, Dec. 13, 1930, RDP, NYH.

183 "borrowed a Cadillac from his former fiancée": ibid.

183 "'NIPS ANTI-FASCIST PLOT'": Arnaldo Cortesi, "Arrest of 27 Nips Anti-Fascist Plot," *NYT*, Dec. 4, 1930.

183 "'weak Italy at their mercy?'": "Fascist Fear of News, *Manchester Guardian*, Dec. 9, 1930.

184 "the fate of Italian Liberty": "The Situation in Italy," *New York World*, Dec. 28, 1930.

184 "'publication of repugnant libels'": *Il Popolo di Roma*, Dec. 12, 1930.

184 "three-by-five-metre room": "Signora de Bosis Ill," *The Manchester Guardian*, Dec. 11, 1930.

184 "'sincere and fervid devotion'": De Bosis family to Mussolini, Dec. 12, 1930, ACS.

184 "'your false telegram doesn't fool'": Lauro de Bosis to Ruth Draper, Dec. 13, 1930, RDP, NYH.

185 "'unexplainably laconic and unresponsive'": Sylvia Sprigge, "A Statue on the Janiculum," *Encounter*, Feb. 1958, 7.

185 "'the best is yet to come'": Lauro de Bosis to Ruth Draper, Dec. 26, 1930, RDP, NYH.

185 "precisely three o'clock": "I compilatori dell''Alleanza Nazionale' al Tribunale Speciale," *CDS*, Dec. 23, 1930.

186 "manacles around their wrists": Arnaldo Cortesi, "Mrs. De Bosis Freed, 3 Convicted in Rome," *NYT*, Dec. 23, 1930.

187 "'double-crossing each other?'": Sylvia Sprigge, "A Statue on the Janiculum,"*Encounter*, Feb. 1958, 7.

188 "forty minutes of exercise a day": *Italy To-Day*, May 1931, 4, LDP, HLH.

188 "'I always remain untouched'": Lauro de Bosis to Ruth Draper, Dec. 23, 1930, RDP, NYH.

188 "'she is in perfect health'": Lauro de Bosis to Ruth Draper, Dec. 26, 1930, RDP, NYH.

189 "considered Lauro 'a scoundrel'": Lauro de Bosis to Ruth Draper, [undated, mid-January 1931?], RDP, NYH.

189 "Lauro was a double agent": *La Libertà*, Jan. 1, 1931.

CHAPTER 17: THE FLYING CONCIERGE

page

191 "luxurious passenger steamer *ss Rex*": Robert Hughes, *Rome*, 409.

191 "'Ambling Alp'": Professional Boxing Record for Primo Carnera, accessed at BoxRec.com, boxrec.com/en/boxer/12086.

191 "world's top honour for literature": Robert Hughes, *Rome*, 409.

191 "Blériot brought his flying machine": Lucy Hughes-Hallett, *The Pike*, 30.

191 "'dream of Icarus into reality'": R.J.B Bosworth, *Mussolini*, 70.

191 "first Italian-made aircraft": Lucy Hughes-Hallett, *The Pike*, 423.

192 "first person in history": ibid, 380.

192 "6,500 planes": ibid, 441.

192 "emerging from a 1921 crash": R.J.B Bosworth, *Mussolini*, 143.

192 "A Superhuman will'": John P. Diggins, *Mussolini and Fascism*, 72.

192 "title of world's fastest plane": Robert Hughes, *Rome*, 409.

192 "the Airship *Italia* flew from Milan": Garth Cameron, *Umberto Nobile and the Arctic Search for the Airship Italia*, 20.

193 "'the assassination of a priest'": Franco Fucci, *Ali contro Mussolini*, 226.

193 "spartan new headquarters": Claudio G. Segrè, *Italo Balbo: A Fascist Life*, 186.

193 "led a squadron of 61 seaplanes": ibid, 194.

194 "declaring an 'Italo Balbo Day'": Gerald Silk, "Il Primo Pilota," in Claudia Lazzaro, ed., *Donatello Among the Blackshirts*, 72.

194 "appeared in the sky above Milan": Franco Fucci, *Ali contro Mussolini*, 9.

195 "'we prefer to celebrate another flight'": "Un velivolo si fracasso sul Gottardo," *CDS*, July 13, 1930.

195 "thirty hours of flight time": Franco Fucci, *Ali contro Mussolini*, 14.

195 "toss pamphlets out of the cockpit": Caroline Moorehead, *A Bold and Dangerous Family*, 257.

196 "'the bath for number 28!'": Lauro de Bosis to mother, June 26, 1931, LDP, HLH.
196 "'but a little bit shabby'": Lauro de Bosis to Ruth Draper, March 4, 1931, RDP, NYH.
196 "paid 800 francs ($32) a month": ibid, Feb. 5, 1931.
196 "'I chose this hotel for its name'": Lauro de Bosis to Giorgio La Piana, March 9, 1931, GLP, AHT.
197 "an estimated 150,000": Caroline Moorehead, *A Bold and Dangerous Family*, 247.
197 "pulling off a daring motorboat escape": ibid, 235.
197 "'We Italians, and no one else'": ibid, 249.
197 "drop real bombs on Mussolini's offices": ibid, 292.
198 "'they killed them'": ibid, 185.
198 "'realistic vision of things there'": Lauro de Bosis, *Storia della mia morte*, 49.
198 "'tiny blue mood' ": Lauro de Bosis to Ruth Draper, Mar. 19, 1931, RDP, NYH.
199 "declined to write the preface": Iris Origo, *A Need to Testify*, 59.
199 "'guarantee that you'll approve it'": Lauro de Bosis to Giorgio La Piana, March 9, 1931, GLP, AHT.
199 "'It would be glorious!'": Lauro de Bosis to Eric Wood, Dec. 11, 1930, LDP, HLH.
200 "'your best chance for success'": Eric Wood to Lauro de Bosis, Dec. 28, 1930, LDP, HLH.
200 "'enterprise appeals to you'": Lauro de Bosis to Eric Wood, Jan. 17, 1931, LDP, HLH.
201 "'Lauro met me at the station here'": Dorothy Warren, *The Letters of Ruth Draper*, 114.
201 "pedalled off on a bicycle": Lauro de Bosis to mother, June 26, 1931, LDP, HLH.
202 "'The individual is moving to America'": Ministero dell'Interno, "Oggetto: Adolfo de Bosis, detto Lauro," June 30, 1931, ACS.
202 "'On a London tube platform'": Sylvia Sprigge, "A Statue on the Janiculum," *Encounter*, Feb. 1958, 7.
202 "a half million of them": ibid, 8.
202 "'Does Mussolini really believe'": Lauro de Bosis to mother, June 26, 1931, LDP, HLH.
203 "'De Bosis was one of the bravest'": Owen Cathcart-Jones, *Aviation Memoirs*, 221.
204 "this breach of etiquette": ibid, 222.
204 "'lost sight of him in the haze'": ibid, 222.
205 "associate was waiting for him with fuel": Ministero dell'Interno, "Oggetto: de Bosis, Lauro," Aug. 7, 1931, ACS.

CHAPTER 18: MERRILL & MORRIS
page

206 "identified with such code names": Caroline Moorehead, *A Bold and Dangerous Family*, 251.
207 "'scoundrel of a Bino'": Lauro de Bosis to mother, June 26, 1931, LDP, HLH.
207 "one of OVRA's most successful agents": Caroline Moorehead, *A Bold and Dangerous Family*, 283.
207 "'ten thousand minor problems'": Lauro de Bosis to mother, June 26, 1931, LDP, HLH.
207 "'also an act of the will'": Iris Origo, *A Need to Testify*, 112.
207 "'required superhuman willpower'": Gaetano Salvemini, *Scritti sul fascismo*, 449.
208 "staying at the Hôtel de l'Europe": Franco Fucci, *Ali contro Mussolini*, 174.
208 "a baron from the Trentino region": ibid, 172.
209 "'could not one play a duet?'": ibid, 175.
209 "'a beautiful old manor house'": Dorothy Warren, *The Letters of Ruth Draper*, 120.
209 "point an arrow directly at Lauro": Iris Origo, *A Need to Testify*, 112.
209 "wood-framed Messerschmitt M.23b": Richard Sanders Allen, "A Rendezvous with Pegasus," *Aviation Quarterly*, Summer 1988, 246.

209 "longer flying range": "The BFW M.23: A German Light 'Plane with Many Variations," *Flight*, March 21, 1930, 317.

210 "set at eight thousand marks": "L. De Bosis a survolé Rome," undated clipping, *Le Soir* (Brussels), ACS.

210 "'member of Hitler's National Socialist party'": Report from Italian Consulate, Munich, Oct. 13, 1931, ACS.

210 "'Cape Horn for the Flying Dutchman'": Lauro de Bosis to Giorgio La Piana, Aug. 4, 1931, GLP, AHT.

211 "P.G. Wodehouse's short stories": Iris Origo, *A Need to Testify*, 107.

211 "'I've gotten so superstitious'": Dorothy Warren, *The Letters of Ruth Draper*, 123.

211 "Ferrari replies with a coded telegram": Lauro de Bosis to Francesco Ferrari, undated letter from Munich, LDP, HLH.

212 "lighting up the airfield over Cannes": Max Rainer to Ruth Draper, Nov. 4, 1931, LDP, HLH.

212 "local publisher to ask Georg Hirth": Report from Italian Consulate, Munich, Oct. 13, 1931, ACS.

213 "speaks German very badly'": ibid.

213 "'Make sure the machine is here'": Max Rainer to Ruth Draper, Nov. 4, 1931, LDP, HLH.

213 "'I have still on my lips'": Lauro de Bosis to Ruth Draper, Oct. 2, 1931, RDP, NYH.

213 "'You wanted me to play a role'": ibid.

214 "'may he forgive my ruse!'": Lauro de Bosis, *The Story of My Death*, 9.

214 "'desiring its complete annihilation'": ibid, 11.

215 "'worth more dead than alive'": ibid, 16.

216 "'*auf Wiedersehn* at Nice tonight!'": Max Rainer to Ruth Draper, Nov. 4, 1931, LDP, HLH.

CHAPTER 19: BOMBARDING THE BOSS

page

219 "rising to twenty-six degrees". "Bolletino meteorologico," CDS, Oct. 4, 1931.

219 "a St. Martin's Summer": Franco Fucci, *Ali contro Mussolini*, 186.

219 "twice what the unemployed received": E. Lorenz, "Italy in the Storm of the Economic Crisis," *International Press Correspondence*, Oct. 29, 1931, 1000 1.

219 "in a cage midway up the stairs": "Wolf and Eagle Get New Homes in Rome," *NYT*, Apr. 29, 1935.

220 "pouring in from the six regions": "I reparti celere dei Fasci giovanili," CDS, Oct. 2, 1931.

220 "choruses of 'Giovinezza'": "Le celere marce dei Giovani Fascisti," CDS, Oct. 4, 1931.

220 "benefit of dredges or steam shovels": Kenneth M. Murchison, *Architectural Forum*, Oct. 1930, 407.

221 "gendarmes dressed in hooded red burnoose": "La prima Mostra d'arte coloniale," CDS, Oct. 2, 1931.

221 "simulation of an African souk": "La Mostra coloniale a Roma," CDS, Oct. 1, 1931.

221 "'chemicals weapons and the sky'": R.J.B. Bosworth, *Mussolini*, 255.

221 "named Governor-General of Libya": Claudia Lazzaro, ed., *Donatello Among the Blackshirts*, 75.

222 "at the Excelsior in Via Cavour": "Spettacoli d'oggi," CDS, Oct. 3, 1931.

222 "taking its toll on enrolment": Lucia Valentine, *The American Academy in Rome 1894–1969*, 95.

222 "meeting of the Grand Council of Fascism": "Il Gran Consiglio fascista approva la continuità della politica monetaria," CDS, Oct. 2, 1931.

223 "sketched out his route in pencil": Lauro de Bosis, sketch, [Sept. 1931?], LDP, HLH.
223 "clocked his take-off at 3:15": Max Rainer to Ruth Draper, Nov. 4, 1931, LDP, HLH.
223 "thirty thousand automobiles": Spiro Kostoff, The Third Rome, 15.
224 "galloping up the Spanish Steps": Iris Origo, A Need to Testify, 33.
224 "separating in the light breeze": Lauro de Bosis, The Story of My Death, 6.
225 "Next came the Quirinal Palace": Iris Origo, A Need to Testify, 33.
225 "he'd had translated and printed": Lauro de Bosis to Giorgio La Piana, Aug. 12, 1931, GLP, AHT.
225 "For thirty minutes": Lauro de Bosis, The Story of My Death, 6.
225 "a crowd gathered at an outdoor cinema": Iris Origo, A Need to Testify, 33.
226 "the military airfield at Ciampino": Milizia Volontaria S. Nazionale, "Oggetto: Lancio Manifestini sovversivi," Oct. 4, 1931, ACS.
227 "a 'putrefied corpse'": Lauro de Bosis, The Story of My Death, 18.
227 "'its program frightens the regime'": ibid, 19.
227 "Whoever you are": text of third leaflet from Lauro de Bosis, The Story of My Death, 18–19.
228 "he was enraged": William D. Carter, "Report on My Trip from Paris to Rome," Oct. 12, 1931, LDP, HLH.
228 "two airfields, Ciampino and Centocelle": Franco Fucci, Ali contro Mussolini, 184.
229 "Mussolini himself had ordered": "Report on My Trip from Paris to Rome," Oct. 12, 1931, LDP, HLH.
229 "'Roman Fascism is ready'": Il Popolo d'Italia, Oct. 6, 1931, 1.

CHAPTER 20: DOV'È DE BOSIS?
page

230 "'Can you imagine?'": Dorothy Warren, The World of Ruth Draper, 71.
230 "'there is no dictatorship'": "Il valore morale d'un gesto," La Libertà, Oct. 15, 1931.
231 "'rendering me a cause of sadness'": Lauro de Bosis to Ruth Draper, Oct. 2, 1931, RDP, NYH.
231 "kissed her on both cheeks": Dorothy Warren, The Letters of Ruth Draper, 126.
231 "'Italians regard with adoration'": Manchester Guardian Weekly, Oct. 9, 1931.
231 "newborn son Timothy Lauro": Sylvia Sprigge, "A Statue on the Janiculum," Encounter, Feb. 1958, 9.
231 "'It takes the children'": Lauro de Bosis, The Story of My Death, 10.
232 "'Hero of Liberty'": Giustizia e Libertà newsletter No. 30, Oct. 1931.
232 "she'd wired 45,000 francs": William D. Carter, "Report on My Trip from Paris to Rome," Oct. 12, 1931, LDP, HLH.
232 "was eating a croissant in a café in Paris": Dorothy Warren, The World of Ruth Draper, 72.
233 "they'd learned from the radio": Franco Fucci, Ali contro Mussolini, 188.
233 "'He was especially struck'": William D. Carter, "Report on My Trip from Paris to Rome," Oct. 12, 1931, LDP, HLH.
233 "Zanotti Bianco's research": Stephen L. Dyson, Eugénie Sellers Strong, 182.
234 "Lauro might have landed in the trees": William D. Carter to Ruth Draper, Oct. 17, 1931, LDP, HLH.
234 "'My whole state of mind'": Dorothy Warren, The Letters of Ruth Draper, 117.
235 "Lauro's act as 'sheer romanticism'": Nancy Cox McCormack, "La Famiglia de Bosis," part 1, p. 18.
236 "'I wanted none of it!'": ibid, part 5, pg. 2.

236 "five thousand were now foreigners": Matthew Kneale, *Rome: A History in Seven Sackings*, 299.

236 "enough money to feed his horse": Nancy Cox McCormack, "La Famiglia de Bosis," part 6, p. 1.

236 "'a human spider conscious'": ibid, part 7, p. 2.

237 "'The boy was lost at sea": ibid.

238 "been blown into the chimney": Nancy Cox McCormack, handwritten note, 1945, LDP, HLH.

238 "telegrams were sent by provincial prefects": reports from Prefettura di Viterbo (etc), Oct. 6, 1931, ACS.

239 "occurred in the town of Tuscania": report from Lt. Commander, Roncigilione, Oct. 7, 1931, ACS.

239 "the Merchant Marine reported": report from Direzione Generale della Marina Mercantile, Oct. 12, 1931, ACS.

239 "'an 'unverifiable source'": report from Console Generale, Marseilles, Oct. 21, 1931, ACS.

239 "'enterprise of a similar kind'": report from Direttore, Divisione Polizia Politica, Rome, Nov. 6, 1931, ACS.

239 "a seaplane pilot has reported": "Search for Lauro de Bosis," *Times of London*, Oct. 7, 1931.

239 "secretly transported to Rome": reported in *Le Soir* (Brussels), Nov. 8, 1931.

239 "OVRA informant in Marseille": unsigned report from Marseilles, Nov. 11, 1931, ACS.

239 " clipped 'in the American style'": unsigned report from Madrid, July 3, 1931, ACS.

240 "one of the few accounts": Franco Fucci, *Ali contro Mussolini*, 190.

240 "'Smile at Anti-Fascist Leaflets'": *New York Herald Tribune*, Oct. 11, 1931.

240 "'what can ever console us?'": Franco Fucci, *Ali contro Mussolini*, 189.

240 "'I loved my mother more'": Iris Origo, *A Need to Testify*, 55.

240 "'I never failed Adolfo'": Lillian Vernon de Bosis to Nancy Cox McCormack, Nov. 23, 1931, LDP, HLH.

241 "final photo in Lillian's album": photo album, LDP, HLH.

CHAPTER 21: THE NEW AUGUSTUS

page

242 "refer to as the 'years of consensus'": Renzo de Felice, *Gli anni del consenso, 1929–1936*.

243 "declared the Mafia defeated": Christopher Duggan, *The Force of Destiny*, 458.

243 "1929 Lateran Accords": R.J.B. Bosworth, *Mussolini*, 258.

243 "First-grade students were given primers": Christopher Duggan, *The Force of Destiny*, 461.

243 "more than ten children with gold prizes": ibid, 471.

243 "to just 70,000 in 1934": R.J.B. Bosworth, *Mussolini*, 251.

244 "stock market lost a third of its value": ibid, 288.

244 "banned the handshake": Christopher Duggan, *The Force of Destiny*, 510.

244 "high-speed cross of rugby": ibid, 492.

244 "replaced by the Italianate neologisms": R.J.B. Bosworth, *Mussolini*, 344.

244 "gradually embraced 'autarky'": R.J.B. Bosworth, *Mussolini's Italy*, 291.

244 "bloated class of Fascist bureaucrats": Borden W. Painter, Jr., *Mussolini's Rome*, 18.

244 "bread made of mashed chickpeas": Jane Scrivener, *Inside Rome with the Germans*, 144.

245 "redecorated in an angular Rationalist style": Borden W. Painter, Jr., *Mussolini's Rome*, 26.

245 "seven-metre-tall crucifix": from Luce newsreel, "Mostra della Rivoluzione Fascista," Oct. 28, 1932, accessed at patrimonio.archivioluce.com/luce-web/detail/ IL5000009152/2/roma-mostra-della-rivoluzione-fascista.html

245 "Mostra's guests of honour": Borden W. Painter, Jr., *Mussolini's Rome*, 29.

246 "carried 6.2 million automobiles": Joshua Arthurs, *Excavating Modernity*, 62.

246 "pitch-black Apuan marble": Heather Hyde Minor, "Mapping Mussolini," *Imago Mundi*, Vol. 51 (1999), 149.

247 "'stand out in unimagined splendour'": Stewart Bagnani, "Ten Years of Fascism," unpublished article, GBP, TUA.

248 "'did not make a *bella figura*'": Gilbert Bagnani to mother, Dec. 24, 1930, GBP, TUA.

248 "'presumptuous and antifascist'": Ian Begg, "Fascism in the Desert," in Michael L. Galaty, ed., *Archaeology Under Dictatorship*, 36.

248 "discovered next to the railway tracks": Richard Hodges, *Visions of Rome*, 1.

249 "'To us he was more a fellow-Roman'": "Obituary, Dr. Thomas Ashby," *Times* of London, May 26, 1931.

249 "discovered an enormous sanctuary": Gilbert Bagnani, "The Great Egyptian Crocodile Mystery," *Archaeology*, June, 1952.

249 "second-largest cache of papyri": Ian Begg, "Gilbert Bagnani: A Life in Focus," 13.

250 "dispatch 650,000 troops to east Africa": Christopher Duggan, *The Force of Destiny*, 503.

250 "Mussolini's son Vittorio led": R.J.B. Bosworth, *Mussolini*, 307.

250 "*Giornata della Fede*": Borden W. Painter, Jr., *Mussolini's Rome*, 118.

251 "lost only 4,5000 troops": Christopher Duggan, *The Force of Destiny*, 507.

251 "'Our peninsula is too small'": ibid, 493.

251 "typhus in concentration camps": ibid, 496.

251 "on the fated hills of Rome": Joshua Arthurs, *Excavating Modernity*, 125.

251 "Only 3,200 Italian peasants": R.J.B. Bosworth, *Mussolini*, 320.

251 "'eight million bayonets'": Borden W. Painter, Jr., *Mussolini's Rome*, 141.

252 "to make Africa 'fit for Fiats'": Ernest Hemingway, "Wings Always Over Africa," *Esquire*, Jan. 1936.

253 "'would not have existed without the black shirt'": quoted in R.J.B. Bosworth, *Mussolini*, 260.

253 "worst of European blood groups": ibid, 266.

253 "life-sized bust of Il Duce": ibid, 270.

253 "'Thirty centuries of history'": ibid, 282.

253 "his first meeting with Hitler": ibid, 281.

253 "over two hundred Jewish Fascists": Caroline Moorehead, *A Bold and Dangerous Family*, 340.

253 "allowed three thousand German Jews": ibid, 335.

254 "opposing them in 'one unshakeable will'": Christopher Duggan, *The Force of Destiny*, 510.

254 "'Today in Spain, tomorrow in Italy'": R.J.B. Bosworth, *Mussolini*, 318.

255 "pour 50,000 men into Spain": Christopher Duggan, *The Force of Destiny*, 508.

255 "under-equipped and below strength": Matthew Kneale, *Rome: A History in Seven Sackings*," 316.

255 "military power was a 'tragic bluff'": R.J.B. Bosworth, *Mussolini*, 352.

255 "named the 'Lauro de Bosis company'": Charles F. Delzell, *Mussolini's Enemies*, 151.

CHAPTER 22: THE DESPOT'S RAGE

page

256 "'wait and be ready for anything!'": Dorothy Warren, *The Letters of Ruth Draper*, 130.

256 "'Machiavellian in its cruelty'": ibid, 132.

257 "dark-haired young man of Italian appearance": Dorothy Warren, *The World of Ruth Draper*, 78.

257 "'Lauro de Bosis is still alive'": report to Arturo Bocchini from Direttore Generale per i servizi della Propaganda, Jan. 25, 1938, ACS.

257 "carry Ruth's letters to Lillian": Iris Origo, *A Need to Testify*, 117.

258 "'rare really great men are'": Dorothy Warren, *The Letters of Ruth Draper*, 185.

258 "series of a dozen one-week engagements": ibid, 136.

258 "'Lauro and I would have been married'": Dorothy Warren, *The World of Ruth Draper*, 74.

258 "appearances in Capetown and Khartoum": ibid, 81–3.

258 "Salvemini became the first appointee": Iris Origo, *A Need to Testify*, 117.

259 "'I am going there as to prison'": Caroline Moorehead, *A Bold and Dangerous Family*, 338.

259 "'and that is *to kill Mussolini*'": ibid, 342.

259 "Nello was stabbed to death": ibid, 349.

260 "'a superbly gifted writer of polemics": quoted in Mollie della Terza, "Lauro de Bosis," *Harvard Library Bulletin*, July, 1982, 274.

260 "'absolutely a free agent in what he did'": John Haynes Holmes, "The Greatest Single Deed of Heroism in Our Time," 11, LDP, HLH.

260 "'Only pilots can realize the courage'": Owen Cathcart-Jones, *Aviation Memoirs*, 224.

260 "'Italy will never forget him'": quoted in Jean McClure Mudge, *The Poet and the Dictator*, 169.

260 "'I feel a great weight off my heart'". Dorothy Warren, *The Letters of Ruth Draper*, 187.

260 "supporting the widowed Vinciguerra's daughter": Dorothy Warren, *The World of Ruth Draper*, 78.

261 "Vinciguerra continued active resistance": Jean McClure Mudge, *The Poet and the Dictator*, 169.

261 "became the subject of OVRA surveillance": Mollie della Terza, "Lauro de Bosis," *Harvard Library Bulletin*, July, 1982, 276.

261 "'holding our race up to ridicule'": report, Ministero degli Affari Esteri, June 2, 1935, ACS.

262 "'from the first been utterly perfect'": Dorothy Warren, *The World of Ruth Draper*, 80.

262 "enough for one-and-a-half hours": Jean McClure Mudge, *The Poet and the Dictator*, 156.

262 "thirty per cent past its recommended load": "The BFW M.23: A German Light 'Plane with Many Variations," *Flight*, March 21, 1930, 317.

262 "eighteen-kilometers-an-hour at ground level": Jean McClure Mudge, *The Poet and the Dictator*, 157.

263 "German pilots had neglected to replace": Max Rainer to Ruth Draper, Nov. 4, 1931, LDP, HLH.

263 "'Men must reap the things they sow'": Percy Bysshe Shelley, "Lines Written Among the Euganean Hills," *Poems of Percy Bysshe Shelley*, 6.

CHAPTER 23: THE HELL IT CAN'T

page

268 "'grinding it to death under the wheels'": John P. Diggins, *Mussolini and Fascism*, 34.

268 "'Never look back, my friend. Always forward'": "Vanderbilt Tells Mussolini Story," *Lawrence* (Kansas) *Daily Journal*, Feb. 13, 1931.

268 "ordering the first court-martial": "Gen. Butler Freed With A Reprimand As He Voices Regret," *NYT*, Feb. 9, 1931.

268 "'dictator's heretofore almost immaculate image'": David Talbot, *Devil Dog*, 114.

268 "Holed up in a Revolutionary-era house": Mark Greenberg, interview with George Seldes, Oct. 29, 1987, 1.

268 "rejected by editors in New York": John P. Diggins, *Mussolini and Fascism*, 55.

269 "'Reactionary dictators are men'": George Seldes, *Sawdust Caesar*, 381.

269 "'Fascism not only exists'": ibid, xiii.

269 "dismissed it as 'perfect moonshine'": Hans Schmidt, *Maverick Marine*, 224.

269 "putsch was 'actually contemplated'": "Asks Laws to Curb Foreign Agitators," *NYT*, Feb. 16, 1935.

269 "loaned him the money to buy his house": Mark Greenberg, interview with George Seldes, Oct. 29, 1987, 1.

270 "'Fascisti are a kind of American Legion'": Richard Lingeman, *Sinclair Lewis: The Rebel from Main Street*, 187.

270 "shared an apartment with Lewis's wife": ibid, 389.

270 "'In country after country,'": ibid, 393.

270 "covert appointments with his doctor": Erik Larson, *In the Garden of Beasts*, 74.

271 "'two million of my countrymen'": ibid, 106.

271 "'I had to relate every meeting'": Richard Lingeman, *Sinclair Lewis: The Rebel from Main Street*, 402.

271 "two months of twelve-hour days": ibid, 407.

271 "'American sense of humor of a Mark Twain'": Sinclair Lewis, *It Can't Happen Here*, 143.

272 "'America was any more individual than Canada'": ibid, 116.

272 "'That couldn't happen here in America'": ibid, 17.

273 "'one of the most important books'": Clifton Fadiman, "Books: Red Lewis," *New Yorker*, Oct. 26, 1935.

273 "with 320,000 copies sold": Sinclair Lewis, *It Can't Happen Here*, 390.

273 "'address him as "Sinclair Levy'": Richard Lingeman, *Sinclair Lewis: The Rebel from Main Street*, 390.

273 "'dig house' made of mud bricks": Ian Begg, "Gilbert Bagnani: A Life in Focus," 13.

274 "boy known as 'Mohammed the Cat'": Gilbert Bagnani to Stewart Bagnani, March 11, 1931, GBP, TUA.

274 "frescoed with Coptic inscriptions": Gilbert Bagnani to Stewart Bagnani, March 26, 1931, GBP, TUA.

274 "'very delicate fingers and excellent eyesight'": Gilbert Bagnani, "Excavations at Tebtunis," unpublished typescript, GBP, TUA.

274 "'they stank to high heaven'": Gilbert Bagnani: "The Great Egyptian Crocodile Mystery," *Archaeology*, June, 1952.

275 "shoot a gazelle from the window": Gilbert Bagnani to mother, Apr. 7, 1933, GBP, AGO.

275 "looted the Obelisk of Axum": Borden W. Painter, *Mussolini's Rome*, 157.

275 "make a cast of one of the walls": Ian Begg, "Fascism in the Desert," in Michael L. Galaty, ed., *Archaeology Under Dictatorship*, 27.

275 "claiming the discovery of the most significant cache": Ian Begg, "Gilbert Bagnani: A Life in Focus," 17.

276 "on the verge of obtaining his *tessera*": Gilbert Bagnani to mother, Jan. 20, 1935, GBP, AGO.

276 "suffering a heart attack in Toronto": "Mrs. Houston Much Mourned," GAM, Sep. 10, 1935.

276 "declare all his Canadian securities": Ian Begg, "Fascism in the Desert," in Michael L. Galaty, ed., *Archaeology Under Dictatorship*, 28.

277 "gathered to greet him at Le Bourget airfield": Jean McClure Mudge, *The Poet and the Dictator*, 66.

277 "Invited by Hermann Göring": Joyce Milton, *Loss of Eden*, 354.

277 "'the two most virile nations in Europe'": ibid, 357.

277 "senator was a lover of Italian culture": Ron Chernow, *The House of Morgan*, 288.

277 "Book-of-the-Month Club selection": Joyce Milton, *Loss of Eden*, 392.

278 "new director of the American Academy": Lucia and Alan Valentine, *The American Academy in Rome*, 96.

278 "Chester had given a twenty-year-old": Joyce Milton, *Loss of Eden*, 72.

278 "'you who have braved Nazi Germany'": Amey Aldrich to Anne Morrow Lindbergh, Aug. 28, 1936, Amey Aldrich Papers (AAP), BNL.

CHAPTER 24: BACK TO THE ACADEMY

page

279 "sculpture by Robert J. McNight entitled 'Fascist Allegory'": "Americans of Academy Cheer Mussolini As He Opens Show on Washington's Birthday," NYT, Feb. 23, 1923.

279 "greeted him with stiff-armed Roman salutes": Bruce Johnson, *Jazz and Totalitarianism*, 81.

279 "'My place is so damp'": "King Envies Academy Site," NYT, June 3, 1939.

279 "completely shuttered in 1934": Lucia and Alan Valentine, *The American Academy in Rome*, 95.

280 "close friend of Bernard Berenson": ibid, 97.

280 "With the firm Delano and Aldrich": Biographical sketch of Chester Aldrich, Columbia University Archives, accessed at clio.columbia.edu/catalog/6168536/.

280 "charming and spirited sister Amey": Lucia and Alan Valentine, *The American Academy in Rome*, 96.

280 "Amey carried with her a package": Dorothy Warren, The World of Ruth Draper, 83.

280 "'confirmation of all that my heart desires'": ibid.

281 "'go on a lecture tour which you will hear about'": Lauro de Bosis to mother, June 26, 1931, LDP, HLH.

281 "landed in the Littorio airfield": "Linbergh giunto in volo a Roma," CDS, Feb. 2, 1937.

281 "twin-seater capable of making long flights": "Lindbergh Buys British: His New Miles Mohawk Described," Flight, Nov. 5, 1936, 473.

281 "modern history represents the height of civilization": "Linbergh giunto in volo a Roma," CDS, Feb. 2, 1936.

282 "looked out over the city's spires and domes": Anne Morrow Lindbergh, *The Flower and the Nettle*, 139.

282 "the research of Dr. Alexis Carrel": Joyce Milton, *Loss of Eden*, 201.00 "'leaders of nations grown beyond human'": Alexis Carrel, *Man the Unknown*, 262.

282 "'was highly admired by foreigners'": "La Partenza di Lindbergh da Roma," CDS, Feb. 8, 1937.

282 "'turned into a "speck in the sky"": Amey Aldrich to Anne Morrow Lindbergh, Apr. 5, 1937, AAP, BNL.

282 "Lindberghs' landings in Tripoli": "Lindbergh giunto a Tripoli," CDS, Feb. 11, 1937.

283 "Charles would condemn Britain": Joyce Milton, Loss of Eden, 387.

283 "'But not full of Nazi praises'": Amey Aldrich to Anne Morrow Lindbergh, Oct. 22, 1938, AAP, BNL.

284 "found it divertente—entertaining": John Tytell, Ezra Pound: The Solitary Volcano, 229.

284 "'Treat him as artifex'": quoted in Borden W. Painter, Jr., Mussolini's Rome, 8.

284 "'am Roman above all'": ibid, 19.

284 "'a dente cariato'": Joshua Arthurs, Excavating Modernity, 72.

285 "museums in Florence and Paris": ibid, 73.

285 "'May the glories of the past'": ibid, 101.

285 "21,000 plaster casts": Borden W. Painter, Jr., Mussolini's Rome, 75.

285 "Fascist youth dressed in knee-pants": from Luce newsreel, "La Mostra Augustea della Romanità," Sep. 29, 1937, accessed at patrimonio.archivioluce.com/luce-web/detail/IL50023031/2/la-mostra-augustea-della-romanita.html

285 "vast 250:1 scale model": Borden W. Painter, Jr., Mussolini's Rome, 75.

286 "'reawakened in our day under your auspices'": Stephen L. Dyson, Eugénie Sellers Strong, 185.

286 "displayed at the Metropolitan Museum": Joshua Arthurs, Excavating Modernity, 107.

286 "Tiber River was now traversed": Matthew Kneale, Rome: A History in Seven Sackings, 283.

287 "population eventually reaching 1.4 million": Borden W. Painter, Jr., Mussolini's Rome, 17.

287 "Even the sewer grates": Joshua Arthurs, Excavating Modernity, 2.

287 "eight-storey case popolari": Borden W. Painter, Jr., Mussolini's Rome, 97.

287 "'500 Hitler boys were here'": Amey Aldrich to Richard Aldrich, Sep. 26, 1934, AAP, BNL.

288 "arrived in Ostiense station": Borden W. Painter, Jr., Mussolini's Rome, 119.

288 "welcomed with a military salute": ibid, 156.

288 "venerable march invented in Piemonte": Christopher Duggan, The Force of Destiny, 510.

288 "young archaeologist Ranuccio Bianchi Bandinelli": Stephen L. Dyson, Eugénie Sellers Strong, 187.

288 "arranged themselves into a giant M": Borden W. Painter, Jr., Mussolini's Rome, 121.

289 "'Rome is all topsy-turvy'": Amey Aldrich to Anne Morrow Lindbergh, Apr. 29, 1938, AAP, BNL.

289 "'Rome of travertine marble'": Robert Hughes, Rome, 430.

289 "'Jews do not belong to the Italian race'": quoted in R.J.B. Bosworth, Mussolini, 338.

289 "was, in fact, 'Nordic'": ibid, 334.

290 "quietly spirited off to Portugal": ibid, 344.

290 "three years to prepare the country": Borden W. Painter, Jr., Mussolini's Rome, 141.

290 "'from Rome to the Risorgimento'": ibid, 142.

290 "General Rommel's Afrika Korps": ibid, 144.

291 "'we have the worst allies'": quoted in R.J.B. Bosworth, Mussolini, 307.

291 "'It is strange to be living here'": Amey Aldrich to Anne Morrow Lindbergh, Oct. 20, 1940, AAP, BNL.

291 "portrait of the gluttonous Hermann Göring": Cecil Brown, "Letter from Rome," New Yorker, May 17, 1941.

291 "Chester Aldrich died in a Roman hospital": Lucia and Alan Valentine, *The American Academy in Rome*, 90.

292 "'The monuments are sandbagged'": Amey Aldrich to Anne Morrow Lindbergh, Oct. 20, 1940, AAP, BNL.

292 "it was one of the shortest speeches": William L. Vance, *America's Rome Vol. II*, 362.

292 "copy of the *Nuremberg Chronicle*": Pearl McCarthy, "Boldness, Unerring Taste Create a Splendid Art Collection," *The Globe Magazine*, Oct. 26, 1957.

293 "'a typical Canadian farmhouse'": "Lives Lived: Stewart Bagnani," *Globe and Mail*, May 8, 1996.

293 "barred from employment": ibid.

293 "Forbidden to travel without government permission": Ian Begg, "Gilbert Bagnani: A Life in Focus," 17.

293 "inducted into the Royal Society of Canada": E.T. Salmon, "Gilbert Bagnani 1900–1985," *Proceedings of the Royal Society of Canada*, Vol. XXIII, 1985.

294 "now scattered in collections around the world": Ian Begg, "Gilbert Bagnani: A Life in Focus," 18.

294 "'his gestures frozen in the air'": Gilbert Bagnani, undated poem, GBP, TUA.

295 "billeted at the Albergo Maestoso": Gilbert A. Harrison, *The Enthusiast*, 198.

295 "air corps commission was revoked": ibid, 187.

296 "he had flown out of Maine": Penelope Niven, *Thornton Wilder, a Life*, 556.

296 "knack for strategic planning": ibid.

296 "'Today we choose to drop pamphlets'": Robert Katz, *The Battle for Rome*, 11.

296 "waves of B-26 bombers": Robert Hughes, *Rome*, 440.

296 "seven thousand Romans would die": Matthew Kneale, *Rome: A History in Seven Sackings*, 340.

296 "Pope Pius XII visited San Lorenzo": Robert Katz, *The Battle for Rome*, 15.

297 "invited Mussolini to his villa": Matthew Kneale, *Rome: A History in Seven Sackings*, 279.

297 "Il Duce pissed his rumpled blue suit": ibid, 281.

297 "offices of the arch-Fascist newspaper *Il Tevere*": ibid, 282.

298 "abandoned his subjects to their fate": R.J.B. Bosworth, *Mussolini*, 403.

298 "promoted to lieutenant-colonel and transferred to Caserta": Gilbert A. Harrison, *The Enthusiast*, 196.

298 "'gypsy people gone to rot'": R.J.B. Bosworth, *Mussolini's Italy*, 504.

298 "centre of the city into a parking lot": Matthew Kneale, *Rome: A History in Seven Sackings*, 340.

298 "Fascism had eliminated malaria": R.J.B. Bosworth, *Mussolini*, 292.

299 "Finding a gate unlocked": Gilbert A. Harrison, *The Enthusiast*, 199.

299 "slap-up meal at a black-market restaurant": ibid, 200.

300 "'the highest prison in the world'": R.J.B. Bosworth, *Mussolini*, 216.

300 "had already forgotten their Duce": ibid, 21.

300 "the deaths of 400,000 Italians": ibid, 34.

301 "only 610 of whom survived": R.J.B. Bosworth, *Mussolini*, 407.

301 "a million people to an early grave": ibid, 35.

301 "overcome by a brain hemorrhage": Lucy Hughes-Hallett, *The Pike*, 642.

301 "Count Ciano would be dispatched": Christopher Duggan, *The Force of Destiny*, 522.

301 "two-by-two-meter cage": John Tytell, *Ezra Pound: The Solitary Volcano*, 277.

302 "used for clandestine meetings": Iris Origo, *A Need to Testify*, 77.

302 "history-teaching position in Florence": ibid, 180.

303 "'part of his Puritan ancestry'": Giorgio de Santillana, "Lauro de Bosis memoir," 72.

303 "'prepared to yield in principle'": Iris Origo, *A Chill in the Air*, 147.

304 "'vir liberalis et ingenuus'": Giorgio de Santillana, "Lauro de Bosis memoir," 74.

304 "members of the 52nd Garibaldi brigade": Christopher Duggan, *The Force of Destiny*, 529.

304 "bullet-ridden bodies were driven": R.J.B. Bosworth, *Mussolini*, 407.

304 "newly restored Mausoleum of Augustus": R.J.B. Bosworth, *Whispering City*, 188.

304 "hoisted up on a meat hook": Christopher Duggan, *The Force of Destiny*, 532.

EPILOGUE: THE OBELISK

page

307 "'I made him lose his place'": Daniel Lang, "Letter from Rome," *The New Yorker*, June 16, 1944.

307 "by the late eighties had fallen into disrepair": "In Rome, Renovation Worthy of the Medici," *NYT*, June 9, 1994.

308 "middle-aged waiters carry espressos": author's visit to American Academy, Jan. 9, 2017.

308 "'plunged into the Tyrrhenian Sea'": Thornton Wilder, *The Ides of March*, v.

309 "Ruth sent him a letter pointing out": Ruth Draper to Thornton Wilder, undated 1948, TWP, BNL.

309 "the French existentialist Jean-Paul Sartre": Gilbert A. Harrison, *The Enthusiast*, 212.

309 "ignored by the critics": ibid, 219.

310 "bust was dedicated in 1954": Sylvia Sprigge, "A Statue on the Janiculum," *Encounter*, Feb. 1958, 3.

310 "helmeted heads of Il Duce": Matthew Kneale, *Rome: A History in Seven Sackings*, 356.

311 "vandalized during the war": Heather Hyde Minor, "Mapping Mussolini," *Imago Mundi*, Vol. 51 (1999), 155.

311 "chiselled off after the war": Borden W. Painter, Jr., *Mussolini's Rome*, 158.

311 "subject to ritual denunciation": ibid, 157.

311 "an honoured place in a crypt": R.J.B. Bosworth, *Mussolini*, 421.

311 "tattooed on the back of his neck": Tobias Jones, "The Fascist Movement that has Brought Mussolini Back to the Mainstream," *The Guardian*, Feb. 22, 2018.

312 "long power-sharing coalition": Borden W. Painter, Jr., *Mussolini's Rome*, 158.

313 "three hundred tons of Carrara marble": Matthew Kneale, *Rome: A History in Seven Sackings*, 356.

INDEX

IMAGE CREDITS

Lauro De Bosis (5) and plane (217): MS Ital 65 (13), Lauro De Bosis papers, 1917–1933,
    Houghton Library, Harvard University.
Nancy Cox MacCormack (65): Rec ID 1493, Cushman Papers, Sophia Smith Collection,
    Smith College (Northampton, Massachusetts).
Palazzo Braschi (159): Photo code A00053502, Archivio Storico Istituto Luce.
Obelisk (305) courtesy of the author.
Map designed by Tiffany Munro